Conformed to the Image of Christ

Conformed to the Image of Christ

The Image of God in Spiritual Discernment

≈

BRYAN SHULER
Foreword by EVAN B. HOWARD

WIPF & STOCK · Eugene, Oregon

CONFORMED TO THE IMAGE OF CHRIST
The Image of God in Spiritual Discernment

Copyright © 2025 Bryan Shuler. All rights reserved. Except for brief quotations in critical publications or reviews, no part of this book may be reproduced in any manner without prior written permission from the publisher. Write: Permissions, Wipf and Stock Publishers, 199 W. 8th Ave., Suite 3, Eugene, OR 97401.

Wipf & Stock
An Imprint of Wipf and Stock Publishers
199 W. 8th Ave., Suite 3
Eugene, OR 97401

www.wipfandstock.com

PAPERBACK ISBN: 979-8-3852-4710-3
HARDCOVER ISBN: 979-8-3852-4711-0
EBOOK ISBN: 979-8-3852-4712-7

For those God foreknew he also predestined to be conformed to the image of his Son.
—Romans 8:29a

True religion is a union of the soul with God, a real participation of the divine nature, the very image of God drawn upon the soul, or, in the apostle's phrase, "It is Christ formed within us."
—Henry Scougal, *The Life of God in the Soul of Man*

Contents

Foreword xi

Introduction 1
    Research Question, Purpose, and Thesis 1
    Assumptions and Delimitations 3
    Definitions of Terms 5
    Research Context: Spiritual Theology and the Academic Study of
        Spirituality 8
    Importance of the Study 12
    Methodology and Outline 14

Chapter 1–Experience and Its Various Sources: On the Necessity of Discernment 17
    Toward Greater Definitional Clarity: Experience, Experiencing, and a
        Spiritual Experience 18
        Experience and Experiencing 18
        An Experience and a Spiritual Experience 22
        A Summary of Definitions 23
    Evan B. Howard's Model of Human Experience 24
        The Operations 24
        The Stages 28
        The Relationships 31
        The Depths 31
        A Concise Summary of Howard's Model 32
    Fallen Human Experience 32
        The Depths 33
        The Operations 34
        The Stages 36

The Relationships 38
Conclusion: On the Necessity of Spiritual Discernment 40

Chapter 2–Criteria of Spiritual Discernment: On the Necessity of Doctrine for Discernment 43
    A History of Spiritual Discernment and Criteria 45
        The Old and New Testaments 45
        The Early Church 51
        The Middle Ages 54
        The Reformation and Counter-Reformation 62
        Post-Reformation Catholicism and Protestantism 66
            Roman Catholic Theologians 67
            Puritan, Quaker, and Pietist Theologians 69
            John Wesley and Jonathan Edwards 75
    The Criteria of Spiritual Discernment and the Image of God: A Summative Analysis and Critique 77
        The Criterion of Scripture and the Image of God 78
        The Criterion of Christ and the Image of God 80
        The Criteria of the Holy Spirit, Sanctification, and the Image of God 82
    Doctrine and the Plurality of Christian Spiritualities 84
        Christian Spirituality Without Doctrinal Criteria 85
        Unity in Diversity: The Balance of Doctrine and Experience 87
        The Image of God and the Balance of Particularity and Diversity 89

Chapter 3–The Image of God as a Criterion for Discerning Authentic Spiritual Experiences 91
    The Image of God as Creational, Christological, and Teleological: The Biblical Data 92
        Man and Woman: Created in the Image of God 92
        Christ: The Image of God 95
        Christians: Conformed to the Image of God 98
        Excursus: The Image of God in Non-Christians 100
    The Main Systematic Positions on the Image of God 103
        The Structural Image 103
        The Functional Image 106

The Relational Image 108
The Multifaceted Image 110
The Multifaceted Image: A Heuristic Definition 111
Conclusion: Christ, the Image of God and the *Telos* of Christian Spirituality 113

Chapter 4–Principles for Spiritual Discernment: The Three Aspects of the Image of God in the Life of Christ 115
The Structural Aspect of the Image of God 117
Principle (1): Christ's Cognition, Affectivity, and Volition 117
Authentic Spiritual Experiences and Cognition 117
Cognition and the Life of Christ 117
Cognitive Christlikeness in the Life of the Believer 120
Cognition Christlikeness in the Spiritual Traditions 121
Authentic Spiritual Experiences and Affectivity 123
Affectivity and the Life of Christ 123
Affective Christlikeness in the Life of the Believer 125
Affective Christlikeness in the Spiritual Traditions 127
Authentic Spiritual Experiences and Volition 128
Volition and the Life of Christ 128
Volitional Christlikeness in the Life of the Believer 130
Volitional Christlikeness in the Spiritual Traditions 131
The Relational Aspect of the Image of God 133
Principle (2): Christ's Love for God Relationally Expressed 133
Authentic Spiritual Experiences and Relationship with God 134
Christ's Relationship with God 134
The Believer's Relationship with God 135
Relationship with God in the Spiritual Traditions 136
Authentic Spiritual Experiences and Relationships with Others 137
Christ's Relationship with Others 137
The Believer's Relationship with Others 139
Relationship with Others in the Spiritual Traditions 141
Authentic Spiritual Experiences and Relationship with

    Oneself 142
      Christ's Self-Identity 142
      The Believer's Self-Identity 143
      Self-Identity in the Spiritual Traditions 144
  The Functional Aspect of the Image of God 145
    Principle (3): Christ's Threefold Office of Prophet, Priest, and King 145
    Authentic Spiritual Experiences and the Office of King 147
      Christ's Kingly Office 147
      The Believer's Royal Vocation 148
      Royal Vocation in the Spiritual Traditions 150
    Authentic Spiritual Experiences and the Office of Priest 151
      Christ's Priestly Office 151
      The Believer's Priestly Vocation 152
      Priestly Vocation in the Spiritual Traditions 152
    Authentic Spiritual Experiences and the Office of Prophet 154
      Christ's Prophetic Office 154
      The Believer's Prophetic Vocation 154
      Prophetic Vocation in the Spiritual Traditions 155
  Conclusion 157

Conclusion 163

Selected Bibliography 167

Foreword

THE PROFESSOR WHO LED the doctoral seminar in discernment I attended in 1991 was right. She was doubly right, and Bryan Shuler's *Conformed to the Image of Christ* is one more testimony to her double rightness. First, my professor declared that discernment was central to the study of Christian spirituality. "The practice of spiritual direction," I summarize her words, "is vital to our growth in relationship with God. And what we find ourselves talking about most in spiritual direction is discernment." Bingo! Whether we use the language of "spiritual direction" or "discipleship," whether we name it as "discernment" or "hearing God," we Christians talk about recognizing and identifying God all the time. We praise God for a sunrise or a healing, and we express appreciative discernment. We look back at (or forward toward) the Lord's hand in our journey, and we express life discernment. We evaluate a decision, an experience, a trend, and we express situational discernment. Discernment is important—as my professor, my own research, and now the work of Bryan Shuler, proclaim.

Yet, my professor was *doubly* right. One day in the seminar, we got to talking about our doctoral program (we were asking her about how to choose a dissertation topic), and she gave us a bit of wisdom. "Choose a topic you are deeply interested in," she said. "Because you will be living with it for the rest of your life." I had always been interested in the question of "knowing": how we come to know, and how we come to know God. Then to discover how central discernment has been in Christian scripture and history—it just seemed obvious to me. And now here I am, thirty years later, introducing the publication of Shuler's dissertation on discernment. Over the years, and in various chapters and articles, I have developed my own thought on discernment from where I began in that first exploration of *Affirming the Touch of God*. But in all those years, I never explicitly pursued the possibility of using the doctrine of the image of God—as revealed in Christ—as a relevant criterion for guiding discernment; though, as Shuler points out, I did suggest that, "If discernment is the evaluation of what is from God, then Jesus himself is the clearest sign of what 'from God' might look like." In *Conformed to the Image of Christ*, Bryan Shuler has begun with the foundation I laid and has developed it in a direction and to a depth that is unique in the study of Christian spirituality. Reading Shuler's study today, I am still interested.

Bryan Shuler targets his analysis—his subtitle points right to the matter—toward one important aspect of Christian discernment: the evaluation of spiritual experiences. The fact is spiritual experiences happen. We open our Bible, and a single phrase seems to jump off the page into our heart. We listen to a series of sermons, and in the course of that series, a light begins to shine in our understanding. We sit quietly on a hillside, and we sense a deep and cosmic welcome that our parents never provided. We are confronted with an injustice and respond with rage and a need to act, sensing that the rage and compulsion to act are shared—if not inspired—by the God of justice. Shuler himself names a "variety of ways" we encounter spiritual experience: visions, dreams, auditions, "seeing" God in nature or in a miracle, or through being aware of God's mystical presence apart from any sensory perceptions. Accounts of spiritual experiences are ubiquitous in Scripture and history.

Which raises the problem. How do we know whether spiritual experiences are beneficial ("from God") or perhaps harmful (not "from God")? That Bible phrase—in spite of the fact that it jumped off the page—might actually offer the worst possible advice. Another verse could have been more helpful. The series of sermons may have been persuasive but heretical. And so on. Our assessments are fallible, subject to our human limitations. They are also twisted, as Shuler points out so clearly in his summary of fallen human experience. The fact of spiritual experience combined with the frailties of human evaluation reveal the need for discernment. Our solution, Shuler suggests, is neither one of "naive trust" in experiences nor "skeptical despair" of any resolution, but rather "a recognition of the necessity and efficacy of spiritual discernment."

But how do we go about doing spiritual discernment? Discernment method has been a topic of discussion for a very long time. Shuler's treatment of the history of spiritual discernment and criteria surveys this discussion, illustrating the richness of discernment-wisdom from both Roman Catholic and "Protestant" traditions. More specifically, he demonstrates the role many figures throughout history have given doctrinal criteria for discernment. Following the footsteps of writers like Jon Sobrino, Philip Sheldrake, and Kees Waaijman, Shuler argues that Christian doctrine is a valuable measure, helping Christians distinguish authentic from inauthentic experiences. Of course, the inclusion of doctrine as a relevant factor in discernment—along with communal, psycho-spiritual, and biographical factors—does not guarantee discernment "success" in the evaluation of any spiritual experience. Indeed, it simply acknowledges the doctrinal component of our Christian faith and reminds us of the need for careful theology.

Whether we like it or not, we are compelled to evaluate the authenticity of our spiritual experiences in view of our beliefs and, as Christians, most particularly through our understanding of Jesus Christ. Thus Shuler, having now set the stage, presents in chapter three a constructive examination of the doctrine of the image of God—as revealed in Christ—as a criterion for discerning authentic spiritual experiences. Here is where he makes his most original (and to me, his most important) contributions. Shuler wisely avoids taking a rigid stance regarding the much-debated issue of the nature of "the image of God" in human beings, adopting instead what he calls a "weaker claim," that the image of God "consists in or entails structure, function, and relation." This multifaceted approach, linked to his Christ-centered understanding of the doctrine of the image of God, then leads naturally to viewing the Experience of Christ—structure, function, and relation—as a worthy criterion by which Christians can evaluate our spiritual experiences.

And this brings us to Shuler's final chapter. Here he links his understanding of human experience (drawing from my own model) with Christology (opening up windows into Christ's own thinking and feeling; relationships with God, others, and self; along with the classic "offices" of prophet, priest, and king), with the believer's own formation into Christ, and with examples from the richness of the traditions of our Christian community. How do we discern our spiritual experiences in light of the doctrine of the image of God as revealed in Christ? Discernment wisdom often speaks of attending to the beginning, the middle, and the end: how an experience originates, the character of an experience as it is encountered in the present, and where it leads. Shuler's application of doctrine to discernment emphasizes the end. His operative phrase throughout the final chapter is, "Authentic spiritual experiences will conform to or lead to growth in conformity with . . ." (Christ's heart of compassion, Christ's self-giving love toward others, Christ's royal vocation, and so on). What we discover here is an important connection between discernment and formation, a connection that is not immediately noticed. This is why I believe that discernment is at its best when conducted in the context of a loving—and perhaps diverse—Christian community. A diverse and loving Christian community will help me to see where my excitement over that series of sermons leads over time: whether toward spiritual pride or self-giving love. A diverse and loving Christian community will help me perceive whether my rage and desire to act is an authentic sharing of the anger of Christ who turned over the tables of the unjust religious leaders of his own times, or perhaps an unhealthy attachment to current trends. Wise discernment leads to godly formation.

And this is why I think that *Conformed to the Image of Christ* is worth the read. It points us to the heart of the Christian faith. The passion of Jesus enables the life of Christ lived out through the Body of those who follow Christ. As we evaluate our experiences through the lens of the person and work(s) of Christ, we become ever more closely formed to the image of God, and through that growing conformity we discern what it means to live "from God."

As you can see, I still think discernment is both interesting and important.

—Evan B. Howard

Introduction

RESEARCH QUESTION, PURPOSE, AND THESIS

IN RECENT DECADES, THE study of Christian spirituality has burgeoned into a new and distinct field of research marked by a growing variety of methodologies and approaches.[1] One central characteristic shared by the scholars in this field is an explicit emphasis on experience, studying the spiritual life *as* experience and using experience as a source for knowledge of the spiritual life.[2] Additionally, theology and societies in the modern world both have experienced "turns" to experience, elevating the authority of experience in the pursuit of knowledge.[3] Given this current emphasis on experience, various debates surround religious and spiritual experience, such as (1) the nature of experience, especially in regard to it as a source of knowledge for Christian spirituality; (2) the relation between experience and doctrine, both as sources of knowledge for Christian spirituality, often played out in terms of the relation between theology and spirituality; and (3) the criteria needed to evaluate experience.[4]

Within this context of ongoing interest in experience, recent decades also have witnessed increased publications on spiritual discernment within the study of Christian spirituality.[5] Broadly defined, spiritual

---

1. O'Sullivan, "Spirituality," 71–77.

2. Schneiders, "Hermeneutical Approach," 50–54.

3. Gelpi, *Turn to Experience*, 1–8; Trueman, *Rise and Triumph*, 35–72. In society, the "turn" to experience can be seen in what Trueman calls the inward turn to "the psychological self."

4. Sheldrake, *Spirituality and Theology*, 84–95; Sheldrake, "Study of Spirituality," 162–67.

5. Waaijman, "Discernment and Biblical Spirituality," 1–12.

discernment is "a process of coming to 'know' that which is from God."[6] Spiritual discernment applies to a variety of situations, such as deciding between two vocational choices or judging the authenticity of one's spiritual experiences. One central problem that spiritual experience involves, and so one problem that is exacerbated as a result of the "turns" to experience, is that spiritual experiences must be judged for authenticity. An *authentic* spiritual experience is one that truly originates from the triune God of Christianity, and not all spiritual experiences are authentic.[7] Multiple origins of inauthentic spiritual experience exist, such as evil spirits, the world, or oneself, and writings on spiritual discernment long have acknowledged such alternative origins as showing the need for discernment within Christian spirituality.[8] Overall, then, one central problem posed by spiritual experience—the problem of authenticity—is solved by the study of spiritual discernment.[9] One important aspect of spiritual discernment is the development of specific criteria by which experiences can be judged. As such, the study of spiritual discernment includes the following question: What are the criteria by which one can discern whether a spiritual experience is authentic?

As early as John Cassian, Christian writings on spiritual discernment have connected the criteria of discernment, among other things, to the *telos*—the final goal or perfection—of spirituality, assuming that authentic Christian spiritual experiences will result in progress, or growth in sanctification, toward the *telos* of spirituality.[10] This *telos* has been

6. Howard, *Affirming the Touch*, 265.

7. This definition of authenticity assumes that the triune God of Christianity is the one, true God, and that religious pluralism or alethic nonrealism (à la John Hick) is not the case.

8. Origen, *On First Principles*, 3.2.4; Cassian, *Conferences*, 1.20.

9. The use of "problem solving" language indicates that spiritual discernment is focused on the solvable. In other words, as Gabriel Marcel and Andrew Louth reveal, problems and mysteries are distinct entities within theological reasoning. Problems are barriers that need to be defined and removed, whereas a mystery is something that involves the self and invites contemplation, transcending technique. See Marcel, *Being and Having*, 100–101, 117–18; Louth, *Discerning the Mystery*, 69–72. Being mostly oriented toward problem-solving, spiritual discernment does not pertain as much to clarifying the mysteries of God, such as the natures of the Trinity or the incarnation.

10. Cassian, *Conferences*, 1.2–5, 8, 15–20. Cassian stated that the ultimate end of spirituality is to enter the kingdom of God, which necessitates the immediate goal of purity of heart (i.e., sanctification). Purity of heart is achieved through contemplation, but contemplation is hampered by thoughts arriving from various origins other than God. As such, *discerning* the origins of one's thoughts is essential for maintaining purity of heart, for thoughts originating from God will lead to progress in sanctification.

described in a variety of ways, such as glorification, union with God, the vision of God, and perfection.¹¹ The New Testament describes growth in sanctification as growth in conformity to the image of Christ (Rom 8:29; 1 Cor 15:49; 2 Cor 3:18; Col 3:9–10) and states that Christ is the perfect image of God (Col 1:15; Heb 1:3; 2 Cor 4:4). As such, the image of God is connected to the *telos* of Christian spirituality, and conformity to the image of Christ entails conformity to the image of God. The image of God, then, holds creational, christological, and teleological value. All of these considerations—concerning experience, spiritual discernment, and the image of God—lead to this research question: How can the *imago Dei* act as a criterion of spiritual discernment to judge the authenticity of one's spiritual experiences?

I argue that, as christological and teleological, the image of God is able to act as a criterion of spiritual discernment by identifying the specific ways in which conformity to the image of Christ takes on functional, relational, and structural aspects. As such, a spiritual experience must conform to (or move one toward conformity with) the image of God to be counted authentic. In order to defend my thesis, I aim to show the necessity of discerning spiritual experiences, the necessity of doctrine for such discernment, the reasons why the image of God can act as a criterion for discernment, and the principles of discernment gained from the use of the image of God as such a criterion.

ASSUMPTIONS AND DELIMITATIONS

Scholars working within the academic study of Christian spirituality take various positions concerning a theology of religions, some being more open to interreligious (and even nonreligious) positions than others. For example, approaching spirituality from anthropological or hermeneutical perspectives, Christian scholars such as Sandra Schneiders and Celia Kourie view spirituality primarily as a universal human phenomenon.¹² As will be shown below, such approaches are common within the academic study of Christian spirituality, with many Christian scholars drawing upon the writings and experiences of non-Christians to understand better spirituality. Furthermore, given the works of scholars

---

11. Allen, *Spiritual Theology*, 23.

12. Schneiders, "Spirituality as Discipline," 13; Schneiders, "Hermeneutical Approach," 49–53; Kourie and Ruthenberg, "Contemporary Christian Spirituality," 81.

such as Raimundo Panikkar, John Hick, and Paul Knitter, religious pluralism has grown in popularity and influence, providing support for the interreligious study of spirituality.[13]

Religious pluralism is the view that "all religions (or at least the 'major' ones) are in their own ways complex historically and culturally conditioned human responses to the one ultimate Reality."[14] Christian particularism, on the other hand, upholds the unique particularity of Jesus Christ's atonement and the universal human need for this atonement.[15] Throughout my research project, I will assume that particularism is the case. I hold to particularism for various reasons, some of which are more philosophical and apologetic. First, I am convinced that good philosophical arguments exist for the existence of an almighty and personal God. Second, I am further convinced that the best explanation for the historical data surrounding the crucifixion and resurrection of Christ is that Christ really was resurrected from the dead by God as a sign of God's approval on the life, ministry, and teachings of Christ. Third, as such, the worldview Christ taught, which Christians take as their own worldview, is how the world actually is.[16] Ergo, Christ is the only way to salvation, and Christianity is the one true religion. Furthermore, the truth claims made by the Christian religion do, in fact, correspond and cohere with reality. As such, I also reject the alethic nonrealism intrinsic within pluralism, the idea that "religious doctrines never describe or point to any objectively existing spiritual Reality."[17] Overall, then, throughout my research, I will assume that Christianity is the one true religion and that the truth claims of Christianity describe and point to the one true God.

These assumptions hold implications for how I will go about answering my research question and defending my thesis. First, these assumptions imply that a distinction exists between the spiritualities of Christians and non-Christians. The Christian discernment of spiritual experiences, then, can be divided into two parts: the discernment of experiences had by Christians and the discernment of experiences had by non-Christians. This distinction leads to the following delimitation. While non-Christians are able to have authentic experiences of God, and

13. For their respective positions on religious pluralism, see Panikkar, *Unknown Christ*; Hick, *Interpretation of Religion*; Knitter, *Without Buddha*.
14. Netland, *Encountering Religious Pluralism*, 54.
15. Stewart, "Can Only One," 10.
16. This argument comes from Habermas, *Risen Jesus*, 3–172.
17. Clark, *To Know*, 334.

presumably do at times have such experiences on the way to redemption, I will be focusing on the spiritual experiences of Christians, not non-Christians.

While the discernment of non-Christian spiritual experiences from a Christian perspective is a legitimate research question to ask, I will not be pursuing that question, focusing instead on how the image of God acts as a criterion of spiritual discernment for Christians in particular. Furthermore, I will not be engaging with the more general philosophical question of the epistemic justification of religious experience (à la William Alston and Alvin Plantinga). My goal is not to justify the rationality of religious experience but rather to explore authentic Christian experience, assuming its rationality. The one question concerning non-Christians that I will pursue is how conformity to the image of God as a soteriological process coheres with the reality that every human being is made in the image of God. This problem pertains to one of the central arguments of my paper, whereas the application of my research project to the question of non-Christian spiritual experiences is left best for further research at another time.

DEFINITIONS OF TERMS

Various terms occur frequently throughout this book and merit preliminary definitions. First, three uses of *spirituality* relate to three levels of definition. First, spirituality can refer to "the real or existential level" lived out by a person. When using the term *spirituality* without any modifier, I will be referring to this level of definition. Second, spirituality also can denote "the formulation of a teaching about the lived reality, often under the influence of some outstanding spiritual person," such as Ignatian spirituality. When I refer to *Christian spirituality* I will be referring to this second level. Third, spirituality can indicate "the study by scholars of the first and especially of the second levels of spirituality."[18] When I use the term *spiritual theology* or *the academic study of spirituality*, I am referring to this third definitional level.

To define *spirituality* is not an easy task. Many definitions for the term exist. Sandra Schneiders defined *spirituality* as "the experience of conscious involvement in the project of life-integration through

---

18. Principe, "Toward Defining Spirituality," 47–48. This taxonomy is generally accepted as noncontroversial.

self-transcendence toward the ultimate value one perceives."[19] This definition leaves open the possibility of secular spiritualities. Jordan Aumann defined *spirituality* in two ways. Defined in terms of comparative religions and religious psychology, which is similar to Schneiders's anthropological definition, *spirituality* refers to "any religious or ethical value that is concretized as an attitude or spirit from which one's actions flow. ... It applies to any person who has a belief in the divine or transcendent, and fashions a lifestyle according to one's religious convictions."[20] This definition of spirituality lies outside the realm of theology. Aumann argued that spirituality becomes an area for theological study when, citing Paul Evdokimov, it concerns "the life of man facing his God, participating in the life of God; the spirit of man listening for the Spirit of God."[21] Aumann is correct to distinguish between these two types of definitions. As such, Schneiders's definition is too broad for my current purposes.

While this study holds implications for non-Christian religions and spiritualities, they are not my immediate concern. The immediate focus of this study is on Christian spirituality. Alister McGrath stated that Christian spirituality "concerns the quest for a fulfilled and authentic Christian existence, involving the bringing together of the fundamental ideas of Christianity and the whole experience of living on the basis of and within the scope of the Christian faith" to "foster and sustain [one's] relationship with Christ" and "deepen [one's] experience of God."[22] J. I. Packer concisely defined Christian spirituality as "the life of communion with God."[23] Packer's definition can be viewed as a concise encapsulation of McGrath's and Evdokimov's definitions, and when I use the terms *Christian spirituality* and *spirituality*, unless otherwise noted, these terms will refer to Packer's definition, delimiting this study to Christian spirituality and leaving non-Christian spiritualities for further research at a later time.

Second, spiritual theology can be defined in two manners. Broadly conceived, spiritual theology is the application of theology within the realm of spirituality. Narrowly and more robustly conceived, as a distinct theological discipline, spiritual theology is a theological approach to the

---

19. Schneiders, "Theology and Spirituality," 266.
20. Aumann, *Spiritual Theology*, 17.
21. Evdokimov, *Struggle with God*, 41; cited in Aumann, *Spiritual Theology*, 17.
22. McGrath, *Christian Spirituality*, 2–3.
23. Packer, "Towards a Systematic Spirituality," 1–14.

study of Christian spirituality. One of the most widely cited definitions comes from Jordan Aumann:

> Spiritual theology is that part of theology that, proceeding from the truths of divine revelation and the religious experience of individual persons, defines the nature of the supernatural life, formulates directives for its growth and development, and explains the process by which souls advance from the beginning of the spiritual life to its full perfection.[24]

Building off this definition, John Coe defined spiritual theology as follows:

> Spiritual Theology is that part of theology that brings together ... (1) a study of the truths of Scripture with (2) a study of the ministry of the Holy Spirit in the experience of human beings, in order to (a) define the *nature* of this supernatural life in Christ (derived from the Bible and theology as the primary data), (b) explain the *process* of growth by which persons advance from the beginning of the spiritual life to its full perfection in the next life (derived from the data of the Bible, theology and experience) and (c) formulate *directives* for spiritual growth and development (derived from the data of the Bible, theology and experience).[25]

Both definitions incorporate the data of Scripture and experience into the study of Christian spirituality, and they both accurately define the task of spiritual theology.

Third, experience can be defined in various ways. Experience can be understood as "practical wisdom gained through life," as "our observation of external sensible objects or of internal mental operations," or as "a particular stage in the human process."[26] In the broadest sense, human experience, constituted by cognitive, affective, and volitional operations, is a fundamental metaphysical category, "a way of describing the very nature of reality" in which "all reality is seen within experience and as experience."[27] Evan B. Howard's work on experience will be a focus of chapter 1, and greater definitional clarity of the term *experience* will be given at that time.

---

24. Aumann, *Spiritual Theology*, 22.
25. Coe, "Spiritual Theology," 12.
26. Howard, *Brazos Introduction*, 78.
27. Howard, *Brazos Introduction*, 78, 84–85.

Fourth, the definition of the image of God is a controversial matter. Any defense of a definition requires multiple pages of explanation. For now, I simply will state the definition I hold to, while elaborating on it further in chapter 3. The image of God in humanity consists of, or entails, at least three aspects. First, the image of God is structural, being a set of capacities within the human person or being regarded as the whole human person, enabling the potentiality for humans to image God and be set apart from other creatures. Second, the image of God is functional, being a human function unique to human beings, such as representing God's presence on earth through exercising dominion over the earth. Third, the image of God is relational, consisting of the unique relationships humans are capable of having with God, one another, and creation.[28]

RESEARCH CONTEXT: SPIRITUAL THEOLOGY AND THE ACADEMIC STUDY OF SPIRITUALITY

The issue of spiritual discernment has been discussed for millennia. Nevertheless, to understand the context of current discussions on spiritual discernment, one must understand the present academic field of Christian spirituality and its predecessor to which it is reacting and that it is developing out of—namely, Roman Catholic spiritual theology from the seventeenth to the twentieth century. As such, to set the context, I will explain briefly the current academic study of Christian spirituality and its relationship to Roman Catholic spiritual theology while seeking to make two points concerning the need for another work of spiritual theology on spiritual discernment. First, as the current field of Christian spirituality is focusing more on anthropological or historical approaches to the study, a need exists for more spiritual theology to be written. Second, given that experience has become increasingly more important and central to the academic study of Christian spirituality, the issue of spiritual discernment is critical for the current field of research, creating an ongoing need for research on spiritual discernment from a theological perspective.

The current academic study of Christian spirituality, in various ways, builds off of and reacts against Roman Catholic spiritual theology. From the seventeenth to the twentieth century, Roman Catholic spiritual

---

28. Cortez, *Theological Anthropology*, 18–28. See also King, *Beauty of the Lord*, 113–24.

theology was the theoretical study of the life of perfection, divided into three stages (purgation, illumination, union). Over time the study became focused on the division between the active life (asceticism) and the passive life (mysticism), and it was structured as a subdiscipline of dogmatic theology, being deductive, scholastic, and speculative (e.g., the works of Joseph de Guibert, Etienne Gilson, Louis Bouyer, Yves Congar, and Adolphe Tanquerey).[29] In the mid-twentieth century, especially after Vatican II, a shift occurred. The study of Christian perfection began to be labeled *spiritual theology* or simply *spirituality*. This shift involved an inductive focus on the personal and experiential, the universal call to holiness, as well as sociocultural context, viewing the older study as overly systematized, elitist, and prescriptive (e.g., the works of Hans Urs von Balthasar, Jean Mouroux, Michel de Certeau, and Albert Besnard).[30]

The academic study of Christian spirituality continued to develop and proliferate into the twenty-first century, maintaining its movement away from deductive theology and toward an inductive study of experience, context (à la Michel de Certeau), and self-implication, viewing theology as founded upon and sustained by spiritual experience.[31] In recent decades, this study within Roman Catholic and mainline Protestant circles has been led by scholars such as Bernard McGinn, Sandra Schneiders, and Philip Sheldrake. Schneiders's definition of the academic study of spirituality, in particular, has been influential. She defines the study of spirituality based on its material and formal objects. The material object is the lived experience of Christian faith, and the formal object is spirituality as religious experience.[32] As mentioned earlier, this new emphasis on experience heightens the need for research on spiritual discernment.

The current study of Christian spirituality is interdisciplinary, often descriptive-critical instead of prescriptive-normative, at times inclusive of nonreligious spirituality and frequently impacted by the linguistic-hermeneutical turn.[33] Instead of system building, the field mostly publishes

29. Sheldrake, *Spirituality and Theology*, 54; Schneiders, "Approaches to the Study," 23; Megyer, "Spiritual Theology Today," 58; Steggink, "Study in Spirituality," 6–8.

30. McGinn, "Letter and the Spirit," 15; Megyer, "Spiritual Theology Today," 59–63; Steggink, "Study in Spirituality," 11–14; Endean, "Spirituality and the University," 74; Schneiders, "Approaches to the Study," 23.

31. Sheldrake, *Spirituality and Theology*, 57–61; Sheldrake, "Study of Spirituality," 164–68.

32. Schneiders, "Approaches to the Study," 15–17.

33. Sheldrake, "Study of Spirituality," 163, 169; Steggink, "Study in Spirituality," 20–21; Schneiders, "Approaches to the Study," 17; Kourie, "Spirituality and the University,"

through paper collections, encyclopedia articles, and narrowly focused monographs.[34] Evangelicals have contributed to this movement while holding to evangelical priorities. The *Zondervan Dictionary of Christian Spirituality*, edited by Glen Scorgie, and *For All the Saints*, edited by Timothy George and Alister McGrath, are representative of the evangelical contribution. Many of the evangelical contributions fit within a more normative-prescriptive theological approach to Christian spirituality compared with the more postmodern-influenced descriptive-critical approach taken by scholars such as Schneiders.

At least three main approaches to the study of Christian spirituality exist, all of which contain a spectrum of variety dependent on their context of practice. First, the historical approach seeks to explain the history of a given spiritual phenomenon and understand the phenomenon itself through the tools of historical research. This approach acknowledges the contextual situatedness of spirituality and focuses on description over normativity.[35] Second, the anthropological approach, represented by and later developed by Schneiders into the "hermeneutical" approach, situates spirituality within human nature in general as self-transcendence toward some ultimate value. Most of the publications in spirituality are written from within this approach. This approach is often postmodern, cross-cultural, and interreligious, dialoguing extensively with various fields such as psychology, sociology, and feminist studies while still holding to some sort of Christian context and yet moving beyond confessional boundaries.[36] The third approach is theological, labeled either *theological spirituality* or *spiritual theology*, depending on the degree to which one's method is deductive or inductive.[37] This current spiritual theology is similar to the mid-to-late twentieth-century Roman Catholic spiritual theology, working from within an explicit doctrinal framework

---

152, 158.

34. Sheldrake, "Study of Spirituality," 169.

35. McGinn, "Letter and the Spirit," 18–19; Schneiders, "Approaches to the Study," 19–21; Kourie, "Spirituality and the University," 162–63.

36. Schneiders, "Approaches to the Study," 16–17, 26–28; Kourie, "Spirituality and the University," 159–60; McGinn, "Letter and the Spirit," 17.

37. Schneiders, "Approaches to the Study," 23–26. "Theological spirituality" works within a framework established by Scripture and doctrine but is not as concerned with theory building or deductive-prescriptive argumentation, placing the emphasis more on an inductive study of spiritual experience, rather than doctrinal application. "Spiritual theology," on the other hand, is used to describe the more deductive-prescriptive-normative approach taken by scholars such as Chan and McGrath.

while often starting inductively with particular religious experiences.[38] For example, evangelicals such as Simon Chan, Alister McGrath, and J. I. Packer frequently use a theological approach to the study of Christian spirituality that is on the normative-prescriptive side of the spectrum.

Most of the writing on Christian spirituality currently is done within the anthropological or historical approaches to the study. A need for more theological approaches to Christian spirituality exists, specifically from a prescriptive-normative stance—i.e., spiritual theology.[39] Yet, not all will agree that spiritual theology is a valuable approach to the study of Christian spirituality. Certain scholars, such as Schneiders, argue that the study of spirituality, while related to theology, is autonomous and separate, viewing spirituality as an equal partner with theology that goes beyond the borders set by theology.[40] Others, such as McGinn and Sheldrake, argue for a closer connection. McGinn sees spirituality as autonomous, while yet a discipline within theology. Thus, while spirituality has priority over theology, theology supplies criteria for interpreting spirituality.[41] Sheldrake, seeking to provide a *via media*, argues that the relationship is fundamental but that spirituality is a distinct field that should not be squeezed into the "tidy" systems of systematic theology or spiritual theology. As such, while spirituality is dependent on theology, the spiritual theology model is rejected as too rigid. Spirituality cannot be understood fully by theology or subsumed into the structures of doctrinal theology. Furthermore, Sheldrake sees spiritual traditions as historically arising out of experiences, not doctrine.[42] Still others, often evangelicals

38. McGinn, "Letter and the Spirit," 16; Schneiders, "Approaches to the Study," 22–23; Kourie, "Spirituality and the University," 161–62. While this threefold division commonly is discussed, various scholars have organized the current field around different categories. See Kourie, "Spirituality and the University," 165–66; Howard, *Brazos Introduction*, 25; Downey, *Understanding Christian Spirituality*, 123–31; Demarest, *Satisfy Your Soul*, 74–79.

39. Concerning theological approaches to spiritual discernment, Howard notes, "There have been relatively few publications which have sought to explore the nature of discernment explicitly from within the discipline of Christian theology." See Howard, *Affirming the Touch*, 19–20.

40. Sandra Schneiders's position is set out fully over a number of various articles. Other than those already cited, see Schneiders, "Spirituality in the Academy," 676–97; Schneiders, "Spirituality as Academic Discipline," 10–15. See also Sheldrake, "Study of Spirituality," 166; Endean, "Spirituality and the University," 77.

41. Sheldrake, "Study of Spirituality," 166; Sheldrake, *Spirituality and Theology*, 84; McGinn, "Letter and the Spirit," 13–22.

42. Sheldrake, "Study of Spirituality," 166–67; Sheldrake, *Spirituality and Theology*, 85–87, 95.

such as Simon Chan, posit an even closer relationship between theology and spirituality. Chan argues that spiritual theology builds off of systematic theology, drawing out its implications. Doctrines, arising out of the historic church's experience of God, regulate the church's ongoing experience of God.[43] Alister McGrath, J. I. Packer, and Diogenes Allen all similarly put forward positions in which spirituality and doctrine are intimately connected, doctrine guiding and controlling spirituality and spirituality keeping theology to its proper purpose.[44]

Given the influence of McGinn, Sheldrake, and Schneiders, many scholars have followed them in leaving behind the older spiritual theology in which theology regulates the ongoing experience of God. Yet, if theological realism is true and Scripture reveals the one, true, triune God, then the doctrine contained in Scripture should guide and control spirituality. In fact, the history of spiritual discernment shows the necessity of doctrine for judging spiritual experience, as will be shown in chapter 2. If a close relationship between biblical doctrine and Christian spirituality is not maintained, the ability to discern authentic spiritual experiences will be weakened, if not made completely impossible. Furthermore, for individuals who hold to the authority of Scripture and to theological realism, the application of doctrine within spiritual life will be of great importance. As such, with the current field mostly focusing on other approaches to the study of Christian spirituality, a need exists for more studies on spiritual theology.

IMPORTANCE OF THE STUDY

My contribution to the study of spiritual discernment involves using the image of God as a christological (and thus teleological) criterion of discernment through the application of the three aspects of the image of God to spiritual experience. This research builds off of the valuable tradition of spiritual discernment that already exists and develops it by bringing together the studies of spiritual discernment, contemporary

---

43. Chan, *Spiritual Theology*, 17–20; Chan, "Spiritual Theology," 52. This difference between Sheldrake and Chan broadly shows a key difference between "theological spirituality" and "spiritual theology."

44. Allen, *Spiritual Theology*, 152–60; McGrath, *Christian Spirituality*, 30; McGrath, *For All the Saints*, 13–17; McGrath, *Studies in Doctrine*, 232–76; Packer, "Towards a Systematic Spirituality," 1–2, 5–14; Packer, "Introduction," 6–7. See also Coe, "Spiritual Theology," 7, 10–15; 33.

theological anthropology, Christology, and the psychology and philosophy of human experience. This project contributes to the field of research by filling a gap in research and by meeting the continued need for more theological studies on spiritual discernment.

First, this study fills a gap in research and contributes to the academic study of Christian spirituality. No extended treatment exists yet on the image of God as a criterion of spiritual discernment that applies contemporary theological anthropology and a model of the psychology and philosophy of human experience to spirituality in order to draw out the three aspects of the image of God as teleological criteria in correlation with Christ as the perfect image of God. Much has been written already on the criteria of spiritual discernment—especially on the criteria of doctrine, Christ, and the fruit of the Spirit—as will be shown in chapter 2, and this study builds upon and develops out of these writings. To a certain extent, then, this study is not putting forward a grand claim that would revolutionize a field of research as much as a modest claim that draws out and develops implications from various areas of established scholarship. Furthermore, as most research is being done from an anthropological, hermeneutical, or historical perspective, recent literature on the study of Christian spirituality is comparatively lacking in the continued development of spiritual theology through the direct application of contemporary doctrinal formulations within the realm of spirituality. My use of the image of God, as a theological concept clarified within contemporary theological anthropology, addresses the need for more spiritual theology.

Second, this study helps meet the continued need for the development and application of spiritual discernment within the lives of Christians. As experience continues to rise in authority in theology, society, and spirituality, a great need exists for the development of the study of spiritual discernment. One cannot presume that the historic formulations of spiritual discernment can be adapted meaningfully to one's current situation without also translating them into one's context, especially through the use of contemporary doctrinal formulas. In particular, as globalization increases and the Christian church is confronted by a plurality of religious and spiritual influences, whether from other religions or nonreligious spiritualities, Christians must be equipped with the tools to discern between the various "spirits" within modern society. As such, this study will aid readers in judging and discerning their own spiritual experiences. The task of spiritual discernment is shared universally by all Christians, so this study will apply to all Christians. Furthermore, this study will equip theologians and ministers within the church with the conceptual clarity needed to discern, identify, and teach on the nature of experience and spiritual discernment within Christian spirituality. In other words, as pluralism continues to confront the church, this study will hold to the particularity of Jesus Christ, using Christ as the normative measurement of spiritual growth and truth and, in so doing, equipping readers with the vocabulary to articulate how this particularity distinguishes authentic Christian spirituality from other non-Christian spiritualities.

METHODOLOGY AND OUTLINE

I primarily will follow an inductive and abductive methodology centered on an exploration of a few key questions, which, when taken all together, will construct a solution to the research question of this study and a defense of my thesis. In chapter 1, "Experience and Its Various Sources: On the Necessity of Discernment," I will explore the following question: What is the nature of experience, and why does it necessitate discernment? To answer this question, I will survey Christian theologians who have written on the nature of human experience, such as Evan B. Howard, Bernard Lonergan, Donald Gelpi, and others, all of whom have written on the psychology and philosophy of human experience from within the context of Christian spirituality.

Concerning the nature of experience, first, I will seek mostly to show that experiences are ambiguous, and individuals must interpret the raw data of experiences in order for them to hold meaning. The goal of this study of experience will not be to put forward a new model of human experience but rather to show, based on Evan B. Howard's preexisting model, the ways in which experiences originate and necessitate interpretation by the individual undergoing the experience. Second, due to fallen human experience and the resulting ambiguity inherent within experience, this engagement with the works of Howard, Lonergan, and so forth will reveal the ways in which spiritual experiences are able to originate from various sources, which are not necessarily perspicuous, given that the ability to understand and judge rightly one's experiences is impacted by the fallen nature of one's cognitive, affective, and volitional operations. Taken together, the ambiguity of experience and the obscurity of the origin of an experience necessitate the practice of discernment within Christian spirituality.

The second main question, pursued in chapter 2, "Criteria of Spiritual Discernment: On the Necessity of Doctrine for Discernment," is the following: What are the criteria of spiritual discernment? To answer this question, I will present a concise history of spiritual discernment, specifically focusing on the identification of criteria for spiritual discernment. The literature from which I will be drawing will include both classic and contemporary works of Christian spirituality. Beginning with the Old Testament and concluding with recent works on Christian spirituality, I will offer a summative analysis and critique of my findings. The goal of this study will be to show, first, the ways in which certain criteria of spiritual discernment have been oriented around the *telos* of Christian spirituality, growth in sanctification, and Christ, and, second, that doctrine has played a major role in Christian history as a criterion for spiritual discernment.

The answer to this second main question will show the legitimacy of using doctrine, such as the image of God, as criteria for spiritual discernment as well as the lack of detailed work on an examination of the image of God as a criterion for spiritual discernment. One potential objection to the use of doctrine in this way is the argument that doctrine cannot fully comprehend experience and should not be used to dictate what counts as an authentic spiritual experience, given that experience produces doctrine. In response, I will seek to show, based on the history of spiritual discernment, that doctrine is a necessary criterion of spiritual discernment and that, while at times doctrine has been used to construct an overly rigid and narrow view of authentic spirituality, doctrine is able to be used as a criterion of spiritual discernment in a manner that acknowledges the plurality of authentic ways in which Christian spirituality can be expressed.

Having determined that experiences necessitate discernment and that doctrine is a necessary criterion of discernment, the remainder of the book will turn to the doctrine of the image of God. As such, the remaining questions to be explored include the following: First, what is the image of God, and how does the image of God relate to spiritual discernment? Second, what do the three aspects of the image of God reveal about the nature and effects of authentic spiritual experiences? To answer the first question, in chapter 3, "The Image of God as a Criterion for Discerning Authentic Spiritual Experience," turning to Scripture and soteriology,

I will explain the creational, christological, and teleological aspects of the image of God to show that growth in conformity to the image of God is a sign of growth in sanctification and, as such, can act as a criterion of spiritual discernment. Next, I will engage writings within contemporary theological anthropology to explain the main positions currently held on the image of God, specifically the functional, relational, structural, and multifaceted positions. I then will defend a heuristic approach to the multifaceted view of the image of God, arguing that the image of God consists of, involves, or at the least results in human beings having the functional, relational, and structural aspects that the multifaceted view of the image of God posits while showing how the image of God is able to be a criterion of spiritual discernment based on its christological and teleological orientation.

The final question concerning the ways in which the aspects of the image of God help one discern authentic spiritual experiences will be answered in chapter 4, "Principles for Spiritual Discernment: The Three Aspects of the Image of God in the Life of Christ," by applying the content of the three aspects of the image of God to examples drawn from the life of Christ, applied to the life of the believer, and compared and contrasted with the great traditions of Christian spirituality as described, for example, in Richard Foster's *Streams of Living Water*. The goal of this chapter will be to identify general principles from each aspect of the image of God that can be used to guide one through the process of spiritual discernment regarding one's spiritual experiences. These principles are not meant to replace other methods of discernment as much as supplement already existing work on discernment. Overall, then, to explore my research question and defend my thesis, I will seek to show the necessity of spiritual discernment, to defend the necessity of doctrine for spiritual discernment, to explain how the image of God acts as a criterion of spiritual discernment, and to draw out principles from the three aspects of the image of God useful for spiritual discernment.

1

Experience and Its Various Sources
On the Necessity of Discernment

SCHOLARS ON SPIRITUALITY, ACCORDING to Philip Endean, are "united in an insistence that human experience is a genuine source of wisdom and knowledge about God."[1] Nonetheless, formal acknowledgment of experience as such a source is a relatively recent phenomenon for theology, and not all scholars agree on the matter. Ellen Charry, for example, argues that doctrine provides experience with meaning, not the other way around.[2] Furthermore, theologians such as Stanley Grenz and Paul Tillich argue that experience is only the medium through which the sources of theology are received.[3] Without commenting on this debate, the use of experience for a source in the study of Christian spirituality is a different question, given that spiritual theology directly benefits from the study of the lived experiences of past saints to understand devotional practices and shared experiences, such as the dark night of the soul or the habitual awareness of the presence of God.

The use of experience as a source for either spiritual or theological knowledge brings up the following questions. Are all perceived spiritual experiences reliable and trustworthy guides to spiritual or theological realities? In other words, can spiritual experiences always be trusted to provide insight into theological or spiritual matters, or can they be misleading? Before one even can use an experience as a source of spiritual or

1. Endean, "Spirituality and the University," 78.
2. Charry, "Experience," 414–15, 419–23.
3. Grenz, *Theology*, 18–21; Tillich, *Systematic Theology*, 1:40–46.

theological knowledge, one first needs to decide whether it is authentic or not, which raises the question of discernment. If one uses inauthentic experiences as sources for knowledge of the spiritual life, then one will be misguided. In this chapter, I aim to show that the discernment of spiritual experiences is absolutely necessary given the nature of human experience within its fallen state and the consequential ambiguity and obscurity of a spiritual experience's meaning and origin.

In order to show the necessity of discernment, I first will provide greater definitional clarity to such terms as *experience*, *an experience*, and *spiritual experience*. Second, working with Evan B. Howard's model of human experience, I will explore the various aspects of the nature of human experience in its operations, stages, relationships, and depths. Third, I will seek to show the impact of sin upon the nature of human experience and conclude with how spiritual experiences and their origins can be ambiguous and obscure, necessitating discernment. Throughout this chapter, I mostly will be engaging with scholars who are working at the intersections of philosophy, psychology, and theology, and who are attentive to spiritual realities and the impact of sin upon human nature. In particular, the work of Howard will be paramount to this chapter and will hold implications for all the remaining chapters.

TOWARD GREATER DEFINITIONAL CLARITY: EXPERIENCE, EXPERIENCING, AND A SPIRITUAL EXPERIENCE

Experience and Experiencing

Experience is difficult to define, being subjective and, to a certain extent, incommunicable.[4] The term *experience* is used in a variety of ways; it can refer to such things as practical wisdom, sensory knowledge, internal mental operations, uncritical cognition contrasted with understanding and judgment, the entire spectrum of human evaluative responses, or the very nature of reality.[5] In general, theories of human experience fit into two broad categories. First, exclusive theories of human experience identify experience with feeling or emotion in contrast to thought, conceptualization, and judgment. Experience, then, refers to feeling, not

---

4. Schneiders, "Approaches to the Study," 17–18. Some prefer the term *consciousness* over *experience*. See McIntosh, *Mystical Theology*, 31–32.

5. Gelpi, *Turn to Experience*, 2; Howard, *Brazos Introduction*, 78.

thinking.⁶ For example, Alister McGrath equates the "experiential" with the affective (heart) in contrast to the cognitive (mind).⁷ Caroline Davis made a similar claim, arguing that experiences are "undergone," which excludes thinking, calculating, and other cognitive activities.⁸

Second, inclusive theories of human experience define experience broadly in terms of "knowing, doing, and feeling, or ideas, emotions, and institutions."⁹ On this account, experience includes both thinking and feeling as well as other elements constitutive of human existence. For example, John E. Smith wrote, "In its most basic sense, experience is the many-sided product of complex encounters between what there is and a being capable of undergoing, enduring, taking note of, responding to, and expressing it."¹⁰ Experience, then, involves both passive receptivity and active response, involving cognition, affectivity, and volition, not mere subjectivity or emotionalism.¹¹ As Stephen Parker explained, "Experience refers to a complex conscious, affective, physiological phenomenon, involving both cognitive awareness of external events and internal physiological, affective, and conscious reactions to such events."¹²

Building on the findings of experimental psychology and the philosophical works of Donald Gelpi, Evan B. Howard provides a way forward beyond this dichotomy between inclusive and exclusive models, with his distinction between experience as consisting of cognitive, affective, and volitional operations and Experiencing as a stage in the cognitive process.¹³ Defending an inclusive model of experience, Howard views human experience as "the particular presence and interactive entirety of any and all dimensions of human life."¹⁴ Basically, human experience incorporates the entirety of the various dimensions of human life, including one's body, thoughts, feelings, intentions, awareness, perceptions,

---

6. Lash, *Easter in Ordinary*, 133.

7. McGrath, "Theology and Experience," 66–67.

8. Davis, *Evidential Force*, 22.

9. Lash, *Easter in Ordinary*, 133. For an example, see Schleiermacher, *Christian Faith*, 8.

10. Smith, *Experience and God*, 23.

11. Dubay, *Authenticity*, 59; Lane, *Experience of God*, 4–5; Downey, *Understanding Christian Spirituality*, 118.

12. Parker, *Led by the Spirit*, 11.

13. The term "Experiencing," along with the other terms for the stages of the cognitive process, are capitalized by Howard, and I will follow accordingly.

14. Howard, "Experience," 176.

decisions, actions, and relationships within cognitive, affective, and volitional operations.[15]

Yet, much that exclusive models of experience want to accomplish also can be maintained in Howard's inclusive model of experience while avoiding an unnecessary and artificial polarization of thinking and experience (feeling).[16] Exclusive models of experience want to distinguish between passive receptivity and feeling on the one hand and active response, thought, and judgment on the other hand, identifying experience with the former and not the latter. Howard intimates a technically nuanced form of this exclusivist distinction within the stages of the cognitive process. Howard stated that the cognitive process of human experience consists of "generally identifiable stages" through which "human experience ordinarily proceeds."[17] Experience flows "from pre-encounter 'givens' to encounter, to evaluation, and ultimately to a response which, in turn, shapes the givens of subsequent encounters."[18] Howard places Experiencing as a stage prior to Understanding in the cognitive process, with Experiencing involving "stimulus, sensation, perception, and initial memory processing" and Understanding involving thinking "in its various types," such as "conceptual processing" and "general knowledge."[19] In other words, the distinction between experience (feeling) and thinking that exclusive models of experience want to make is, in large part, not rejected but upheld and redefined by Howard as a distinction between the stages of Experiencing and Understanding within the cognitive process. Howard's model thus bridges the gap between inclusive and exclusive models of human experience.

Howard is heavily influenced by the critical realist tradition of Donald Gelpi and develops this definition of experience along metaphysical lines. My argument will focus on other aspects of Howard's model of experience, but this aspect of his work deserves a quick explanation. Alfred North Whitehead used experience as a metaphysical category when he equated reality with process, defined process as "the becoming of experience," and stated that "apart from the experiences of subjects there

---

15. Howard, "Experience," 176; Howard, *Brazos Introduction*, 77–111.

16. The complex and mutually influential relationship between thinking (cognition) and feeling (affectivity) will be explored in the following section.

17. Howard, *Brazos Introduction*, 87.

18. Howard, *Affirming the Touch*, 211.

19. Howard, *Affirming the Touch*, 296.

is nothing, nothing, nothing, bare nothingness."[20] Relying heavily on Charles Peirce, Donald Gelpi reformulated Whitehead's principle within critical realism, arguing, "If whatever appears in experience enjoys reality, then reality and experience would appear to coincide."[21] Following Gelpi, Howard views all of reality "within experience and as experience."[22] Building on Peirce and Gelpi, Howard identifies the three fundamental elements of experience as follows: first, Quality or Evaluation, namely the communication of and evaluative response to qualities; second, Force or Act, which is a confrontation of "a self-negating identification of other"; and third, Tendency or Habit, which is the recognizable patterns of interaction between Quality and Force that evoke meaning.[23]

Whether one shares Howard's metaphysical view of experience, in which one is an experience, or retains the language of subjects that have experiences, the important point to note is that *experience* is an inclusive term that denotes every dimension of human life, involving the whole person. Human experience is irreducibly complex.[24] The complexity in part arises from the fact that experiences are both somatic and psychosomatic, involving encounters with a physical world through a physical body as well as nonphysical, mental awareness and apprehension, or even introspective investigation independent of sensory perception.[25]

Summarizing this complexity, Howard defined human experience in detail as "the somewhat integrated arising of various mental-biological operations or systems of operations, ordinarily occurring within an identifiable pattern or process, developing in time and space within the context of a web of relationships."[26] This definition highlights three aspects of human experience: the operations, the stages (process), and the relationships of experience. Overall, then, Howard's model of human experience is an inclusive theory of human experience that also leaves nuanced room for much that exclusive theories want to maintain, thus providing

20. Whitehead, *Process and Reality*, 252, 254. For an analysis of James, Whitehead, Peirce, and Josiah Royce, see Gelpi, *Gracing of Human Experience*, 276–82.
21. Gelpi, *Gracing of Human Experience*, 279.
22. Howard, *Brazos Introduction*, 78.
23. Howard, *Brazos Introduction*, 78–81.
24. Howard, *Brazos Introduction*, 104.
25. Johnson, *Religious Experience*, 47–48. Cf. Howard, *Brazos Introduction*, 81–84; Lane, *Experience of God*, 5–7; Yandell, *Epistemology of Religious Experience*, 42–43; Rakoczy, "Structures of Discernment Processes," 121; Lash, *Easter in Ordinary*, 92.
26. Howard, *Affirming the Touch*, 293.

a balanced solution to the prima facie dichotomy between inclusive and exclusive theories of human experience.

An Experience and a Spiritual Experience

Before moving on to explain each of these three aspects of human experience and how the fall impacts each aspect, one final note is needed concerning the unique complexity and meaning that attend the term *spiritual experience*. Spiritual discernment is a process by which one judges whether a spiritual experience is or is not authentic, and so discernment operates at the level of an experience that is a spiritual experience. The phrase *an experience* can be defined as "a perceptual encounter that introduces something to human experience more generally."[27] In other words, an experience is an identifiable or specific duration of human experience. The term *spiritual experience* refers to an experience that one has of a spiritual reality, whether that be of God, good angels, or evil spirits.[28]

A spiritual experience of God, in particular, can occur in a variety of ways, whether through visions, dreams, and auditions or through "seeing" God in nature or in a miracle or through being aware of God as direct and present within internal sensations or mystically present in their absence.[29] By an experience of God, William Alston explained that one has an awareness of God that "contrasts with thinking about God, calling up mental images, entertaining propositions, reasoning, engaging in overt or covert conversation, [or] remembering," that "something,

---

27. Howard, "Experience," 176. Cf. Netland, *Religious Experience*, 21–22.

28. I am purposely avoiding the term *religious experience*. Keith Yandell defined religious experience as an "experience doctrinally and soteriologically central to a religious tradition." See Yandell, *Epistemology of Religious Experience*, 15. This definition seems too broad and vague for my purposes at hand, especially since I will be focusing on perceived experiences of God in particular, rather than religious experiences in general. For example, the sudden realization and understanding of a doctrinal truth could count as a religious experience while not counting as an experience of God. Cf. Alston, *Perceiving God*, 34; Wynn, "Concept of Religious Experience," 147–66; Netland, *Religious Experience*, 17–37.

29. Swinburne, *Existence of God*, 298–301; Webb, "Religious Experience." For a list of biblical examples of experiences of God, see Dubay, *Authenticity*, 61–70. One point of a list like Swinburne's is to highlight how an experience of God need not be dramatic or seemingly miraculous. As Michael Rea explained, "There is . . . a kind of widespread and experientially available communication of God's love and presence," as seen in examples of sensing God's majesty in nature, feeling God's love while singing hymns, or feeling forgiveness after confessing one's sins to God. See Rea, *Hiddenness of God*, 91.

namely, God, has been presented or given to [one's] consciousness, in generically the same way as that in which objects in the environment are (apparently) presented to one's consciousness in sense perception."[30] As such, an experience of God is not purely subjective. Rather, it involves God presenting himself to someone. Therefore, like sense perception, the perception (experience) of God involves presentation, but unlike sense perception, the perception of God need not be accompanied by an awareness of sensory qualia.[31] While perception often is defined as essentially involving sensory qualia, the term still can be used in relation to God, at least analogically.[32] What is necessary to perception is presence. Without the presence, or with the absence, of X, one does not have the perception of X.

Based on the multiple ways in which God can be experienced, the presence of God, or his "immediacy," can be experienced to various degrees. William Alston distinguished between mediate (indirect) perception, mediated immediacy (direct perception), and absolute immediacy. Mediate perception is being aware of God by perceiving something other than God, such as a beautiful sunset. Mediated immediacy is being aware of God not by virtue of something else but solely as mediated through consciousness, such as perceiving God directly as good and loving and this being accompanied by joy. Absolute immediacy is being aware of God not through anything else, not even a state of consciousness, such as experiencing mystical union with God or being united with God in eternity.[33]

A Summary of Definitions

Definitional clarity concerning *experience* and other related terms is important to spiritual discernment as a subject. The study of spiritual discernment engages with the experiences of human beings and so benefits from a general definition and model of human experience. Such a model provides the study with an overarching framework in which to

---

30. Alston, *Perceiving God*, 14. Perception can be defined simply as "an awareness of a given objection." See Gavrilyuk, "Encountering God," 47.

31. Alston, *Perceiving God*, 16.

32. Plantinga, *Warranted Christian Belief*, 181.

33. Alston, *Perceiving God*, 21–33. Cf. Lane, *Experience of God*, 18; Dubay, *Authenticity*, 60. Bernard Lonergan held a similar taxonomy of immediacy. See Lonergan, *Method in Theology*, 28–29. Cf. Roy, *Transcendent Experiences*, 138–39.

understand the occurrences and various aspects of individual human experiences. Given that the study of spiritual discernment does not stop at the general level of human experience but proceeds on to engage with individual experiences, the study also benefits from having clear definitions of *an experience* and *spiritual experience*.

Human experience, as defined by Evan B. Howard, refers to the presence and interaction of every dimension of human life, including specific operations, cognitive stages, and relationships. Howard's definition is an inclusive model of experience that incorporates aspects of an exclusive model of experience by how it places Experiencing as a stage in the cognitive process before Understanding. *An experience* is an identifiable duration of human experience, and a *spiritual experience* is an experience of a spiritual reality, whether that be of God, good angels, or evil spirits. Spiritual experiences of the presence of God can occur with various degrees of immediacy (presence) and with or without sensory qualia. A focused engagement with the main aspects of human experience will prepare the way to understand how the fall impacts human experience and leaves spiritual experiences in need of discernment.

EVAN B. HOWARD'S MODEL OF HUMAN EXPERIENCE

The Operations

Howard identifies three specific operations involved in human experience: cognition, affectivity, and volition.[34] Historically, these operations often have been called the faculties of the soul or mind. For example, in *De Anima*, Aristotle delineated between nutritive, perceptual, and intellectual souls and their respective faculties, such as growth, nutrition, sensation, movement, thought, and intellect.[35] Similarly, Aquinas identified five powers of the human soul, including vegetative, sensitive, appetitive, locomotive, and intellectual powers.[36] The vegetative power pertains to the body, making the body exist (generative power), grow (augmentative power), and endure (nutritive power).[37] The sensitive power involves both the external and internal senses, namely the five bodily senses and internal perception, which includes common sense,

---

34. Howard, *Affirming the Touch*, 293.
35. Aristotle, *On the Soul*, 413a22–414a4.
36. Aquinas, *Summa Theologica* I–I, Q 78, A 1.
37. Aquinas, *Summa Theologica* I–I, Q 78, A 2.

imagination, estimative power (intuition), and memory.[38] The appetitive power is divided between natural, sensible, and intellectual appetites. The will, what Howard labels as "volitional operations," is the intellectual appetite, whereas emotion and passions (affectivity) belong to the sensible appetite.[39] Finally, Howard's cognitive operation corresponds with Aquinas's intellectual power as well as the internal senses. Overall, the three categories used by Howard, while evincing variety throughout history, seem to portray accurately the various operations at work in human experience. Even modern psychology continues to use the categories of cognition, emotion, and volition, although Howard notes that the category of volition is now studied often under the psychological categories of choice, decision making, motivation, or habit.[40]

Howard defined the operations or systems of operation of human existence as "the particular physiological or mental tendencies to evaluate, respond, and adapt to that which confronts us."[41] First, cognitive operations (the intellect) involve a "sensitivity to the structure of the environment, of that which confronts" and include such things as "inquiry, judgment, insight, deduction, comparison, [and] synthesis," including category formation and retrieval, language production and recognition, both theoretical and practical judgment, as well as verbal and spatial processing.[42] Cognition includes all that is associated with the intellect, such as reason, imagination, and memory.[43] Furthermore, a distinction can be made between epistemic and practical cognition. Epistemic cognition produces and maintains beliefs, whereas practical cognition evaluates the world, formulates plans and goals, and initiates action.[44]

Second, affective operations involve such things as emotions, feeling, action tendency, attraction, excitement, mood, sentiment, passions, and desires.[45] Instead of being sensitive to the structure of one's environ-

38. Aquinas, *Summa Theologica* I-I, Q 78, A 3.

39. Aquinas, *Summa Theologica* I-I, Q 82, A 1.

40. Howard, *Brazos Introduction*, 86n18. For recent works on cognition, emotion, and volition, see Farmer and Matlin, *Cognition*; Cornelius, *Science of Emotion*; Frith, "Psychology of Volition," 289–99.

41. Howard, *Brazos Introduction*, 84–85. Cf. Howard, *Affirming the Touch*, 139–40; Howard, *Christian Spiritual Formation*, 46–47.

42. Howard, *Affirming the Touch*, 293; Howard, *Brazos Introduction*, 85.

43. Demarest, "Human Personhood," 73; cf. Aizawa, "What Is This Cognition," 759.

44. Pollock, "Evaluative Cognition," 325.

45. Howard, *Affirming the Touch*, 81, 206, 293. Howard excludes bodily sensations such as pain and attributes such as personality traits from affectivity. See Howard,

ment, affections are sensitive to the meaning of relationships between the environment and persons, heavily incorporating physiological processes, phenomenological tone, appraisals of significance, and other such tendencies.[46] Howard uses "emotions" narrowly to mean "particular identifiable patterns of affective operations," and he uses "affectivity" broadly "to include emotions as well as other affective phenomena," such as "operations like mood, wish, desire, feeling, passion, urge, drive, intuition, hunch, wonder, and others insofar as they are used not simply to indicate mental attitudes, states, inclinations that are not affective."[47] Affective operations occur in response to the perceived significance and meaning of a situation, insofar as it addresses an individual's needs, goals, plans, or concerns.[48]

Third, volitional operations (the will), subsidiary to cognitive and affective operations, are concerned with intentionality, deliberative action, and self-control.[49] Volition moves in and through cognition and affectivity, whether involving a choice to adopt a belief, take an action, or cultivate a desire.[50] In other words, the will is not so much an independent system outside of the intellect or the affections but more of an expression of an agent's autonomy and self-determination within "the movement/inclination of cognitive or affective process insofar as initiated by the self."[51] Overall, volition is that by which an agent moves from

---

Affirming the Touch, 208.

46. Howard, *Brazos Introduction*, 85; Howard, *Affirming the Touch*, 293.

47. Howard, *Affirming the Touch*, 204; cf. 205. Howard uses the term *wish* as an example of a term that can be used or not used in an affective sense. *Wish* could refer to "mere preference" (non-affective) or "felt inclination" toward an object (affective). In other words, affections incline one toward or away from an object and act as motivations for actions. Cf. Willard, *Renovation of the Heart*, 32; Elliott, "Affections," 249. At times, Howard seems to use *emotion* and *affection* as synonyms. See Howard, *Brazos Introduction*, 85. In general, no widely accepted definitions exist for the terms *emotion*, *affection*, and *feeling*. Some scholars use them more or less as synonyms. Others make distinctions of the same kind as Howard's. For example, some scholars use *affect* to refer to nonintentional feelings such as anxiety or fatigue and *feeling* to refer to intentional feelings such as joy, hope, or fear. See Izard, "Basic Emotions," 260; Studzinski, "Feelings," 392; Doran, "Affect, Affectivity," 12; Roy, *Transcendent Experiences*, 136; Lonergan, *Method in Theology*, 30–34.

48. Howard, *Affirming the Touch*, 208.

49. Howard, *Affirming the Touch*, 293; Howard, *Brazos Introduction*, 85.

50. Howard, *Brazos Introduction*, 86.

51. Howard, *Affirming the Touch*, 316. Cf. Willard, *Renovation of the Heart*, 33; Demarest, "Human Personhood," 73; Plantinga, *Warranted Christian Belief*, 208–9. Some scholars hold that neuroscience has shown that free will is illusory. For a recent example

deliberation to decision and then action, forming the intention to act, deciding to act, and initiating and sustaining the act.[52]

Howard distinguishes between operations and systems of human experience. Systems are simply "sets of interrelated operations."[53] For example, cognitive operations come together to form the cognitive system. Furthermore, each system is interrelated. The cognitive system incorporates both affective and volitional operations. The affective system likewise incorporates cognitive and volitional operations.[54] The systems work together and cooperate. They are not three independent and separate "faculties."[55] Affect, intellect, and will always work together. As Dallas Willard explained, "There is no feeling without something being before the mind in thought and no thought without some positive or negative feeling toward what is contemplated" and no choice without "some object or concept before the mind and some feeling for or against it."[56]

Affections are always, in part, cognitive, being connected with how one judges and perceives the world and the relation of the world to one's goals and plans.[57] Likewise, cognition is always affective.[58] Simeon Zahl noted this complex relationship: "The way we receive and process ideas and whether we find them compelling is significantly affected by the affective texture and atmosphere in which we encounter them, by our personal history and temperament, by our social context, even by our mood."[59] Cognition and affectivity also impact volition. Affections

---

of this position, see Ota, "Neuroscientific Threat," 109–30. Cf. Schlosser, "Neuroscientific Study," 245–62; Zhong, "What Does Neuroscience," 287–310. For a response to this sort of argument, see Rescher, "Evidentiating Free Will," 79–106; Goetz, "Substance Dualism," 47–53. Rescher's main point is that neuroscience cannot tell one whether free will exists; it can tell one only what occurs in the brain during putatively free-will decisions. See Rescher, "Evidentiating Free Will," 90–91.

52. Zhu, "Intention and Volition," 177–80.
53. Howard, *Affirming the Touch*, 293.
54. Howard, *Affirming the Touch*, 293.
55. Howard, *Affirming the Touch*, 214, 226, 294; Parker, *Led by the Spirit*, 11.
56. Willard, *Renovation of the Heart*, 33–34. For a recent example of a neurocomputational model that shows how the brain integrates cognition, affectivity, and decision making, see Thagard, "Moral Psychology," 370–72.
57. Nussbaum, *Upheavals of Thought*, 19, 23–24, 27–31; Zahl, *Holy Spirit*, 44. Affections are also always embodied. See Luhrmann, *When God Talks Back*, 110; Maiese, "How Can Emotions," 513–31.
58. Au and Au, *Discerning Heart*, 50–51; Peterson, "Emotions," 198–200.
59. Zahl, *Holy Spirit*, 14; cf. Smith, *Desiring the Kingdom*, 71.

motivate one toward a perceived good, and one's acts are based on one's beliefs.[60]

These operations of human experience hold implications for spirituality and discernment. First, like all human experience, the experience of God has cognitive, affective, and volitional elements. The experience of God, in order to be an experience, will cohere with the operations of human experience rather than negate them.[61] Second, the process of discernment involves the operations of human experience. In order to discern, one must use one's intellect, affections, and will; insofar as these operations are fallen or unbalanced, one's ability to discern will be hindered.[62]

The Stages

According to Howard, all of these operations occur within the cycle of human experience, the cognitive process, and he identifies the six stages of this process as Being Aware, Experiencing, Understanding, Judging, Deciding and Acting, and Worldview Adjusting.[63] He developed these stages based on the works of Bernard Lonergan, Donald Gelpi, and cognitive psychology. For Lonergan, cognition passes through experiencing, understanding, judging, and deciding.[64] By placing experiencing as the first stage of cognition, Lonergan meant that experience begins with bare consciousness before proceeding on toward an understanding of its unity and relatedness, a judgment of its truth and reality, and finally responsible action.[65] For Gelpi, experiences similarly involve experiencing, which is sensation and perception, then imagining, thinking, judging, and finally deciding.[66] Modern cognitive psychology, as Howard notes, similarly structures human experience around the stages of perception, memory,

60. Moses, "'Keeping the Heart,'" 615, 625; Izard, "Basic Emotions," 260. Recent studies in neuroscience show that beliefs affect intention and motivation, as indicated by a change in preconscious motor preparations for decisions. See Rigoni et al., "Inducing Disbelief," 613–18.

61. Mouroux, *Christian Experience*, 15–17; Muto, "Formative Spirituality," 8–16; Wolff, *Discernment*, 9–10.

62. Wolff, *Discernment*, 4–7; Rakoczy, "Structures of Discernment Processes," 53–54; Liebert, *Way of Discernment*, 41–144; Howard, *Affirming the Touch*, 324.

63. Howard, *Affirming the Touch*, 295–97.

64. Lonergan, *Method in Theology*, 3–25. See also Lonergan, *Insight*, 271–347.

65. Lonergan, *Method in Theology*, 12–15.

66. Gelpi, *Turn to Experience*, 126–30.

inquiry and categorization, language, problem solving, and decision making.[67] What each of these schemes shows is that the evaluative stages of the cognitive process add meaning to sensations and perceptions.[68] The process of experience is one in which an act of evaluation emerges over the progression of the stages of experience, assigning structure and meaning to the data from stimuli, sensations, and perceptions. A look at each of the six stages of the cognitive process in Howard's model will show how this act of evaluation is the case.

First, the stage of Being Aware consists of bare consciousness and initial awareness. Awareness can vary in range (open to restricted), intensity (dull to alert), energy (relaxed to tense), and level (conscious to unconscious).[69] Consciousness is "the raw material upon which all of human experience arises." Second, Experiencing consists of "stimulus, sensation, perception, and initial memory processing."[70] Contrasted with Being Aware, Experiencing is more active, involving "selection, pattern recognition, evaluation and more."[71] At this stage, sensory experience is structured into cognitive perceptions, memories, and images, and the affective identification of elements of concern.[72] Third, Understanding pertains to the various types of thinking, conceptual processing, language processing, general knowledge, and the appraisal and regulation of emotion.[73] Using hypothesis, inquiry, and insight, this stage answers the question "What is the case?"[74]

Fourth, Judging moves from asking "What is the case?" to "Is it really the case?" relying heavily on deduction and induction.[75] Judging

---

67. Howard, *Brazos Introduction*, 87. See Farmer and Matlin, *Cognition*, v–xiv. Howard made the point that these six stages commonly are identifiable in the standard textbooks of cognitive psychology by looking at their table of contents. Looking at the Contents of Farmer and Matlin's *Cognition*, one indeed can see a general arc that passes through the stages outlined by Howard, beginning with perception and progressing through memory, language, problem solving, and decision making.

68. Howard, *Affirming the Touch*, 258–59. Cf. Liebert, "Supervisions as Widening," 128–29, 135.

69. Howard, *Affirming the Touch*, 295; Howard, *Brazos Introduction*, 87–88.

70. Howard, *Affirming the Touch*, 296.

71. Howard, *Affirming the Touch*, 296.

72. Howard, *Brazos Introduction*, 88–89.

73. Howard, *Affirming the Touch*, 296.

74. Howard, *Brazos Introduction*, 89.

75. Howard, *Affirming the Touch*, 296–97. Howard places abduction mostly in Understanding.

incorporates both intellect and affect within the verification and demonstration of the truth and reality of the meaning of an experience.[76] Fifth, Deciding and Acting is the stage of decision making, in which one entrusts oneself to the previous judgment in both belief formation and action, moving from deliberation to decision to action.[77] Sixth, Worldview Adjusting, or Integrating, involves taking responsibility for an area of life, shaping one's character of consciousness in relation to a body of knowledge, habits, and sociohistorical conditioning.[78] Paradigm shifts, changes of horizon, conversions, revolutions, and worldview adjustments all happen at this stage. Once integration occurs, new possibilities of evaluation and action are made possible, and the overall shape of Being Aware is made new.[79]

The six stages of the cognitive process indicate that, first, experience is active.[80] Second, experience is, in part, preconditioned. At the stage of Being Aware, reality is experienced as given and prior to oneself, and one's activity within each stage of the cognitive process will grow out of one's historical, cultural, communal, and linguistic context.[81] Third, experience is an interpreted reality, in which one filters the raw data of consciousness through one's pre-understanding, actively shaping and forming it and making sense of it through conceptual thought, language, and other cognitive activities.[82] Finally, while one progresses through the various stages of the cognitive process in order to achieve truth about reality and to live in response to that truth, the cognitive process will not lead reliably to truth insofar as it contains flaws within its stages or one holds to a faulty pre-understanding of an experience.

---

76. Howard, *Brazos Introduction*, 90.

77. Howard, *Affirming the Touch*, 297; Howard, *Brazos Introduction*, 90.

78. Howard, *Affirming the Touch*, 297.

79. Howard, *Brazos Introduction*, 90–91. For paradigm shifts, see Kuhn, *Structure of Scientific Revolutions*. For changes of horizon, see Thiselton, *Two Horizons*.

80. Mouroux, *Christian Experience*, 11, 16; Lane, *Experience of God*, 5.

81. Lane, *Experience of God*, 6–8; Johnson, *Religious Experience*, 54.

82. Johnson, *Religious Experience*, 49; Moser, *Understanding Religious Experience*, 46, 50–51. Moser made the helpful distinction between *de re* and *de dicto* elements of experience. The *de re* element refers to whatever is presented directly to one in experience, such as redness in the experience of redness. The *de dicto* element is the active judgment and concept formation in response to the *de re* element, which can misrepresent the *de re* element.

The Relationships

The operations and stages of experience would be inactive if it were not for the web of relationships in which experience takes place. Explaining this web of relationships, Howard wrote, "Our thoughts, feelings, [and] choices only arise within the context of a complex network of 'others' to whom we relate."[83] These "others" are the perceived causes of one's experience and the content of one's experience. These relationships are perceived at the stage of Experiencing. At the stages of Understanding and Judging, they are the material out of which one forms thoughts, feelings, and decisions, and at the stage of Deciding and Acting, they are that upon which one acts.[84] These "others" that form the web of relationships within experience include nature, oneself, other humans, spiritual realities, and specifically God. Concerning nature, human experience is embodied and ecological. Concerning oneself, one's thoughts, feelings, and choices can become the objects of one's thoughts, feelings, and choices. Concerning other humans, human experience is interpersonal, social, political, and economic. Concerning spiritual realities, humans can relate experientially to angels and demons, and even the one true God.[85]

The Depths

Howard uses the term *depth* to refer to "levels of significance within human experience or degrees of influence on the whole of human experience."[86] He identifies four levels of depth, each pertaining to cognition, affectivity, and volition. At the first level are shallow thoughts, simple feelings, and simple choices and actions. The second level of depth occurs when thoughts, feelings, and choices become patterns and habits, whether patterns of thinking and cognitive beliefs, feeling tendencies, or habitual choices and actions. At the third level, Howard places one's worldview that structures one's cognitive patterns, one's nuclear concerns that drive one's feeling tendencies and emotional patterns, and one's lifestyles. The fourth level is the center of the person at which cognition, affectivity,

---

83. Howard, *Affirming the Touch*, 299.
84. Howard, *Affirming the Touch*, 299; Howard, *Brazos Introduction*, 92–93.
85. Howard, *Affirming the Touch*, 300–301; Howard, *Brazos Introduction*, 93–94. Howard also noted that experience can be a corporate reality, not just an individual reality.
86. Howard, *Brazos Introduction*, 100.

and volition are joined entirely and inseparable.[87] The importance of this scheme is to show that, first, a change within a deeper level of experience will hold a greater impact on one's experience than a change at a shallower level.[88] For example, a change in one's worldview will impact one's patterns of thought and one's shallow thoughts. Second, the depth of experience makes experience irreducibly complex.[89]

A Concise Summary of Howard's Model

Evan B. Howard views human experience as the integrated occurrence of cognitive, affective, and volitional operations. These operations ordinarily occur within and progress through the stages of the cognitive process—Being Aware, Experiencing, Understanding, Judging, Deciding and Acting, and Worldview Adjusting (Integrating). These operations and this cognitive process occur only within a web of relationships that is constituted by a set of "others" that are the objects and perceived causes of one's experiences, including nature, oneself, other humans, and spiritual realities, including God. Finally, human experience contains various depths or levels of significance: first, simple thoughts, feelings, and actions; second, patterns and habits of thoughts, feelings, and actions; third, the worldviews, nuclear concerns, and lifestyles that structure and drive such patterns and habits; and fourth, the center of personhood at which cognition, affectivity, and volition are united.

FALLEN HUMAN EXPERIENCE

When humanity fell into sin, human experience became corrupt in its operations, process, and relationships at every level of depth. Scripture uses a myriad of symbols to depict this point, as Heather Thompson noted: "Humanity is corrupt (Genesis 6:11–13; Jeremiah 17:9), stained or blemished (Psalm 51:2,7), lost or strayed (Psalm 119:176; Isaiah 53:6), burdened or heavy-laden (Matthew 11:28), hard-hearted (Ezekiel 3:7; Mark 3:5), captive or servile (Romans 7:23; Galatians 5:1), dead

---

87. Howard, *Brazos Introduction*, 100–102. Concerning levels of affectivity, see Wolff, *Discernment*, 38–41; Benner, *Desiring God's Will*, 107.

88. Howard, *Christian Spiritual Formation*, 52–53.

89. Poling and Miller, *Practical Theology of Ministry*, 67.

(Ephesians 2:1,5; Colossians 2:13), and blind (Luke 4:18; John 9:40–1)."[90] While Christ has brought new life and transformation to believers, believers continue to live in the already-not-yet tension of salvation. Believers are able to overcome sin by the power of the Holy Spirit, but they still continue to struggle with sin and their fallen human nature until they are glorified in eternity.[91] Therefore, in order to understand why discernment is necessary for believers, one must understand the ways in which human experience, and thus the experience of God and spiritual realities, has been impacted by sin.

The Depths

While sin can be understood as individual infractions against the divine will, sin also "involves a disorganization of humankind's exquisite complexity, with functions, instincts and powers given to uncontrollable divergence."[92] Explaining the fallen state of human experience, Howard wrote, "Human experience is twisted through covenant unfaithfulness and sin, plagued by threatening social forces, and subject to evil spiritual powers."[93] This matrix of corruption and fallenness in which human experience now exists can be summarized by reference to the flesh, the world, and the devil.[94]

At times, the flesh (σαρξ)—particularly within the context of sin and corruption in Paul's writings—refers to the impact of sin upon one's embodied existence and the various aspects of human existence that are fallen and set against the things of God (Rom 7:18, 25; 8:3–8; Gal 5:16–24).[95] When human beings fell into sin, all the various aspects of human experience became corrupt and twisted at the various depths of human experience. Sin, then, is not solely isolated actions, feelings, and thoughts or patterns of such but also "godless worldviews," "a deep core of selfishness," and "a lifestyle lived apart from God."[96] Ultimately, sin

---

90. Thompson, "Fallen Image," 71.

91. Quarles, "New Creation," 98; Skaug and Morgan, "Tensions in Spirituality," 107–8. Cf. Laato, "*Simul Iustus et Peccator*," 735–66; Chang, "Christian Life," 257–80.

92. Blocher, *Original Sin*, 90; cf. Gathercole, "'Sins' in Paul," 143–61.

93. Howard, *Brazos Introduction*, 154.

94. Morgan and McLendon, "Trajectory of Spirituality," 40; Howard, *Brazos Introduction*, 154; cf. Lovelace, *Dynamics of Spiritual Life*, 140.

95. Howard, *Brazos Introduction*, 160. Cf. Bauer et al., *Greek-English Lexicon*, 915.

96. Howard, *Brazos Introduction*, 161.

reaches to the deepest parts of human nature and the very core of human experience.[97]

The Operations

Scripture describes fallen humanity, among other things, as being in a state of foolishness, rebellion, disobedience, hardness of heart, darkness and death, slavery to sin, error, and ignorance (Rom 1:18–24; 2:5; 6:23; 7:5; 8:7; Eph 2:1–5; 4:18; Col 1:21).[98] All such descriptions, when taken together, show that sin and fallen human nature—insofar as believers are not yet perfect—twist and corrupt human cognition, affectivity, and volition.[99] Human cognition is blinded by sin, unable to tell reliably right from wrong, good from bad, and beauty from ugliness. This cognitive blindness limits the human ability to know God and to identify his presence and activity.[100] This blindness is a lack of knowledge, the possession of flawed knowledge, as well as a willed suppression of knowledge (Rom 1:20).[101] Rather than being formed by God and the things of God, the intellect is formed by bias, prejudice, and self-centeredness. Knowledge becomes about self-preservation, and spiritual truths appear foolish (1 Cor 2:14; 2 Cor 4:4; Eph 4:17–18).[102] Sin ultimately leads to a cognitive idolatry in which the intellect grows in independence from God's authority to develop control, self-importance, and self-gratification.[103]

Similar to cognition, human affectivity is subject to "biases, gaps, and lacunas," faultily oriented around the self rather than God.[104] Fallen affectivity is beset with a litany of faults, including pride, lust, egoism,

---

97. Lovelace, *Dynamics of Spiritual Life*, 88.

98. Berkouwer, *Man*, 143–44; Quarles, "New Creation," 80–82.

99. Plantinga, *Not the Way*, 31. Cf. Plantinga, *Warranted Christian Belief*, 207; Berkouwer, *Man*, 132, 141; Skaug and Morgan, "Tensions in Spirituality," 123.

100. Plantinga, *Warranted Christian Belief*, 207, 216–17; Lovelace, *Dynamics of Spiritual Life*, 79–80.

101. Sutanto, "Questioning Bonaventure's Augustinianism," 415.

102. Howard, *Brazos Introduction*, 160; Demarest, "Human Personhood," 74.

103. Moser, *Elusive God*, 101–105; Willard, *Renovation of the Heart*, 54. Cf. Smith, "Perception," 592; Vandici, "Reading the Rules," 180, 190. Vandici makes the point that the degeneration of the imagination into a fascination with worldly things or with fearful ruminations about the future is a byproduct of the noetic effects of sin. Additionally, this description of the corrupt intellect indicates further that the intellect is influenced by the will and one's desires. See Johnston, "Authority of Affect," 181.

104. Howard, *Affirming the Touch*, 211; Howard, *Brazos Introduction*, 160.

arrogance, envy, cowardice, fear, anxiety, insecurity, and greed (Jas 3:16; 4:1–2; 2 Tim 3:2–6).[105] In general, love is misordered away from God and the eternal toward self and the temporal.[106] One cares about self-preservation more than the glory of God, and what one cares about impacts one's emotions, as emotions deal with the perceived significance of a situation. Emotions, then, become structured either around self-centered ideals or around the deceptive or misperceived significance of situations. Being interpretive, emotions can be wrong, especially when considering the way in which one's fallen intellect impacts one's perception of a situation.[107] Overall, one's desires lead away from God, influenced by selfish loves, cares, and emotions. Even self-deception can occur when one becomes misguided by one's disordered and unregulated desires, trusting something to be from God only because it aligns with one's desire.[108]

Finally, volition (the will) also is corrupted by sin and, as a result, is predisposed to sinful intentions, decisions, and actions. Unregenerate human beings have a will that is in complete bondage to sin (Rom 6:16–17).[109] While believers have been released from this slavery, their will continues to be drawn, in part, toward sin. The intentions, decisions, and actions of believers are not always and continually aligned with the will of God. Fallen human beings do not naturally intend the good, as Dallas Willard explained:

> The drive toward good, which is naturally implanted in the human will by its Creator, is splintered, corrupted, and eventually turned against itself as a result of practical self-deification and all that accompanies it. . . . Manipulation, deception, seduction, and malice replace transparency, sincerity, and goodwill, as exaltation of self replaces submission and service to God.[110]

---

105. Mouroux, *Christian Experience*, 252–54; Demarest, "Human Personhood," 74; Willard, *Renovation of the Heart*, 121–22; Elliott, "Affections," 248–49; J. White, "Personality of Sin," 85–92.

106. Mouroux, *Christian Experience*, 260; Plantinga, *Warranted Christian Belief*, 205–208; Sumner, "Gravity of Sin," 266–73.

107. Roberts, *Spiritual Emotions*, 11; Studzinski, "Feelings," 394; Luhrmann, *When God Talks Back*, 105.

108. Liebert, *Way of Discernment*, 25; Smith, *Voice of Jesus*, 19–20; McDonough, "Fall and Fallenness," 189; Lane, "Lust," 31.

109. Blocher, *Original Sin*, 90; Demarest, "Human Personhood," 74.

110. Willard, *Renovation of the Heart*, 145–46. Cf. Martínez, *Discernimiento personal y communitario*, 30–31; Vroom, "Sin and Decent Society," 475.

The will oftentimes simply follows the greatest desire of one's corrupt affectivity, ignoring everything that does not relate to self-preservation.[111]

In relation to spiritual discernment, due to the continued, partial corruption of their cognitive, affective, and volitional operations, believers will not always know the truth of their spiritual experiences, perceive the situational significance of them, or choose and act upon the good within them. In other words, the operations of human experience—in their fallen state—cannot always be trusted to clarify and perceive accurately the nature and origins of one's spiritual experiences, due to flawed beliefs, errant emotions and desires, or bad decisions and actions, necessitating discernment.

The Stages

When focusing on the impact of sin upon the operations of human experience, one already can begin to understand the necessity of discernment. Nevertheless, when one follows the course of these operations through each stage of the cognitive process, seeing how each stage is impacted by sin and the fallen operations, the necessity of discernment becomes even more evident. At the stages of Being Aware and Experiencing, sin keeps one from being open to deeper and wider levels of awareness, making one comfortable with a shallow range of experience.[112] Beyond sin, one's cultural and personal context as well as the defects within the operations of one's experience precondition how one receives or rejects stimuli, possibly skewing the cognitive process from its very beginning.[113]

At the stage of Understanding, sin creates dishonest inquiry and poorly considered insights, keeping one trapped in fear and wrong motives.[114] Furthermore, one interprets and assigns meaning to an experience based on the background beliefs that one already holds. Therefore, prior values, assumptions, and dispositions all impact how an experience is understood.[115] Due to flaws in one's thinking, one can misunderstand an experience. Dallas Willard explained the relationship between thought and the meaning assigned to an experience: "Ideas and images are also a

---

111. Willard, *Renovation of the Heart*, 147; Azadegan, "Divine Hiddenness," 82–83.
112. Howard, *Brazos Introduction*, 160.
113. Howard, *Affirming the Touch*, 207. Cf. Salamon, "Cognitive Validity," 10–11.
114. Howard, *Brazos Introduction*, 161.
115. Davis, *Evidential Force*, 27; Netland, *Religious Experience*, 22, 50.

primary stronghold of evil in the human self and in society. They determine how we 'take' the things and events of ordinary life. They control the meanings we assign to what we deal with, and they can even blind us to what lies plainly before us."[116] Even more than experiences of the physical world, emotional, moral, and especially spiritual experiences all require interpretation.[117] Accurately understanding a spiritual experience requires, to a great extent, that one hold to the doctrines and beliefs that supply the horizon in which to understand the experience, that one is not being misled by the defects in one's cognitive, affective, and volitional operations, and that the stages of Being Aware and Experiencing are deep and wide enough to receive and shape adequately the experience.[118] Due to such complexity, the misunderstanding of a spiritual experience is a real possibility.

Similar issues are apparent at the stages of Judging, Deciding and Acting, and Worldview Adjusting. At the stage of Judging, the impact of sin appears when one is overly stubborn, unwilling to change one's mind, afraid to admit one's mistake, or when one inadequately grounds judgments in little to no criteria of verity.[119] Misjudgment basically occurs from such things as prejudice, haste and a lack of deliberation, illusion, vanity, peer-pressure, and unfounded conclusions.[120] If one's judgment of an experience is wrong, then one's decisions, actions, and worldview adjusting also will be flawed. Furthermore, the stage of Deciding and Acting is fraught with foolish decisions, a lack of discernment, selfishness, and unethical concerns. Additionally, the stage of Worldview Adjusting, due to sin, moves away from the incorporation of God or even the incorporation of all of one's beliefs into a coherent whole, inadequately setting the preconditions upon which Being Aware and Experiencing work.[121]

Altogether, while the cognitive process is meant to lead one to a correct understanding and judgment of an experience as well as wise decisions and worldviews based on those experiences, the cognitive process does not always lead to truth in its fallen state. Each stage of the cognitive process holds its own flaws, and each successive stage retains and

---

116. Willard, *Renovation of the Heart*, 99.
117. Netland, *Religious Experience*, 50.
118. Lane, *Experience of God*, 21–22.
119. Howard, *Brazos Introduction*, 161.
120. Waaijman, *Spirituality*, 539; Netland, *Religious Experience*, 22; Dubay, *Authenticity*, 26, 35–39.
121. Howard, *Brazos Introduction*, 161.

preserves "the defects, limitations, [and] distortions present on preceding levels."[122] Entire stages of the cognitive process even can be skipped. For example, some can have a tendency of skipping from Experiencing straight to Judging or even Deciding and Acting.[123] Overall, sin and the unbalanced and twisted operations of human experience impact the cognitive process, and the entire process becomes unreliable, especially in relation to nonphysical or spiritual experiences. Therefore, if the stages of the cognitive process are unreliable in their fallen states, then discernment is absolutely necessary as a guide and aid to Understanding, Judging, and Deciding and Acting.

The Relationships

The operations and stages of human experience indicate in and of themselves that the discernment of spiritual experiences is necessary. Nevertheless, the case for such necessity is strengthened further by understanding the impact of sin upon the relationships of human experience. Furthermore, when discussing discernment within the context of the authenticity of an experience of God, understanding the impact of sin upon the web of relationships that make up human experience will show why the nature and origins of a spiritual experience are often ambiguous and obscure.

The results of sin are seen through the various relationships of human experience in such things as "social bigotry, ecological neglect and abuse, personal woundedness, and spiritual rebelling."[124] Sin is an alienating force, separating humans from God, each other, the earth, and even themselves.[125] This alienation from nature manifests itself in the domination and abuse of the world by human beings.[126] Alienation from self is seen in neuroses and psychoses as well as one's general lack of self-understanding.[127] Human beings simply do not understand all of their emotions, desires, intentions, and so forth. Alienation from others entails broken relationships, both at the individual and communal levels,

---

122. Rulla, "Discernment of Spirits," 553.
123. Howard, *Brazos Introduction*, 161.
124. Howard, *Brazos Introduction*, 100.
125. Plantinga, *Not the Way*, 29–30.
126. Howard, *Affirming the Touch*, 302; Thompson, "Fallen Image," 66.
127. Howard, *Brazos Introduction*, 161.

involving wars, economic divisions, family separations, manipulation, abuse, selfish competition, rejection, misunderstanding, and divisions of all sorts.[128] Sin also alienates one from God, moving one away from God and moving one to replace God with other things.[129] This sinful separation from God is a chief cause of the misinterpretation of divine experience, involving a refusal to accept God's love and an obfuscation of the perception of exactly what one is refusing.[130]

Complicating the situation all the more is the human relationship to the world and the devil. By world, I narrowly mean "the total system of corporate flesh operating on earth under satanic control, with all its incentives of reward and restraints of loss, its characteristic patterns of behavior, and its anti-Christian structures, methods, goals and ideologies."[131] In this sense, the world is a sort of suprahuman entity that is at odds with God. These evil systems and structures "warp our thinking and will in unconscious ways and make it difficult to tell good from bad."[132] As Howard explained, "Directly by attack, the thoughts, feelings, actions, decisions, relationships, and such that flow from and lead to God are minimized, persecuted, or prevented from expression. . . . Indirectly, by attraction, people are drawn further and further from expressing the heart of God, from living out their co-dominionship of reconciliation on the earth."[133]

Acting within the world, the devil disguises himself as an angel of light to deceive believers into perceiving him as good (2 Cor 11:14). Of course, all that is said about the devil also applies to evil spirits. Due to alienation from spiritual realities, spiritual warfare and potential spiritual deception always is present.[134] The strategies of the devil, to draw people away from God, include such things as temptation, deception, accusation, possession, physical attack, and oppression (Matt 9:32–33;

---

128. Howard, *Brazos Introduction*, 161; Roberts, "Toward a Theological Anthropology," 144; Willard, *Renovation of the Heart*, 180–81; Plantinga, *Warranted Christian Belief*, 214.

129. McGrath, "Theology and Experience," 69–73; Howard, *Brazos Introduction*, 160–61; Porter, "Gradual Nature of Sanctification," 473–74.

130. Fransen, "Divine Revelation," 33.

131. Lovelace, *Dynamics of Spiritual Life*, 94. Cf. Porter, "Gradual Nature of Sanctification," 472; McRorie, "Moral Reasoning," 227.

132. Larkin, *Silent Presence*, 8.

133. Howard, *Brazos Introduction*, 167.

134. Howard, *Brazos Introduction*, 161.

17:14-18; Luke 4:1-13; 8:26-33; Rev 12:9-10).[135] The devil also works to corrupt further the operations of human experience through deception and lies (cognition), anger and bitterness (affectivity), and temptation (volition).[136] Overall, the voice of the Spirit is not the only voice that one hears, and so discernment is necessary to separate the voice of God from those of the world and the devil.[137]

CONCLUSION: ON THE NECESSITY OF SPIRITUAL DISCERNMENT

To conclude, based on the fallen nature of human experience that believers continue in part to struggle against as well as the realities of the world and the devil, spiritual experiences are often ambiguous, with obscure origins, making the practice of spiritual discernment absolutely necessary. Due to the impact of sin upon the operations, stages, relationships, and depths of human experience, believers can be left unsure about the authenticity of a possible experience of God. The true meaning of the experience evades them, and they are left unable to identify the actual origin of the experience, whether it be God, the world, the devil, or their imagination.[138]

All experiences are to a certain extent ambiguous, involving the interpretation of uncertain or unclear significances within a fallen interpretive process. Simply put, the meaning one ascribes to an experience can vary from the true meaning held within that experience.[139] The

---

135. Lovelace, *Dynamics of Spiritual Life*, 137-40.
136. Howard, *Brazos Introduction*, 172.
137. Malatesta, *Discernment of Spirits*, 9; Smith, "Discernment," 404-5.
138. Dubay, *Authenticity*, 81.
139. Moser, *Understanding Religious Experience*, 50-51. Epistemologists might be wondering how this description of the ambiguity of spiritual experience correlates with Swinburne's principle of credulity. Swinburne stated, "It is a principle of rationality that (in the absence of special considerations) if it seems (epistemically) to a subject that x is present (and has some characteristic), then probably x is present (and has that characteristic); what one seems to perceive is probably so." See Swinburne, *Existence of God*, 303. The special conditions that Swinburne noted include (1) conditions that raise the probability of unreliability (such as drugs), (2) circumstances in which similar claims in the past have proven false, (3) background evidence that makes such perception highly improbable, or (4) high probability that something else caused the perception. See Swinburne, *Existence of God*, 310-14. Sin, fallen human nature, and so on would count as the first type of special condition. The third and fourth types of special conditions correspond to criteria of authenticity, which will be treated in the next chapter. In

possibility of such a misunderstanding is simply a byproduct of the necessity to interpret all experience while being a fallen human being. Yet, spiritual experiences are particularly ambiguous. The unique difficulty that besets the interpretation of spiritual experiences is the seeming inability to verify the meaning of an experience, given the invisibility or lack of availability of the purported spiritual cause of the experience.[140] Additionally, the world and the devil work against one's relationship with God, causing greater confusion and deception concerning the meaning of a spiritual experience.

On the one hand, if believers blindly trust in their fallen human nature to interpret and judge a purported experience of God, the understanding of that experience will lie open to all of the defects and corruptions of fallen human experience as well as possible misdirection from the world and the devil.[141] On the other hand, individuals who approach spiritual experiences with great skepticism still must deal somehow with the ambiguity and obscure origins of the experience. Put differently, one's response to this problem should be neither naive trust nor skeptical despair. Naive trust ignores the continued realities of sin and fallenness within the lives of believers, whereas skeptical despair neglects the grace of God in sanctification and the aid of discernment. Instead, one's response to the problem of the ambiguity and obscurity of spiritual experiences and their origins should be a recognition of the necessity and efficacy of spiritual discernment.[142]

The practice of spiritual discernment identifies the ways in which the nature and various origins of spiritual experiences are identified. As a process of knowing, spiritual discernment is aimed at gaining truth and understanding by guiding the operations and stages of human experience

---

other words, given the special conditions of sin and fallen human experience, spiritual experiences contain a probability of unreliability, necessitating further inquiry into criteria of authenticity that help determine the probability or improbability of their authenticity.

140. Johnson, *Religious Experience*, 53. John of the Cross made a similar argument. See John of the Cross, *Ascent of Mount Carmel*, 3.8.3. Cf. Larkin, *Silent Presence*, 7–8.

141. Dubay, *Authenticity*, 90–92, 99; Plantinga, *Warranted Christian Belief*, 210.

142. Howard, *Affirming the Touch*, 311; Dubay, *Authenticity*, 94; Barry, *Spiritual Direction*, 34. The process of discernment, as an act of knowing, will be impacted also by one's fallen human experience. Thus, certainty must give way to fallibilism, even within spiritual discernment. Nonetheless, as will be seen in the following chapter, spiritual discernment is not a process relying solely on subjectivity; it also relies heavily on objective criteria that mitigate the impact of sin and fallenness on the process of discernment.

so that one can understand and judge rightly the value of one's experiences as well as identify their origins, whether good or bad. In other words, spiritual discernment acts as a guide to one's cognitive process and the operations of human experience to aid one in overcoming the limitations of one's fallen human experience. As will be seen in the following chapter, one way in which spiritual discernment guides one's Understanding, Judging, and Deciding and Acting is by offering up specific subjective and objective criteria by which one may discern the authenticity of a spiritual experience.

2

Criteria of Spiritual Discernment
On the Necessity of Doctrine for Discernment

THROUGHOUT HISTORY, CHRISTIAN THEOLOGIANS have acknowledged the necessity of spiritual discernment. As such, the corpus of writings on spiritual discernment is vast. Rather than presenting one unified tradition, this corpus acts more like "an ongoing dialogue throughout history between various emphases concerning the means by which that which is significantly related to God is to be identified."[1] The various emphases within spiritual discernment literature often correspond to different kinds or elements of discernment. For example, the various kinds of spiritual discernment include the discernment of doctrine, prophecy, the movements of spirits, mystical experiences, internal impulses and affections, God's will, the reflection of God in creation, and the principalities and powers of the world, to name only a few.[2] Furthermore, the multiple elements of discernment include its prerequisites, focuses, functions, sources, structures, processes, criteria, contexts, and goals, among other things.[3]

Consistent within all forms of spiritual discernment, though, is the need for criteria by which one judges the authenticity of one's object of

---

1. Howard, *Affirming the Touch*, 19.

2. Rakoczy, "Structures of Discernment Processes," 6–7; Toner, *Spirit of Light*, 11; Wink, *Engaging the Powers*. See also Houdek, *Guided by the Spirit*, 114; Challies, *Discipline*, 61; Anderson, *All That's Good*; Waaijman, *Spirituality*, 499.

3. Rakoczy, "Structures of Discernment Processes," 39–184; Howard, *Brazos Introduction*, 382–84.

inquiry. Criteria of spiritual discernment can be defined as "conditions that, when met, serve to signify that something is (or is not) of God" by identifying "the real tendencies of the character or work of God which can be recognized with consistency in human experience."[4] Criteria cannot be used reliably in absentia of the necessary prerequisites of discernment, such as humility, prayer, community, time spent in reflection, honesty, and self-discipline.[5] In other words, criteria are only one part of a comprehensive understanding of spiritual discernment. Nonetheless, every kind of spiritual discernment is "a process of critical clarification" that "requires criteria that attempt to perform the role of making such awareness available."[6] Concerning the authenticity of spiritual experiences, criteria—whether doctrinal, ethical, or psychological—are used in order to clarify both the origins and *telos* of such experiences and to understand better the meaning and direction of spiritual experiences.[7]

The main goal of this chapter is to show the necessity of doctrinal criteria for discerning authentic spiritual experiences by surveying selected historical and contemporary works on spiritual discernment and by analyzing and synthesizing their conclusions concerning the criteria used in spiritual discernment. In doing so, I aim to support the legitimacy and necessity of using doctrine as a criterion of discernment by revealing the crucial role that doctrine has played within writings on spiritual discernment and by showing how criteria often have related to the *telos* of Christian spirituality. Through this survey and analysis, four doctrinal criteria in particular will stand out as being attested frequently and consistently within discernment literature—namely Scripture, Christ, the Holy Spirit, and sanctification.[8] Based on the findings from the survey, I will correlate these four criteria with the image of God to justify the use of the image of God as a criterion of spiritual discernment by showing how it inheres within and grows out of the four criteria. This justification

---

4. Howard, *Brazos Introduction*, 391–92; Howard, *Affirming the Touch*, 356.

5. Barry, "Theology of Discernment," 139.

6. Libanio, *Spiritual Discernment and Politics*, 121.

7. Gelpi, *Charism and Sacrament*, 91; Houdek, *Guided by the Spirit*, 115; cf. Rakoczy, "Structures of Discernment Processes," 19; Farnham et al., *Listening Hearts*, 23.

8. At first, to say that the Holy Spirit is a criterion of an authentic spiritual experience might seem redundant, as if one is stating that the Holy Spirit is a criterion of an experience of the Holy Spirit. Yet, in saying that the Holy Spirit has been used as a criterion of authentic spiritual experience, I mean theologians have looked to the nature and work of the Holy Spirit, especially within redemption and the fruit of the Holy Spirit, to elucidate what authentic spiritual experiences will consist of and lead toward.

will set the context for chapter 3, which will define the image of God and show the unique and important contribution to spiritual discernment the criterion of the image of God can make. Before concluding the chapter, I will respond to one possible objection to the use of doctrine as a criterion of spiritual discernment.

A HISTORY OF SPIRITUAL DISCERNMENT AND CRITERIA

The Old and New Testaments

The terms *discernment of spirits* and *spiritual discernment* do not appear in the Old Testament. Nonetheless, instances of spiritual discernment are seen during times of choice, such as when Abraham listened to the voice of God and left Haran (Gen 12:1–4) or when Elisha decided to follow Elijah after Elijah threw his cloak on Elisha (1 Kgs 19:19–21). In such choices, individuals took a step of faith into the unknown, making a "discriminating judgment" and "a discernment" of the will or voice of God.[9] Furthermore, the influence of good and evil spirits is also evident in numerous places in the Old Testament, revealing the need for discernment and the possibility of deception and misleading. In 1 Samuel, an evil spirit from the Lord came upon Saul and influenced his mood and behavior (16:14–23; 18:10–11; 19:9–10), and in Numbers, the Spirit of the Lord rested upon the seventy elders so that they prophesied (11:25). These examples are just two of many passages in which the Old Testament indicates that the spiritual world was active within the experiences of human beings.[10]

The most prevalent type of discernment in the Old Testament deals with true and false prophets and prophecy. False prophets were an accepted reality in the Old Testament. These individuals often clashed with legitimate prophets such as Elijah, Isaiah, Micah, and Jeremiah.[11] Interestingly, Ezekiel described such false prophets as prophesying from their own "heart" (לֵב), following "after their own spirit," and seeing "nothing" (13:2–3). The לֵב of a human is his or her inner self, including the mind

---

9. Malatesta, *Discernment of Spirits*, 17–18.

10. Malatesta, *Discernment of Spirits*, 19–20. See also Judg 3:10; 6:34; 9:23; 14:6; 15:14; 1 Sam 16:13; 1 Kgs 19:7; 22:19–23; Isa 19:14; 29:10.

11. McNamara, "Discernment Criteria," 6. See also 1 Kgs 18:20–40; 22:13–28; Mic 2:11; 3:5–12; Jer 28; 29:8–9, 21–23, 29–32.

(or intellect), affections, and will.[12] These false prophets saw false visions and divinations and yet waited expectantly for their prophecies to be fulfilled (Ezek 13:6). The implication is that these false prophets, along with those who are led to prophesy by a deceitful or evil spirit, lacked spiritual discernment.[13] The source of their visions and divinations was not God but was either evil spirits or their own inner self.

Criteria for discerning between true and false prophets are given in multiple passages in the Old Testament. In Deut 13:1-3, false prophets are identified by their endorsement of idolatry. Even if their prophecies are accompanied by signs, wonders, and the eventual coming to pass of whatever was prophesied, all prophets are false who promote the worship of false gods. This criterion is a doctrinal criterion, implying that the prophet must teach that which is faithful to Israelite religion. Furthermore, if a prophet's prophecy does not come to pass, then that prophet has not spoken an authentic word from the Lord (Deut 18:22).

Jeremiah made the general point that all who practice oppression, falsehood, and evil do not know God (Jer 4:22; 9:2-5). The Lord, on the other hand, acts with love, justice, and righteousness (Jer 9:22-23).[14] This moral criterion is reiterated in Jer 23:11, 14. Going further, Jeremiah noted that false prophets are identified by how they do not turn people away from evil (23:14b, 17, 22)—declaring peace instead of God's judgment over sin (28:8-9)—and by how their message is not from God (23:16, 18, 21, 22), for they never have stood in "the council of the Lord" (Jer 23:18, 22).[15] Overall, the prophet's orthodoxy and morality as well as the nature and content of the prophet's message—whether it leads to repentance or complacency— are signs by which one can tell whether the prophet is receptive to God's will and word or not.[16] Michael Buckley succinctly summarized these Old Testament criteria: "Prophets were to be judged by their orthodoxy, the fulfillment of their prophecy, the contents of their prophecy, and the morality of their lives."[17] Already, within these Old Testament criteria, one sees both doctrinal and teleological criteria. True prophets and their prophecies align with the teachings of Israelite

---

12. Brown et al., *Hebrew and English Lexicon*, 524.
13. Malatesta, *Discernment of Spirits*, 20.
14. Moberly, *Prophecy and Discernment*, 67-68.
15. Moberly, *Prophecy and Discernment*, 76; Fretheim, *Jeremiah*, 342.
16. Moberly, *Prophecy and Discernment*, 130.
17. Buckley, "Discernment of Spirits," 275.

religion, in particular the worship of Yahweh. Furthermore, they lead individuals toward God and away from sin and idolatry.

The warnings against false prophets and deceiving spirits are continued in the New Testament, being compounded with the possibility of false messiahs and teachers.[18] Furthermore, the New Testament discriminates between two ways, contrasting the ways of God and the world.[19] Ultimately, Christians are to test all things (1 Thess 5:21) to see that which belongs to the spirit of death and slavery and that which belongs to the Spirit of God (Rom 8:13–16; 1 Cor 2:12–15). While the New Testament continues the discernment tradition of the Old Testament, the New Testament supplements that tradition by identifying Jesus Christ and the Holy Spirit as reliable criteria of discernment.

In the New Testament, Jesus continued the Old Testament tradition of discernment. In Matt 7:15–20, Jesus acknowledged the reality of false prophets and stated that one knows a false prophet by his fruit.[20] In the context of the chapter, bad fruit is known by how it does not align with the will of God, being built upon lawlessness (7:21–23) rather than the word of God (7:24–27). Furthermore, Jesus's message called people to discern his identity and the kingdom of God. The goal of this discernment was "to discover who Jesus is, what he is doing, where his adversary is and what he is plotting."[21] For example, in Matt 11:2–6, Jesus guided John's process of discernment by pointing to the fruit and power of his ministry, and in Matt 12:22–32, the Pharisees failed to discern the source of Jesus's power, despite how the presence of the Holy Spirit was evident in Jesus's work through the signs of "miracles, cures, [and Jesus's] power over sin, evil, suffering."[22] Furthermore, a sign of being led by the Holy Spirit, as demonstrated in both the Gospels and Acts, is the imitation of the life and sufferings of Christ, whether that entails testifying of Christ at the cost of one's life (Mark 13:9–13) or sharing in the ministry of Christ through such things as signs and wonders (Acts 2:43; 5:12), the proclamation of the gospel (Acts 2:14–41; 4:5–13, 29–31; 5:17–21;

---

18. Anderson, "Free Spirits," 27–29. See Matt 7:15–16; Mark 13:3–6, 21–22; Acts 13:6; 1 Cor 14:29; 12:10; 2 Cor 11:14; Gal 1:6–9; 1 Tim 4:1; 2 Pet 2:1; 1 John 4:1–3; Rev 2:20; 16:13; 19:20.

19. Dubay, *Authenticity*, 103–7. See John 8:23; 17:14–16; 1 John 2:15; 1 Cor 2:12; Jas 4:4.

20. Moberly, *Prophecy and Discernment*, 152–55.

21. Malatesta, *Discernment of Spirits*, 33.

22. Malatesta, *Discernment of Spirits*, 36.

6:8–10; 8:35–39; 28:30–31), or joy in persecution (Acts 5:40–41; 13:48–52; 21:12–14).[23] Both the Gospels and Acts are clear that Christ and the Holy Spirit are essential criteria for discerning authenticity.

The importance of Scripture, Christ, and the Holy Spirit as criteria of spiritual discernment is seen especially in the writings of Paul. In 1 Cor 12–14, at least three criteria of discernment can be identified, the first being former revelation and apostolic tradition—namely, Scripture and doctrine (1 Cor 12:3).[24] Beginning a prolonged discussion concerning how one is able to identify authentic gifts and movements of the Holy Spirit, Paul stated that individuals moved by the Spirit will confess Christ as Lord. Conversely, Paul noted elsewhere that people who proclaim another gospel other than Christ are not moved by the Holy Spirit (Gal 1:8; 2 Cor 11:4; cf. 1 John 2:22–24; 4:1–3; 5:1).

In 1 Cor 12:10, Paul listed διακρίσεις πνευμάτων as a gift of the Holy Spirit. While some amount of disagreement exists over what Paul meant by the term, most understand it to relate to the evaluation of spirits and the determination of whether a spirit is good or evil.[25] Paul and early Christians were quite aware that not all inspirations or spiritual experiences are authentic or caused by the Holy Spirit.[26] As such, Paul put forward the doctrinal criterion of the confession of Christ as a sign of the Holy Spirit. One sees this criterion played out in the life of Paul, given that all of his Christian teaching and ministry efforts were catalyzed by his experience of Jesus Christ on the road to Damascus (Acts 9:3–19). For Paul, authentic experiences of the Holy Spirit always will cohere with the revelation of Jesus Christ as Lord.[27] Furthermore, they also will involve the experiences of adoption as a child of God (Rom 8:15–16) and of being shaped into conformity with "the image of God in Christ" (2 Cor 3:18), which tie into a second criterion from 1 Corinthians.[28]

The criteria of the Old Testament concerning the character of a prophet and the fruit of his prophecies are implied by Paul's use of love

---

23. Malatesta, *Discernment of Spirits*, 40.

24. Munzinger, *Discerning the Spirits*, 142.

25. Munzinger, *Discerning the Spirits*, 47–54. See also Grudem, *Gift of Prophecy*, 263–88.

26. Dunn, "Discernment of Spirits," 80.

27. Dunn, "Discernment of Spirits," 84–85. See also Malatesta, *Discernment of Spirits*, 48; Buckley, "Discernment of Spirits," 276.

28. Dunn, *Theology of Paul*, 433.

in 1 Cor 13.[29] Paul was clear that without love, prophets are nothing and prophetic utterances are worthless. The implication is that one must test the nature of a spiritual gift and the character and motivation of the individual, for love is the supreme mark of authentic spirituality. In other words, an authentic spiritual gift or experience of the Holy Spirit will manifest love in one's life.[30] For Paul, love is a fruit of the Holy Spirit. As such, Paul's criterion of love relates to Paul's wider teaching on the fruit of the Spirit and the general criterion that spirits are recognized by their fruit (Gal 5:19–24; Eph 5:8–10).[31]

When worked out along Paul's soteriology, Paul's criterion of love is a pneumatological and christological criterion oriented around sanctification. If one is being influenced by the Holy Spirit, then the fruit of the Spirit—such as love, joy, and peace—will be evident. If one is being influenced instead by the flesh or a deceptive spirit, then immorality and impurity will be manifest.[32] Discernment and the testing of spiritual things involve holding fast to what is good, namely the things of the Spirit, and forsaking all that is evil (1 Thess 5:19–22).[33] Paul's criterion of love, then, is a criterion of sanctification, in which spiritual authenticity is identified with the work of the Holy Spirit, which is to conform believers to the image of Christ, uniting them with Christ in his death and resurrection (Rom 6:5; 2 Cor 3:18; 5:14; Phil 3:10).[34]

Finally, in 1 Cor 14, Paul addressed another criterion, the edification and building up of the church.[35] Authentic gifts of the Spirit are known by how they edify the church (1 Cor 14:12, 26). As Paul stated earlier, the manifestation of the Spirit is given to individuals for the common good (1 Cor 12:7), and so a sign of authentic gifts and experiences of the Holy Spirit will be how they contribute to the body of Christ.[36] This sign of authenticity does not mean that everything that comes from the

29. Munzinger, *Discerning the Spirits*, 142.

30. Dunn, *Theology of Paul*, 433; Dunn, "Discernment of Spirits," 83–84.

31. Malatesta, *Discernment of Spirits*, 45–47; Buckley, "Discernment of Spirits," 276–77.

32. Au and Au, *Discerning Heart*, 39–40. Au and Au point out that Ignatius picks up on this criterion from Paul when discussing the concepts of consolation and desolation within his *Spiritual Exercises*.

33. Moberly, *Prophecy and Discernment*, 170.

34. Johnson, *Scripture and Discernment*, 120; Dunn, *Theology of Paul*, 487; Moberly, *Prophecy and Discernment*, 190.

35. Munzinger, *Discerning the Spirits*, 142; Dunn, "Discernment of Spirits," 86.

36. Malatesta, *Discernment of Spirits*, 45.

Spirit will directly edify the church.³⁷ Paul even stated that Christians who speak in tongues build themselves up unless someone interprets the tongues. Nevertheless, Paul also desired that all would speak in tongues. So the inability for tongues to edify the church without an interpreter does not disqualify it from being an authentic gift of the Spirit. To summarize, in Paul, one sees at least three criteria for spiritual discernment: Scripture, love, and the edification of the church. These Pauline criteria incorporate the general criteria of doctrine, the Holy Spirit, Jesus Christ, and sanctification.

In the writings of John, one finds similar criteria. John acknowledged the real possibility of inauthentic spiritual experiences, which necessitates the use of discernment to test the spirits (1 John 4:1). First, the confession that Jesus has come in the flesh indicates that a spirit is from God. Once again, this criterion is a doctrinal criterion. While this confession entails the rejection of docetism, it goes further to indicate that Jesus's mission on earth is definitive for the knowledge of God.³⁸ Authentic spiritual experiences always will uphold the particularity and finality of Jesus Christ's identity and mission. John identified himself with the confession of Christ and reiterated this doctrinal criterion when he stated, "We are from God. The one who knows God listens to us" (1 John 4:6). Second, John put forward a criterion of love when he stated that God is love and whoever does not love does not know God (1 John 4:8). His point was that individuals who know God will display the qualities of God, of which love is supreme.³⁹ A third criterion is the gift of the Holy Spirit (1 John 4:13; cf. 3:24), for all who abide in God will have the Holy Spirit. The Holy Spirit, furthermore, brings boldness before God, for perfect love casts out fear (1 John 4:17–18). The Spirit also brings truth (doctrine), testifying of the Son and the eternal life in the Son (1 John 5:6–12), for abiding in God entails abiding in the truths of God (1 John 2:24). Finally, the life of abiding in the Spirit will be a life of obedience to the commandments of Christ (1 John 2:3–6; 3:10).⁴⁰ Taken altogether, "the presence of God's spirit, confession of Jesus, and the enacting of love are different facets, or modes of expressing, the one rich reality of the knowledge of God."⁴¹

37. Johnson, *Scripture and Discernment*, 119.
38. Moberly, *Prophecy and Discernment*, 159–60.
39. Moberly, *Prophecy and Discernment*, 162.
40. Malatesta, *Discernment of Spirits*, 52.
41. Moberly, *Prophecy and Discernment*, 164.

In summary, multiple criteria of discernment can be gleaned from Scripture. In the Old Testament, true and false prophets are discerned based on their orthodoxy (doctrine), morality, and the content and fulfillment of their prophecy. In the Gospels and Acts, spiritual realities are identified by whether their fruit aligns with God's will or with lawlessness, by the Holy Spirit and the signs of his ministry, and by the imitation of Christ's life and suffering. In both Paul and John, the confession of Christ (doctrine) and the presence of love—which, for Paul, related to the fruit of the Holy Spirit, the image of Christ, and sanctification—are central criteria for spiritual discernment. Paul also pointed to the edification of the church and John to the gift of the Holy Spirit and the boldness, truth (doctrine), and obedience the Spirit brings. One can see how doctrine is an essential criterion for spiritual discernment in Scripture. Furthermore, the *telos* of spirituality plays a significant role in these criteria, seen in how a prophet's message is discerned by how it leads either toward God or toward sin and seen in the role of Christ and the Holy Spirit within the sanctification of the one undergoing the spiritual experience.

The Early Church

Building off of Scripture, criteria of discernment in the early church emphasized faith in Christ and adherence to apostolic teaching (doctrine) as well as love and the fruit of the Holy Spirit in one's actions and affections (morality).[42] The subject of spiritual discernment appeared early in post-canonical literature. *The Shepherd of Hermas*, written sometime during the second century, posited that two angels exist within every human being, one of righteousness and the other of iniquity. One knows the angel of righteousness by his gentle, modest, meek, and peaceful nature and by how he directs toward righteousness, purity, and virtue. The angel of iniquity, on the other hand, is wrathful, bitter, and foolish, leading to iniquity, pride, and death.[43] Origen (c. 185–254) likewise identified the various spirits that influence one, the various sources of one's thoughts, and the criteria by which to distinguish between them. He held that one's thoughts can proceed from oneself, opposing powers, or God and holy angels. The source of one's thoughts is revealed in how it either excites

---

42. Rakoczy, "Structures of Discernment Processes," 159.
43 See Svigel and Buie, *Shepherd of Hermas*, 188–89.

one toward good and divine things or evil and heretical things.[44] Similar to Origen, Athanasius (c. 296–373) viewed the spiritual life as a struggle between good and evil spirits, as seen in his *Life of St. Anthony*. Athanasius presented Anthony as one who fought against the devil, one who had the spiritual gift of discerning spirits, and one to whom many came to learn how to discern between spirits.[45] According to Anthony, good spirits will be attended by joy, goodness, and the things of God, whereas evil spirits will be accompanied by confusion, fear, and vice.[46] Anthony's point was that the experience of a spirit will be comparable to the character of the spirit experienced.

Augustine (354–430) made a similar point that good spirits instruct and evil spirits deceive. While evil spirits disguise themselves as angels of light, they ultimately reveal their true nature when they lead "against good character or the rule of faith" (*"contra bonos mores vel regulam fide"*). The ability to judge an evil spirit immediately for what it is requires the spiritual gift of discernment (*discretio*).[47] For each of these authors, good spirits uphold the truths of God (doctrine) and are accompanied by and lead toward the good things of the Holy Spirit, such as love and joy (morality and holy affections).

John Cassian (c. 360–c. 430) is well known for his work on spiritual discernment. In *The Conferences*, he presented the ideal of the Egyptian desert monk as one who practices discretion.[48] Monks must practice discernment in order to become perfected in love and purity and to reach the kingdom of God by avoiding the pitfalls of extreme practices and doctrines.[49] He distinguished between the kingdom of God as a place

---

44. Origen, *On First Principles*, 3.2.4; cf. 3.3.4. Origen even cited *The Shepherd of Hermas* as support for his position.

45. Athanasius, *Life of Antony*, §5–6, 8–9, 21–23, 39–41; 51–53; 88.

46. Athanasius, *Life of Antony*, §35–37; cf. Cyril of Jerusalem, *Catechetical Lectures*, 16.15–16.

47. Augustine, *De Genesi*, 12.13–14.

48. Morris and Olsen, *Discerning God's Will Together*, 18–19.

49. Cassian, *Conferences*, 1.4; Waaijman, "Discernment," 19. Cassian applied the categories of discernment mostly to doctrine and spiritual disciplines, especially in the attempt to avoid negative extremes, whether of asceticism or apathy. Cf. John Climacus, *Ladder of Divine Ascent*, 26.1. Climacus viewed discernment as an essential aspect of spiritual growth. In fact, he distinguished between three types of discernment, based on whether an individual is spiritually a beginner, an intermediate, or perfect. For the beginner, discernment is self-knowledge. To the intermediate, discernment is the spiritual sense to distinguish between the good, the natural, and the bad. In the perfect, discernment is a divine illumination to see into the hearts of others and to perceive the

of righteousness, peace, and joy, and the kingdom of the devil as a place of unrighteousness, discord, and a sadness that produces death. The joy of the kingdom of God is not a joy in some vague object but in only that which is of the Holy Spirit.[50] Cassian identified three sources of one's thoughts and criteria for identifying them. First, thoughts are able to originate from God, and they are known to come from God "when he deigns to visit us by the illumination of the Holy Spirit, which raises us up to a higher level of progress; and when we have made little gain or have acted lazily and been overcome and he chastens us with a most salutary compunction; and when he opens to us the heavenly sacraments and changes our chosen orientation to better acts and to a better will."[51] Thoughts from God are known by their *telos*.[52] They lead toward sanctification, for through them the Holy Spirit illuminates, corrects, and guides one toward goodness. Thoughts from the devil, on the other hand, deceptively subvert one's growth in sanctification, leading to a delight in wickedness.[53] Thoughts that originate from oneself occur, for example, when one spontaneously remembers the things that one is doing or has done or has heard.[54]

In light of the various sources of one's thoughts, Cassian argued that, in order to make sure one is acting on the thoughts that lead to sanctification, one must trace the origins, causes, and authors of one's thoughts. He compared this process to a money changer who, when looking at a coin, is able to tell four things: (1) whether the coin is made of pure gold or common brass, (2) whether the coin is stamped with the effigy of the true king

---

divine will in all circumstances.
50. Cassian, *Conferences*, 1.13.
51. Cassian, *Conferences*, 1.19.1.
52. Waaijman, "Discernment," 22.
53. Cassian, *Conferences*, 1.19.3; cf. Climacus, *Ladder of Divine Ascent*, 26.152; Diadochos of Photiki, "On Spiritual Knowledge," 1:262–63. Climacus distinguished between holy and unholy joy, noting that unholy joy is accompanied by confusion. Diadochos made a similar distinction between the thoughts that come from God or the devil. True grace impels one toward love, consisting of uninterrupted joy in which one's soul ineffably clings solely to God in delight. Deceptive joy is interrupted by doubt or unclean thoughts, leading to spiritual pride in which one believes oneself to be holy when one is not. In other words, true grace and true joy so enrapture the heart that all of one's thoughts are unwaveringly focused on God. Diadochos's position seems a bit extreme, for true grace is not destroyed by human finitude within the "already-not-yet" tension of soteriology. This unwavering focus that Diadochos talks about seems reserved for the beatific vision. Cf. Aquinas, *Summa Theologica*, II-II, Q 184, A 2, co.
54. Cassian, *Conferences*, 1.19.4.

or a usurper, (3) whether the coin comes from a counterfeit mint despite being stamped with the effigy of the true king, and (4) whether the coin is of a correct weight.[55] In other words, first, discernment involves the ability to distinguish between that which is of true value, leading to life, and that which is deceptive and worthless, leading to death. Second, one must seek to identify when something good is twisted for evil, like Scripture in the mouth of Satan when tempting Christ.[56] Third, ideas, doctrines, and practices might have the look of piety and yet merely have the external façade of true religion while being products of "Jewish superstition" or prideful and "worldly philosophy."[57] Fourth, one must check—by the acts and writings of the prophets and apostles—for the proper weights of common goodness and the fear of God, contrasted with the improper human weights of ostentation, presumption, and pride.[58] For Cassian, discernment is a virtue that one develops over time through humility and submission to one's elders.[59] The necessity of humility and submission for discernment implies that one must adhere to the doctrine and practices of the church, as handed down from the apostles, stamped with the effigy of Christ, and properly weighted with the things of the Holy Spirit, in order to grow in sanctification toward the *telos* of the kingdom of God.

The Middle Ages

After John Cassian and Augustine, the subject of spiritual discernment was not developed much until the late Middle Ages, beginning in the twelfth century.[60] These centuries saw waves of spiritualism sweep through Europe, resulting in multitudes of self-appointed prophets, visionaries, and mystics. Susan Schreiner explained that, during these movements in the late medieval period,

---

55. Cassian, *Conferences*, 1.20.
56. Cassian, *Conferences*, 1.20.4.
57. Cassian, *Conferences*, 1.20.2; cf. 1.20.6.
58. Cassian, *Conferences*, 1.21.2; cf. 1.22.1.
59. Cassian, *Conferences*, 2.10; cf. Climacus, *Ladder of Divine Ascent*, 4.105. See also Howard, *Brazos Introduction*, 377; Malatesta, *Discernment of Spirits*, 59–60.
60. Anderson, "Free Spirits," 20–21. Much of the following research—from Henry of Friemar until Jean Gerson—draws heavily from Anderson's material. Her work covers these pivotal figures in great detail, including their criteriologies, and she helpfully identifies the critical editions in which one is able to find their original works.

reformers, visionaries, beatas, and mystics all claimed illumination and thereby created suspicion and the need to test the authenticity of their experiences. Added to this phenomenon were the religious controversies that were shattering the unity of Western Christendom, bringing in their wake the crisis of authority, the need for certainty, and the appeals to the Spirit.[61]

Scholars interested in maintaining the traditions and orthodoxy of the Roman Catholic Church wrote much on spiritual discernment (*discretio spirituum*), turning to miracles and Scripture to support their positions.[62] As such, spiritual discernment became a matter of religious authority, depending upon such things as "confessorial or communal approval, demonstrated virtue, episcopal blessings, Scriptural prooftexts, parallels in saints' lives, miracles, fulfilled predictions, patristic writings, gender (in several different ways), theologians' determinations, papal decrees, canon law, and (last but not least) the charismatic verdict of the Holy Spirit."[63]

Both Bernard of Clairvaux and Thomas Aquinas wrote on spiritual discernment, uniting it with prudence and the pursuit of a balanced life.[64] In his *Sermones de Diversis*, Bernard stated that one's thoughts occur within a conversation between oneself and a variety of possible spirits, such as evil spirits, including the devil, the flesh, the world, and wickedness; or good spirits, including God and good angels.[65] Evil spirits are revealed by their suggestions and provocations toward carnal comforts, worldly vanities, malicious bitterness, anger, impatience, and envy. Good spirits turn one's thoughts instead toward virtuous things such as "castigating the body, humbling the heart, preserving unity, and showing charity to the brother."[66] Citing Jas 3:17, Bernard pointed out that the wisdom from God is chaste, displaying virtue, and peaceable, being approved by one's superiors and spiritual brothers. As such, thoughts from God also will be chaste and peaceable.[67] Furthermore, one can be sure that something

---

61. Schreiner, *Are You Alone Wise*, 270. A beata was a woman who pursued mystical experiences.

62. Anderson, "Free Spirits," 20; Malatesta, *Discernment of Spirits*, 65.

63. Anderson, "Free Spirits," 14.

64. Howard, *Brazos Introduction*, 378.

65. Bernard of Clairvaux, *Monastic Sermons*, 23.130. This citation refers to Bernard's sermon number and the page numbers of the book. This book is a modern translation of Bernard's *Sermones de Diversis*.

66. Bernard of Clairvaux, *Monastic Sermons*, 23.131–32.

67. Bernard of Clairvaux, *Monastic Sermons*, 24.136. Cf. Gerson, *De probatione*

is of God when it clearly is supported by Scripture or the Spirit's work of prompting one toward virtues such as love, humility, and purity.[68]

For Aquinas, discernment (*discretio*) is an aspect of prudence, and beyond this point, he wrote little about it.[69] He acknowledged that an individual is able to be influenced by evil spirits. He clarified, though, that the will is the direct cause of sin. While the devil is a cause of sin by persuasion, offering objects of temptation to one's affective appetites and passions, he is not a direct or sufficient cause of sin.[70] The devil does not create thoughts directly in someone's mind, nor does he move an individual's will as if he were inwardly the agent of that will. Rather, he offers objects to the will and seeks to persuade the will of an apparent good within the offered object.[71]

One popular and influential work, dating back around the first decade of the fourteenth century, was Henry of Friemar's *De quattuor instinctibus*, in which Henry sought to present a comprehensive treatment of criteria for spiritual discernment.[72] He identified four instincts, or interior motions, that impact human beings: the divine, the angelic, the diabolic, and the natural. First, the divine instinct leads one to grow in conformity to Christ and the saints, in humility, in spiritual consolation and strength, and in virtue.[73] Second, the signs of an angelic instinct include a desolation that is followed by consolation and joy, hiddenness followed by later revelation, encouragement toward that which is good and useful, and an urging on to good will.[74] Both of these instincts, the divine and the angelic, are teleological, based on whether an interior motion moves one toward growth in sanctification or not. Conversely, the diabolic and natural instincts lead away from sanctification. The diabolic instinct goes against conformity to Christ and the saints, resulting in pride, weakness, and vice, and—contra the *instinctus angelicus*—it consists of an initial joy and security followed by sorrow, doubt, and the

---

spirituum, 9:181.

68. Bernard of Clairvaux, *Monastic Sermons*, 26.148; cf. 88.331; Waaijman, *Spirituality*, 497. See also Gerson, *Collation factum est*, 5:319.

69. Aquinas, *Summa Theologica* I–II, Q 65, A 1, co.

70. Aquinas, *Summa Theologica* I–II, Q 80, A 1, co.; cf. I, Q 111, A 2, ad 2.

71. Aquinas, *Summa Theologica* I–II, Q 80, A 1, co.; cf. A 2, co.; A 4, s.c.

72. Anderson, "Free Spirits," 106.

73. Henry of Friemar, *De quattuor instinctibus*, 155–65; Malatesta, *Discernment of Spirits*, 69–70.

74. Henry of Friemar, *De quattuor instinctibus*, 166–75.

extinction of both good will and charity.⁷⁵ Furthermore, the natural instinct consists of mental disunity, an inflated self-image, and an apathy toward spiritual growth, opposing growth in sanctification and the love of God.⁷⁶

For Henry of Friemar, then, many of the criteria of discernment can be summarized by whether or not an interior motion within one's soul leads one toward or away from growth in sanctification, which involves conformity to Christ and growth in humility and the virtues.⁷⁷ The importance of Henry's work can be seen in how Denis the Carthusian (1402–1471) felt the need to critique the *De quattuor instinctibus* over a hundred years after its publication. Denis agreed with much that Henry wrote, including the enumeration of the four instincts. However, Denis argued, first, that Henry's signs for the divine instinct also fit the angelic instinct, given that both lead to growth in sanctification. Second, Denis denied the idea that the angelic instinct is identified always by a movement from fear to joy or hiddenness to revelation.⁷⁸ Third, Denis held to a more positive view of human nature than did Henry, arguing that the natural instinct, incorporating natural law and reason, tends toward what is good and true, leading to the love of God.⁷⁹ Nonetheless, Denis still held to the more general principle that growth in sanctification is able to act as a criterion of discernment.

At the turn of the fourteenth century, the writings of a French Beguine mystic—Marguerite Porete—swept across Europe, creating upheaval due to its seemingly unorthodox teachings, including a deification without distinction, antinomianism, and anti-ecclesiasticism. Porete's writings were condemned at the Council of Vienne in 1311, and

75. Henry of Friemar, *De quattuor instinctibus*, 174–95.

76. Henry of Friemar, *De quattuor instinctibus*, 198–235.

77. Cf. Denis the Carthusian, *Discretione et examinatione spirituum*, 40:269.

78. Denis the Carthusian, *Discretione et examinatione spirituum*, 282–84. Jean Gerson, on the other hand, held to the idea that an experience of an angelic spirit begins with a certain horror, "not of abomination but of vehement admiration, reverence and stupor" ("*non abominationis sed vehementis admirationis, reverentiae et stuporis*") that is replaced by consolation. See Gerson, *Collation factum est*, 5:316.

79. Denis the Carthusian, *Discretione et examinatione spirituum*, 298–99. See Malatesta, *Discernment of Spirits*, 70. Interestingly, Thomas à Kempis seemed to side with Henry on this point, holding that human nature is inclined toward evil and selfishness, while grace directs one toward God. See Thomas à Kempis, *Imitation of Christ*, 3.54–55; cf. Bernard of Clairvaux, *Monastic Sermons*, 23.132. To a certain extent, *The Imitation of Christ*, in its entirety, is a work of practical discernment, basing discernment on the imitation of Christ. See Morris and Olsen, *Discerning God's Will Together*, 21.

individuals associated with her positions were called "the sect of the Free Spirit."[80] After the German mystic Meister Eckhart was condemned by the church as being a proponent of the Free Spirit movement, his disciples Henry Suso (1295–1366) and Johannes Tauler (c. 1300–1361) wrote fervently on spiritual discernment to defend Eckhart by enumerating the signs that distinguish true and false mystics.[81]

For Suso, genuine visions are intellectual and free of images, leading to order and the perception of rational distinction.[82] At the beginning of the allegory of Suso's *Little Book of Truth*, the "man in Christ" asks "eternal Truth" how to distinguish between true and false mystics—namely those whose goal is simplicity contrasted with those who aim at unrestrained liberty, such as the antinomianism of the Free Spirit sect. In response, the eternal Truth directs the man in Christ to the "core of holy scripture out of which eternal Truth speaks."[83] For Suso, then, Scripture is a clear criterion of authentic spirituality, and individuals who are enlightened by the truths of Scripture are able to perceive spiritual distinctions between true and false spirituality.

Johannes Tauler, like Suso, held that the pure light of genuine visions, consisting of God's greatness, does not consist of images but occurs within the ground (*grunt*) of the soul, leading the visionary to become humble.[84] In other words, authentic experiences of God's greatness lead to growth in virtues such as humility. Individuals who truly love God will cultivate the virtues in fear of God's judgment, whereas individuals who have not truly experienced God will lack virtue and will be identified by their deluded claims to have freedom of the spirit, such as the antinomianism of the Free Spirit sect.[85] The natural light, Tauler wrote, "reflects pride, conceit, and delights in the praise of others and in the applause and approval of the world," whereas the divine light "makes the soul bend down deeply to the ground, because it feels itself the least, the most insignificant, the weakest and blindest among all creatures."[86] Tauler's point

---

80. McGinn, *Flowering of Mysticism*, 244–46. Beguines were semi-monastic communities of devout women, originating in twelfth-century Europe. See Howard, "Beguine Option," 93–116.

81. Anderson, "Free Spirits," 21.

82. Suso, *Life of the Servant*, 195; Suso, *Little Book of Truth*, 329.

83. Suso, *Little Book of Truth*, 308.

84. Tauler, *Predigten Taulers*, 249–50.

85. Tauler, *Predigten Taulers*, 167–68.

86. Tauler, *Johannes Tauler*, 71. The fourteenth-century *Theologia Deutsch* made a

was that the authenticity of a spiritual experience is known by how it leads to humility and obedience to God. If the joy of a spiritual experience fades away into restlessness and disobedience, then the source of that joy was not God.[87]

Many other writers contributed to the subject of spiritual discernment in the fourteenth century, such as Birgitta of Sweden, Catherine of Siena, Henry of Langenstein, John of Ruysbroeck, and Walter Hilton, all of whom provided criteria for distinguishing between the various spirits. While a variety of differing emphases can be noted in their writings, they built off of and cohered with much that already had been written and continued the tradition of pointing to Jesus Christ, the Holy Spirit, Scripture, and sanctification—especially the *teloi* of love, humility, virtue, and the imitation of Christ—as criteria of discernment. Birgitta (d. 1373) identified seven signs of the Holy Spirit and seven signs of the evil spirit, which can be summarized by saying that the Spirit of God makes one despise the world and desire God, and the evil spirit makes one despise God and love the flesh and the world.[88] Catherine of Siena (1347–1380) likewise joined discernment with the virtues, viewing it as engrafted with love and humility and separated from sin.[89] The signs of the Holy Spirit include joy, virtue, humility, and charity, whereas delusion produces a hunger for consolation that is devoid of the love of God, leading to a gladness that lacks virtue and that eventually is replaced by pain.[90] Generally, for both Birgitta and Catherine, authentic spiritual experiences involve growth in virtue.

Building off of Henry of Friemar, Henry of Langenstein (1325–1397) identified four "substantial spirits" that influence humans: one's soul,

---

similar distinction between the true and false light. True light leads to a life of righteousness, shaped according to Christ's life and teaching. False light leads to self-centered pride and undisciplined freedom. See Hoffman, *Theologia Germanica*, 92–95, 115–29.

87. Tauler, *Johannes Tauler*, 71. The anonymously written *Buch von Geistlicher Armuth*—which may or may not have been written by Tauler—made a similar distinction between spiritual experiences: spiritual experiences from God will inspire good deeds, humility, virtue, and moderation; those from nature will lead one to be self-centered; and those from the devil will lead to superfluous things, such as friendship with the wealthy, over-indulgence, or excessive fasts. See Denifle, *Buch von geistlicher Armuth*, 13–16.

88. Birgitta of Sweden, *Revelaciones*, Book IV, 23.11–14, 27–31.

89. Catherine of Siena, *Dialogue*, 9.40–41; 11.44; cf. 4.30–32; 97.183; 98.184–100.192. These citations refer to the section followed by the page numbers.

90. Catherine of Siena, *Dialogue*, 106.198–99.

the Holy Spirit, good angels, and evil angels.[91] He put forward a general principle of discernment that is teleological: what is doubtful in origin must be proven by its end, for "an outcome manifests many times what an origin was hiding."[92] In particular, the Holy Spirit leads toward the ends of internal consolation, a fear that gives way to joy, purity, growth in love, submission to God, conviction over sin, divine truth, and the imitation of Christ.[93]

Like Suso and Tauler, John of Ruysbroeck (1293–1381) sought to distinguish between true and false mystics. In *The Adornment of the Spiritual Marriage*, he stated that visions and dreams may be trusted only insofar as they conform to Scripture and truth, for the Holy Spirit never will contradict the teachings of Christ.[94] He also presented three signs for identifying individuals who deceptively appear enlightened by God, being skilled in rhetorical persuasion but lacking in charity.[95] Truly enlightened individuals possess a simple and stable mind, wisdom from God, the ability to distinguish truth, and a love that pours out into all things. Individuals who are not enlightened are filled with a restless and curious mind that lacks unity, producing and holding to sudden and unfruitful ideas in spiritual pride and intellectual condescension while lacking all virtue, love, and humility.[96]

Continuing the theme of viewing growth in virtue as a criterion of discernment, Walter Hilton (1340–1396) acknowledged that a spiritual feeling may come from God or the devil. If a feeling of delight leads one

---

91. Henry of Langenstein, *De discretione spirituum*, 52–54. Henry also identified twelve "spirits" of the human soul that correspond to such things as one's habits, sexual desires, and bodily senses, and twelve spirits of the evil angel that lead to corruption.

92. Henry of Langenstein, *De discretione spirituum*, 62; "Exitus enim multitotiens manifestat, quod origo occultabat."

93. Henry of Langenstein, *De discretione spirituum*, 62–64, 90–96, 102–8.

94. John of Ruysbroeck, *Adornment*, 78, 162–63.

95. Henry of Langenstein, *De discretione spirituum*, 107. Elsewhere, John distinguished between true and false mystics by stating that mystics who truly have experienced the Holy Spirit rest in the enjoyment of God and work the works of God, while those who have not been drawn or enlightened by God rest in emptiness, lack the desire of God, and selfishly seek a consolation and sweetness that leads to pride, sin, and a life in opposition to God. See John of Ruysbroeck, *Spiritual Espousals*, 165–70. Cf. John of Ruysbroeck, *De Quatuor Tentationibus*, 356–64.

96. John of Ruysbroeck, *Adornment*, 107–8. Pierre d'Ailly similarly stated that false prophets and prophecies are known by their fruit. See Pierre d'Ailly, *De falsis prophetis*, 1:497–99, 511–25. Bernardino of Siena (1380–1444) likewise wrote that divine inspirations are known by their fruit, namely goodness of mind, good works, and the glory of God. See Bernardino of Siena, *De inspirationibus*, 3:135.

away from prayer and spiritual discipline because one is focusing on the feeling in order to keep it and delight in it, then that feeling is not from God. However, if a feeling leads to greater virtue—spiritual discipline, humility, and a love for God—then that feeling is from God.[97] For Hilton, authentic spirituality is identified by the distinction between the image of sin and the image of Jesus, for true spirituality consists of seeking to recover a likeness to the image of God.[98] At this point, Hilton is one of the few to use the image of God as a criterion of discernment. The image of sin is a "false disordered love for yourself" (pride), out of which flows the seven deadly sins.[99] The image of Jesus, which is the image of God, "is made of virtues, with humility and perfect love and charity."[100] Therefore, the image of God is a criterion of discernment based on how authentic spirituality will consist of growth in the virtues of the image of Jesus.

Jean Gerson (1363–1429) was a prominent Catholic theologian during the early fifteenth century and a student of both Langenstein and d'Ailly, who is known for having influenced the Council of Constance, written against the canonization of Birgitta of Sweden, interrogated John Hus, and written multiple important works on spiritual discernment.[101] The criteria of discernment Gerson provided are doctrinal, experiential, and moral. He held that there is no single rule or method that one can infallibly use in matters of discernment.[102] Nonetheless, borrowing imagery from Cassian, Gerson compared spiritual revelations to coins, which must be examined for weight (humility), malleability (discretion), durability (patience), conformability (truth), and color (charity).[103] In particular, the "stamp" of truth requires that true prophecies must come true as intended, unless a second revelation occurs explaining whether the first revelation is to be taken as conditional, mystical, or literal. Furthermore, they must not be contrary to good morals or sincere faith unless, like Abraham, the revelation occurs in such a way that it cannot be

---

97. Hilton, *Scale of Perfection*, 83–84.

98. Hilton, *Scale of Perfection*, 118. For Hilton, the image of God corresponds to the soul and not the body, being constituted by memory, will, and reason. See Hilton, *Scale of Perfection*, 102, 193.

99. Hilton, *Scale of Perfection*, 126; cf. 154–55.

100. Hilton, *Scale of Perfection*, 155–60.

101. Schreiner, *Are You Alone Wise*, 263; Anderson, "Free Spirits," 22–23, 270.

102. Gerson, "On Distinguishing," 334–64.

103. Gerson, "On Distinguishing," 338.

doubted.[104] As such, discernment is based on experiential illumination (intimate taste), morality, and doctrine.[105]

Finally, almost exactly as did Denis the Carthusian, Gerson identified three ways to test the spirits: by Scripture (doctrine); by intimate inspiration, internal taste, and the experience of sweetness that drives away doubt (experience); and by the gift of spiritual discernment as it is tied to church hierarchy (office).[106] Gerson also added that one must look to the actions (the fruit) of the individual who is claiming to be moved by the Spirit of God, for "by their fruits you will know them."[107] Overall, then, for Gerson and many of the theologians writing on spiritual discernment in the Middle Ages, criteria such as Scripture, experiential knowledge, conformity to Christ, growth in sanctification, and the fruit of the Holy Spirit, including virtue, morality, and good works, are essential for spiritual discernment.

The Reformation and Counter-Reformation

The question of spiritual discernment continued to be a matter of importance through the Reformation until the modern day. Debates focused on identifying the sources of discernment, with various groups emphasizing sources such as Scripture, tradition, reason, experience, and the local community.[108] For Martin Luther (1483–1546), spiritual discernment involved the identification of the true natures of the gospel and the church, including its sacraments and various ministries.[109] The devil disguises himself as an angel of light to mimic and pervert the church, and this reality makes discernment absolutely necessary.[110] Luther identified both external and internal criteria.[111] Externally, Christ and the Word are the

---

104. Gerson, "On Distinguishing," 349–50.

105. Gerson, "On Distinguishing," 350, 362–63. As Gerson concluded, "We are to cling to God and to the scriptures, through which and in which God once and for all spoke to us. This revelation he will not repeat." On morality as a criterion, Gerson elsewhere identified thirty signs of evil based on the conduct of an individual. See Gerson, *De signis*, 9:162–66.

106. Gerson, *De probatione spirituum*, 178; Denis the Carthusian, *Discretione et examinatione spirituum*, 270.

107. Gerson, *De probatione spirituum*, 180. "*A fructibus eorum cognoscetis eos.*"

108. Howard, *Brazos Introduction*, 379–80.

109. Schreiner, *Are You Alone Wise*, 300.

110. Luther, *Gospel of St. John*, 312; Luther, *Sermon on the Mount*, 212.

111. Bockmuehl, *God Who Speaks*, 126.

main criteria of discernment, for the true Spirit comes in the name of Christ and teaches nothing but Christ.[112] As Michael Protera pointed out, "Luther's radical import is in the standards which he brought to judge reality, that is, what distinguishes between what ought to be respected and what must be rejected. His challenge is that we re-understand ourselves in terms of divine grace. And the terms of divine grace are simply the Word."[113] Internally, the work of the devil and of the true Spirit can be distinguished by certain characteristics. The work of the devil creates ignorance, hatred and contempt for God, overt sins, an unwillingness to reform doctrine, and doubt and anxiety.[114] On the other hand, the Holy Spirit directs one toward the gospel of Christ, removing doubt and condemnation and leaving in its place comfort, courage, and holiness.[115]

Similar criteria are seen in the writings of John Calvin (1509–1564), such as in his *Institutes of the Christian Religion*. Calvin wrote on spiritual discernment as a response to individuals who sought to bypass Scripture for a different route to God (libertines) and individuals who sought to use the Spirit to defend an antinomian sinfulness (Anabaptists). Calvin argued that the Spirit of Christ cannot be separated from the Spirit as seen in Scripture—the Spirit who led the apostles to revere Scripture and the Spirit who always points to Christ and the gospel.[116] Thus, any spirit that proclaims a new doctrine or something at odds with the Spirit as revealed in Scripture should be rejected as false. For Calvin, Scripture is the one infallible mark by which the Spirit of God is identified, and it is the instrument by which the Spirit's illumination is dispensed.[117] Additionally, the Holy Spirit is given for sanctification and never will lead away from sanctification. Therefore, deceptive spirits are known by how they lead away from holiness, love, and purity.[118]

Despite Calvin's particularly negative view of the Anabaptists, Anabaptist theologians also developed scriptural criteria by which one could discern the spirits and detect the work of the devil and false prophets. For

---

112. Luther, *Gospel of St. John*, 176–77.
113. Protera, *Homo spiritualis*, 22.
114. Luther, *Gospel of St. John*, 12–13; *Lectures on Galatians*, 41, 66.
115. Luther, *Gospel of St. John*, 12–13, 142–43, 294–96.
116. Calvin, *Institutes*, 1.9.1.
117. Calvin, *Institutes*, 1.9.2–3. See Bockmuehl, *God Who Speaks*, 126–32; Berthoud "Discerning Spirituality," 57–58. Calvin was also clear that one cannot discern spiritual truths without the illumination of the Holy Spirit. See Calvin, *Institutes*, 2.2.18–21.
118. Calvin, *Institutes*, 3.3.14.

example, Pilgram Marpeck (c. 1495-1556) acknowledged that miracles, signs, and wonders are able to deceive; that Scripture regularly warns believers of the possibility of being deceived by false teachers; and that Scripture must be used for discernment.[119] In particular, Marpeck pointed out that Christ taught that prophets are recognized by their fruits, not their miracles (Matt 7) and that Christians must discern such individuals by the criteria of the fruit of the Holy Spirit (Gal 5). The fruit of the Spirit manifests not for selfish gain but for the common good (1 Cor 12), the edification of others (1 Cor 14; Eph 4), and the service of others (1 Pet 4).[120] Individuals who have the Spirit of Christ proclaim the teachings of Christ—the gospel. Without the Spirit, there is no sanctification, truth, or instruction but only error and confusion.[121]

In the counter-reformation, Ignatius of Loyola (1491-1556), Teresa of Ávila (1515-1582), and John of the Cross (1542-1591) became well-established authorities on spiritual discernment within Roman Catholic theology. In his *Spiritual Exercises*, consolidating and building off of much from the tradition of spiritual discernment, Ignatius identified three unique times of decision (or election) that are made in processes of discernment. The first time occurs when God so moves that he leaves no room for doubt or the inability to carry out his proposal. The second time occurs when discernment arises through clarity from the experience of consolation or desolation. The third time occurs in tranquility, when one is not moved toward or away from consolation but instead must rely upon one's natural faculties, including one's intellect.[122] Through each of these elections, good spirits always act for the sanctification of the soul and evil angels for the opposite.[123] Furthermore, internal criteria of discernment must be balanced with the external criteria of Scripture, doctrine, and tradition.[124]

Ignatius applied the concepts of desolation and consolation to the context of a person's life concerning whether an individual is growing toward God or away from God. His point was that discernment criteria

---

119. Marpeck, *Writings*, 49, 54.

120. Marpeck, *Writings*, 51-53.

121. Marpeck, *Writings*, 53. See also Hubmaier, *Theologian of Anabaptism*, 300-313.

122. Ignatius, *Spiritual Exercises*, §175-77; Au and Au, *Discerning Heart*, 53-55.

123. Ignatius, *Spiritual Exercises*, §331-33. Cf. de Paz, *De perfecta contemplatione*, lib. 5, part. 4, cap. 1, ind. 2; de la Reguera, *Praxis theologiae mysticae*, lib. 9, q. 1, sec. 1, n. 26.

124. Ignatius, *Spiritual Exercises*, §363.

apply to the affective fruit produced by spiritual experiences, and this fruit is perceived differently for different people.[125] For individuals living in sin, evil spirits and evil thoughts will feel pleasurable and exciting, whereas influences from good spirits and thoughts will bring remorse and doubt. Conversely, for the individual pursuing holiness, the influence of a good spirit will bring peace, consolation, and growth in holiness, whereas evil influences will bring about anxiety, desolation, and a desire for base and earthly things.[126]

Neither Teresa of Avila nor John of the Cross systematically developed a theory of spiritual discernment like Ignatius did, but they did hold to sanctification and Scripture as central criteria of spiritual discernment similar to Ignatius. Teresa held that authentic experiences of God, including divine communications (locutions) and visions, are known by their production of internal good and a contempt for evil things.[127] They strengthen the soul, making it tender and receptive to God, and implant virtue, humility, godly fear, and truth within the soul, leading to a peaceful, loving, and delightful desire for God, prayer, and spiritual growth.[128] The devil cannot produce such internal benefits and peace but leaves behind such evil results as disquiet, temptation, distress, terror, and disgust, or a false assurance that one is safe from falling back into past sins.[129] In *Ascent of Mount Carmel*, John put forward the general principle that authentic experiences of God will aid one to grow closer in union with God.[130] These experiences are known by the effects they inevitably leave behind, such as a purgative desolation that casts light upon one's failings and gives way to a consoling perception of the good given by God.[131] The "locutions" of the devil, on the other hand, incline the will toward

---

125. Cf. McIntosh, *Discernment and Truth*, 95–98; Rakoczy, "Structures of Discernment Processes," 161; Buckley, "Discernment of Spirits," 279; Larkin, *Silent Presence*, 20; Smith, *Voice of Jesus*, 39; Chan, *Spiritual Theology*, 207.

126. Ignatius, *Spiritual Exercises*, §314–27. Cf. Suarez, *De divina gratia*, Proleg. III, c. 5, n. 39–41. Suarez (1548–1617) stated these criteria of discernment: Scripture, doctrine, morality, and movement toward perfection.

127. Teresa of Avila, *Interior Castle*, 6.8.3.

128. Teresa of Avila, *Interior Castle*, 5.3.6–7; 6.2.6–8; 6.3.8; 6.10.7; 7.2.9; 7.3.4–6; Teresa of Avila, *Book of Her Life*, 15.13–15; 25.3; 28.13.

129. Teresa of Avila, *Interior Castle*, 6.8.7; *Book of Her Life*, 25.10–11; Teresa of Avila, *Way of Perfection*, 39.4.

130. John of the Cross, *Ascent of Mount Carmel*, 2.31.2.

131. John of the Cross, *Ascent of Mount Carmel*, 2.11.6; John of the Cross, *Dark Night*, 2.13.10.

dryness concerning the love of God, intellectual vanity, false humility, self-love, and self-esteem.[132] Furthermore, whereas God leads one to grow in repugnance for that which brings oneself honor and readiness for that which involves humility and faithfulness, the devil instigates the opposite.[133]

The ultimate criteria for both Teresa and John were Scripture and church dogma, for if anything contradicts Scripture or established doctrine, then it cannot be a product of the Holy Spirit. Teresa was clear that "a locution bears the credentials of being from God if it is in conformity with Sacred Scripture. And if it should deviate from Scripture just a little, I would have incomparably greater assurance that it comes from the devil than I now have that it comes from God, however, great this latter assurance may be."[134] John went so far as to say that, given the high probability of deception, one should doubt all spiritual locutions, revelations, and visions and simply rely upon the law of Christ and the teachings of the church.[135]

Post-Reformation Catholicism and Protestantism

At this point in the survey, a lot of space could be spent explaining the many Catholic writers who continued on the tradition of spiritual discernment from Ignatius and pre-Reformational figures as well as the many ways in which spiritual discernment took on unique shapes and emphases within the rhetorical and social contexts of the many newly forming denominations of Protestantism. Nevertheless, from what has been written so far, while admitting of a degree of diversity and development, one can see that a certain consistency concerning the criteria of spiritual discernment was maintained from biblical times through the early church, the Middle Ages, and the upheavals of the Reformation and Counter-Reformation, centered on the criteria of Christ, the Holy Spirit, Scripture, and the *telos* of sanctification. This consistent criteriology reveals the major role that doctrine played in the history of spiritual

132. John of the Cross, *Ascent of Mount Carmel*, 2.29.11.

133. John of the Cross, *Ascent of Mount Carmel*, 2.30.3–4. See also *Dark Night*, 1.9 for signs by which one can distinguish the dark night of the soul from imperfection and lukewarmness. The desolation that John of the Cross talked about should not be mistaken for the desolation that Ignatius discussed.

134. Teresa of Avila, *Book of Her Life*, 25.13.

135. John of the Cross, *Ascent of Mount Carmel*, 2.22.7; 2.27.6; 2.29.12.

discernment as well as the necessity of using doctrinal criteria, often aligned with the *telos* of spirituality, for spiritual discernment. All that is needed now is to show that in the main a similar criteriology continued to be upheld in important representational figures and movements within post-Reformational Catholicism and Protestantism.

Roman Catholic Theologians

In the seventeenth and eighteenth centuries, all the nuances of previous periods concerning spiritual discernment were upheld and developed within the challenges and demands of the early modern world, whether in the face of scientific revolutions, revival movements, modern philosophy, or other such difficulties.[136] Continuity with preceding writings on spiritual discernment is seen immediately in the works of Catholic theologians such as Giovanni Bona (1609–1674) and Giovanni Battista Scaramelli (1687–1752), who, in one way or another, sought to assert only that "which has been handed down from the holy Fathers and other approved writers on the discernment of spirits."[137] Even in more recent years, nineteenth- and twentieth-century Roman Catholic theologians such as Adolphe Tanquerey (1854–1932), Joseph de Guibert (1877–1942), Jean Mouroux (1901–1973), Yves Congar (1904–1995), and Jordan Aumann (1916–2007) maintained a robust continuity with the traditional literature of spiritual discernment.

Adolphe Tanquerey enumerated the sources of spiritual promptings in a way similar to earlier authors while noting that, in practice, the important thing to know is whether a prompting urges one to good or to

---

136. Howard, *Brazos Introduction*, 380. The term "early modern," as used here, refers to the sixteenth and seventeenth centuries.

137. Bona, *Tractatus*, 1.1. The Latin text reads, "*Que à sanctis Patribus, aliisque probatis Scriptoribus de Discretione Spirituum tradita sunt.*" Joseph Pegon made the point that very little actual development on the topic of spiritual discernment occurred within Catholicism during the seventeenth and eighteenth centuries. Bona's work is considered to be of unparalleled importance during this period, and he mostly sought to reiterate the teachings of the patristics and medievals. Scaramelli's *Discernimento degli spiriti* (1753) was also an important work, but it heavily relied on Bona and Jacobo Àlvarez de Paz (1560–1620). Intently focused on representing the patristic and medieval heritage of spiritual discernment, the writings of these early modern Catholic theologians did not differ greatly from their predecessors. See Malatesta, *Discernment of Spirits*, 79, 91, 96. For Bona's and Scaramelli's criteriologies, see the following: Bona, *Tractatus*, 6.1–3; 14.1–7; Scaramelli, *Discernimento de' spiriti*, 6.1–10.9.

evil. Concerning specific rules for discernment, he simply directed readers to Ignatius's writings.[138]

Joseph de Guibert explicitly stated that he sought to create a list of rules for discernment based on the traditional doctrine of discernment, which also can be seen in his engagement with the works of de Paz, Ignatius, Aquinas, de Sales, Bona, Scaramelli, and more. At the same time, he also correlated the tradition with new findings from psychology and the study of the subconscious, acknowledging a difficulty in identifying the true origins of one's spiritual impulses and thoughts, especially given potential unconscious factors.[139] As such, he was critical of Ignatius's idea of a consolation without prior cause, and he preferred to base discernment on "the great fruits of sanctity" that spiritual impulses from good sources produce.[140]

Guibert reiterated the criteriology of Scaramelli and divided the criteria generally between good and bad spirits. The fruits of good spirits include an illumined intellect, discretion, humility, interior peace, trust in God, distrust of self, an openness to God, pure intentions, patience, interior mortification, simplicity, zeal for the imitation of Christ, and charity; whereas the fruits of bad spirits include a futile and darkened intellect filled with vain preoccupations, deception, obstinacy, excesses, pride, vanity, a perturbed and disquieted will, despair, hardness of heart, devious intentions, impatience, rebellious passions, duplicity, earthly concerns, estrangement from Christ, and pharisaical zeal.[141] Beyond these criteria, he also held that anything contrary to the doctrine of the church cannot be from God.[142]

Jean Mouroux and Yves Congar both relied upon dogma and Christ in their criteriologies.[143] Mouroux developed his criteria relying upon the foundational works of Ignatius and Scaramelli.[144] Congar, on the other

---

138. Tanquerey, *Spiritual Life*, 450–52. Karl Rahner also based his approach to spiritual discernment on Ignatius's writings, focusing in particular on Ignatius's idea that a consolation without prior cause must be from God. See Rahner, "Logic," 85–170.

139. de Guibert, *Theology*, 129–36. Cf. Congar, *I Believe*, 181. Congar admitted the need for a healthy demythologization that does not "see the demon at work in everything that is no more than human."

140. de Guibert, *Theology*, 136.

141. de Guibert, *Theology*, 137–38.

142. de Guibert, *Theology*, 139. Cf. Poulain, *Graces of Interior Prayer*, 318–44; Nissen, *Eene zachte aanraking*, 27–29.

143. Mouroux, *Christian Experience*, 179; Congar, *I Believe*, 180.

144. Mouroux, *Christian Experience*, 299–300.

hand, adapted Gérard Therrien's work, placing the criteria of spiritual discernment into three categories.[145] First, doctrinal and objective criteria include the word of God, the teaching of the church and spiritual masters, the duties of one's state, the observation of the commandments (1 John 2:3–5), obedience, and Christology. Second, subjective and personal criteria include one's quality of life as a Christian, the fruit of the Spirit (Gal 5:22), and Ignatius's rules concerning consolation and desolation. Third, communal criteria include a Spirit-led community, the edification of the community, the needs of the church, the communal experience of the Spirit, and the approval of the *ecclesia*.[146]

Jordan Aumann reiterated that "God always inclines us to the good, working either directly or through secondary causes; the devil always inclines us to evil, working by his own power or through the allurements of the things of the world; the human spirit may be inclined to evil or to good, depending upon whether the individual follows right reason or self desires."[147] He enumerated the signs by which one can identify each spirit, and his criteria are quite similar to those in Guibert's work, implying that Aumann, while not explicitly stating so, was relying also on traditional sources such as Ignatius and Scaramelli, continuing the tradition of spiritual discernment handed down to him from previous periods.[148]

Puritan, Quaker, and Pietist Theologians

Discernment of the Spirit was not an exclusive Roman Catholic concern after the Reformation.[149] One can note a similar concern in the writings of Protestants, including Puritans, Quakers, and Pietists. Noting the resurgence of prophecy in the seventeenth and eighteenth centuries, Walter Grossmann argued that it led to "an outpouring of controversial writings among radical Puritans in England, French Protestants in the Camisard Wars and later in exile, and radical German Pietists."[150] In the midst of this milieu, Puritans championed the need to discern the authenticity of spiritual movements and impulses based on the criteria of Scripture and

145. Congar stated that he adapted these categories from Gérard Therrien. Therrien, "discernement spirituel," 16–25; Therrien, *discernement*.
146. Congar, *I Believe*, 182–83.
147. Aumann, *Spiritual Theology*, 401.
148. Aumann, *Spiritual Theology*, 402–14.
149. Lovelace, "Evangelical Spirituality," 221.
150. Grossmann, "True and False Inspiration," 363.

reason.¹⁵¹ John Owen wrote that "upon the ceasing of extraordinary gifts really given from God, the gift also of discerning spirits ceased, and we are left unto the Word alone for the trial of any that shall pretend unto them."¹⁵² He also saw the doctrine of the Holy Spirit and his works as providing a foundation upon which to identify the delusions of Satan's counterfeiting actions and inspirations. Overall, he held that spiritual discernment consists of a knowledge of the truth (doctrine) and dependence on the Holy Spirit, who accords with the Word.¹⁵³

In answering the question whether the Spirit is to be tried by Scripture or Scripture by the Spirit, Richard Baxter put forward the following response. First, the Spirit is more excellent than Scripture, being God, rather than a work of God. Second, the operation of the Spirit in the apostles was more excellent and infallible than that operation of the Spirit now in Christians. Third, therefore, the Holy Scriptures are more infallible and perfect dictates of the Spirit than any of one's apprehensions that come by the same Spirit. Fourth, therefore, one must try one's spiritual apprehensions by the Scriptures, and not vice versa. Fifth, this response is not to put Scripture above the Spirit but to try the Spirit by the Spirit, namely by the Spirit's operations in the apostles as recorded in Scripture.¹⁵⁴ This sentiment was shared among the Puritans, who held that Scripture is the means through which the Spirit moves and speaks to Christians.¹⁵⁵

Puritans also held that reason and conscience are able to act as guides to discern spiritual movements. They held that the Spirit moves according to the principles of human personhood. In other words, the Spirit moves through the means of one's reason and conscience, rather than negating or circumventing them.¹⁵⁶ However, while associating the Spirit with reason and conscience, the Puritans did not equate the Spirit with them, viewing the Spirit as superior to both.¹⁵⁷

---

151. Nuttall, *Holy Spirit*, 34–47. Many of the following citations from Puritan and Quaker sources can be found in Nuttall's work.
152. Owen, Πνευματολογία, 1.1.22; cf. 1.1.31.
153. Owen, Πνευματολογία, 1.1.22.
154. Baxter, *Practical Works*, 5:559.
155. Baxter, *Practical Works*, 2:193; Sibbes, *Complete*, 3:434; 7:193, 199.
156. Nuttall, *Holy Spirit*, 36. See Baxter, *Practical Works*, 2:193; Sibbes, *Complete Works*, 1:197; *Records*, 115–16.
157. Nuttall, *Holy Spirit*, 36. See Sterry, *Spirit Convincing*, 11–16; Goodwin, *Works*, 4:304.

In the works of Richard Sibbes (1577–1635), one can see a more systematic criteriology for the discernment of spirits. Sibbes argued that one must ask the following questions to discern whether an experience of joy and peace is from God or not: first, "What went before it?" second, "What accompanies it?" and third, "What follows after it?" If it be from God, the experience of joy and peace will be preceded by a faithful and obedient assent to Scripture, a deep humiliation and abasement, self-denial, often a victory over conflict, and spiritual strength in holy duties. What accompanies such an experience will be a desire for the ordinances, a spiritual illumination, a liberty and boldness with God, and often the malice and opposition of Satan. Finally, a true and holy experience of joy and peace will leave the soul more humble with less affection for earthly things, an increase of spiritual mettle seen in an encouragement and comfort within duty and suffering, and a joy and comfort when thinking of one's latter end.[158] The general principles behind this system, for Sibbes, were that good motions from God will bring one to God, will involve growth in sanctification, and will agree with Scripture.[159]

The Quaker insistence on being led by an inner light of the Spirit led to unique challenges concerning the discernment of spirits. At times, Quakers acted similar to Puritans; as Geoffry Nuttall explained, "So long as the Quakers sought to realize a true identity between the Spirit in the apostles, as manifested in the written word, and the Spirit in themselves, and so long as, whenever any discrepancy occurred, they gave the primacy to the Spirit in the apostles as regulative, they must be regarded as within the bounds of Puritanism."[160] Still, Quakers had a tendency to contrast, if not set in opposition, the Spirit in themselves and the Word, treating the former as the authority over the latter.[161]

Michael Sheeran identified five criteria of discernment used in early Quaker writings.[162] First, Quakers turned to the cross and to Christ.[163] For Quakers, one knows the will of God by how it makes one bear a cross

---

158. Sibbes, *Complete Works*, 5:441–44.
159. Sibbes, *Complete Works*, 5:427.
160. Nuttall, *Holy Spirit*, 29. See *Register*, 73.
161. Nuttall, *Holy Spirit*, 30. See *Records*, 115–16.
162. Sheeran, *Beyond Majority Rule*, 24–28; cf. Sheeran, "Ignatius and the Quakers," 90. The following engagement with Quaker criteria of discernment draws heavily from Sheeran.
163. Sheeran, *Beyond Majority Rule*, 24–25. Sheeran's first criterion is just the cross, but this criterion fits well with Fox's insistence that the inner light is of Christ.

within one's will. As George Fox (1624-1691) put it, "To speak of truth, when ye are moved, it is a cross to the will; if ye live in the truth which ye speak, ye live in the cross to your own wills."[164] The inner light of the Spirit is supernatural and is of Christ, so it involves a self-denial that is characterized as a cross to one's will. Furthermore, it is a light that reveals one's sins and trespasses, one's need for Christ, and the reality that Christ is the only way to salvation.[165]

Second, Quakers used Scripture as a criterion for spiritual discernment.[166] In theory, at times, Quakers argued that the inner light of the Spirit was not to be tried by Scripture, as much as Scripture by the Spirit. In reply to an individual who had argued that Scripture was to be used to try all doctrines, religions, and opinions, George Fox recorded his response: "I could not hold, but was made to cry out and say, 'O no, it is not the Scriptures'; and I told them what it was, namely, the Holy Spirit, by which the holy men of God gave forth the Scriptures, whereby opinions, religions, and judgments were to be tried; for it led into all truth, and so gave the knowledge of all truth."[167] For this reason, the criterion of Scripture was not always prioritized, held consistently, or applied as supreme.[168] Still, the Quaker tendency to reject Scripture as a criterion often was balanced by their other teachings and practices. Nuttall made this point when he wrote that Geroge Fox's "theoretic rejection of Scripture as a spiritual criterion was therefore largely counteracted by his association, in practice, of 'the light within' with Christ."[169] Interestingly, Fox never claimed that a direct inspiration of the Holy Spirit ever revealed to him a doctrine not recorded in Scripture or a doctrine that supersedes Scripture.[170] While he gained knowledge of supernatural matters directly from

---

164. Fox, *Epistles*, 1:38.
165. Fox, *Journal*, 1:362; cf. Penn, *Works*, 2:812.
166. Sheeran, *Beyond Majority Rule*, 25–26.
167. Fox, *Journal*, 1:43.
168. Sheeran, *Beyond Majority Rule*, 25.
169. Nuttall, *Holy Spirit*, 45.

170. King, *George Fox*, 165. Concerning the relationship between experience and doctrine, John Wesley seemed to have sided with the Puritans, rather than the Quakers, in a balanced way. He wrote, "It is objected, First, 'Experience is not sufficient to prove a doctrine which is not founded on Scripture.' This is undoubtedly true; and it is an important truth; but it does not affect the present question; for it has been shown, that this doctrine is founded on Scripture: Therefore, experience is properly alleged to confirm it." See Wesley, "Sermon XI," 129. Thus, while experience cannot prove a doctrine not found in Scripture, it can be used to confirm a doctrine found in Scripture.

the Holy Spirit, Fox also claimed he "had no slight esteem of the holy Scriptures," for he "was in the Spirit by which they were given forth" and what the Lord revealed directly to him was "afterwards found agreeable to them."[171] Fox's habit of seeking to defend the Quaker view of the inner light by Scripture shows that, in practice, the Quakers did use Scripture as a criterion by which their understanding of the divine inner light was deemed true and correct.[172] Robert Barclay (1648–1690) was much clearer on this issue, stating, "Because the Spirit of God is the Fountain of all Truth and sound reason, therefore, we have well said, That it cannot contradict neither the Testimony of the Scripture, nor right reason."[173]

Third, Fox's primary definition of the inner light was "that which shows a man evil."[174] The corollary of this definition is that the true inner light will lead to the fruit of the Holy Spirit, which acts as a criterion of authenticity.[175] The inner light functions to guide an individual to distinguish between good and evil, and this balanced the Quaker fanaticism by directing them continually to Christ and to ethical action.[176] In describing the inner light that all people have, Fox wrote,

> Therefore love the light, which Christ hath enlightened you withal.... Thou that hatest this light, thou hast it; thou knowest that lying, drunkenness, swearing, whoredom, theft, all ungodliness, and all unrighteousness, are evil.... This light, if thou lovest it, will teach thee holiness and righteousness, without which none shall see God; but if thou hatest this light, it is thy condemnation.[177]

Fourth, Quakers are well known for their emphasis on unity, requiring a meeting to have complete unity on a decision in order to move a decision forward.[178] George Fox explained that the light within leads to

---

171. Fox, *Journal*, 1:36; cf. 1:436–37.

172. Fox, *Journal*, 1:369–71. The 1911 Cambridge edition added that Fox told his interlocutor Tombs, "Before I have done with thee I will make thee bende to ye scriptures."

173. Barclay, *Apology*, 2.15, (62).

174. King, *George Fox*, 81; Fox, *Journal*, 1:67, 121.

175. Sheeran, *Beyond Majority Rule*, 27.

176. Farrow, "Discernment in the Quaker Tradition," 59; Nuttall, *Holy Spirit*, 45.

177. Fox, *Journal*, 1:151.

178. Sheeran, *Beyond Majority Rule*, 26–27. For this criterion, Sheeran focused mostly on submission of openings, but his criterion fits well with the Quaker emphasis on unity.

unity and does not contradict itself.[179] Barclay made this point when he stated that "since there is no greater Mark of the People of God, than to be at Peace among themselves; whatsoever tendeth to break that Bond of Love and Peace, must be testified against."[180] Additionally, in pursuit of unity, one was expected to submit one's leadings to others for their opinion on them.[181]

Fifth, within these meetings, as a group sought unity, a test of authenticity was the ability to wait in silence and speak with unadorned speech.[182] Inner silence was viewed as necessary for hearing the voice of God, and for Barclay, the devil could not counterfeit this silent waiting upon God.[183] Through this process of waiting, the use of rhetorical persuasion was not an accepted means of moving toward unity. Rather, plain speech was a criterion of genuine inspiration, which is one reason why William Penn believed that George Fox was sent by God.[184]

Due to their tendency to hold loosely to the objective criterion of Scripture, Quaker criteria were not fully reliable. Inner silence, unadorned speech, unity, and peace all could be fabricated. At times, a greater reliance upon Scripture, reason, and the written tradition of spiritual discernment was lacking in Quaker discernment.[185] An example of a modern Quaker's criteriology, which does not necessarily remain open to this criticism, comes from J. Brent Bill, who holds the following criteria of discernment: sensations of love, caring, beauty, persistence, rightness, feeling in harmony with God, and surrendering of our wills to God.[186] Authentic leadings call one to action, show the way opening, come from within, are often beautiful, are persistent, require waiting, fill one with joy, bring calmness, give one power, help one confront one's weaknesses,

---

179. Fox, *Journal*, 1:257, 265. See also King, *George Fox*, 81, 108–34. King listed dozens of citations from Fox's journal (the 1611 Cambridge edition) where Fox defined the light within either as "that which shows a man evil" or as that "in which is unity," proving the point that these were Fox's primary ways of defining the inner light.

180. Barclay, *Anarchy of the Ranters*, 387.

181. Barbour, *Quakers in Puritan England*, 120.

182. Sheeran, *Beyond Majority Rule*, 27–28

183. Sheeran, *Beyond Majority Rule*, 27; Barclay, *Apology*, 11.12, (370).

184. Sheeran, *Beyond Majority Rule*, 28; William Penn, preface to *Journal of George Fox*, 1:xlvi.

185. Sheeran, *Beyond Majority Rule*, 28–29.

186. Bill, *Sacred Compass*, 50.

bring clarity, never contradict doctrine, demonstrate the fruit of the Spirit, and fit one's teachability.[187]

One example from the Pietist tradition clearly shows how the criteria of Scripture and sanctification were upheld in continuity with the tradition of spiritual discernment. One early Pietist who wrote multiple works on the discernment of true and false inspirations was Eberhard Ludwig Gruber (1665–1728). Gruber was heavily influenced by mystics such as Johannes Tauler.[188] Given this familiarity, Gruber likely read Tauler's work on spiritual discernment as well as other traditional sources on spiritual discernment. For Gruber, the outer words of Scripture are the source for and authority that supports the "inner word."[189] The inner word differs from the outer word only in its manner of revelation. The inner and outer words raise each other up and harmonize (*harmoniren*) and agree (*uberein*) with one another.[190] The purpose of the inner word is to guide each soul in daily instruction and toward eternal salvation.[191] As such, one guided by the true inner word of God will be an instrument of inspiration (*Inspirationswerkzeug*) who is surrendered to God; serving the Holy Spirit; accepting all the trials from God; and daily repenting, improving, and glorifying God.[192]

John Wesley and Jonathan Edwards

Two Protestant figures in particular stand out during the eighteenth century as influential theologians who wrote on spiritual discernment, namely John Wesley (1703–1791) and Jonathan Edwards (1703–1758). In two sermons, both entitled "The Witness of the Spirit," Wesley set out his theology on the inner witness of the Holy Spirit. For Wesley, true Christianity involves a "heartfelt encounter and response to God" that derives from union with the Holy Spirit.[193] Wesley acknowledged the need to discern between the testimony of God's Spirit and the presumption of the

---

187. Bill, *Sacred Compass*, 51–68; cf. 72–76.
188. Grossmann, "True and False Inspiration," 370.
189. Grossmann, "True and False Inspiration," 371.
190. Gruber, *Kurtze*, 78.
191. Gruber, *Kurtze*, 15.
192. Gruber, *Unterschiedliche Erfahrungsvolle Zeugnisse*, 12.
193. Smith, *Listening to God*, 35–36.

natural mind or the delusion of the devil.[194] The two main signs of this union and of the inner witness of the Holy Spirit are a joyful assurance that one is a child of God and the fruit of the Holy Spirit within the moral transformation of growth in sanctification.[195]

First, Wesley argued that the testimony of the Holy Spirit consists of "an inward impression on the soul, whereby the Spirit of God directly witnesses to my spirit, that I am a child of God; that Jesus Christ hath loved me, and given himself for me; and that all my sins are blotted out, and I, even I, am reconciled to God."[196] In other words, the Spirit witnesses to one's salvation and provides assurance that one truly is a child of God. Second, Wesley held that the inner witness of the Holy Spirit and unity with the Holy Spirit are discerned through a consciousness "that we are inwardly conformed, by the Spirit of God, to the image of his Son, and that we walk before him in justice, mercy, and truth, doing the things which are pleasing in his sight."[197] Whereas the natural mind and the deceptions of Satan lack repentance and lead to spiritual pride, a liberty of disobedience, and other forms of sin, the real testimony of the Spirit is preceded by repentance and being born again, accompanied by humble joy and the fruit of the Holy Spirit, and followed by faithful obedience to the commandments of God.[198]

Jonathan Edwards is known for two important works on spiritual discernment, written during the First Great Awakening. For Edwards, true religion, according to Scripture, consists "very much in the Affections; such as Fear, Hope, Love, Hatred, Desire, Joy, Sorrow, Gratitude, Compassion and Zeal"; and since these affections can be counterfeited, they must be tested based on whether they lead to true spiritual growth.[199] In *The Distinguishing Marks of a Work of the Spirit of God* (1741), he stated five signs of a work of the Holy Spirit. A work of the Holy Spirit will raise one's esteem of Christ and confirm the truth of the gospel, will be at odds with Satan's kingdom of sin, will establish the truth and divinity of Scripture, will lead to and convince one of truth, and will consist of the love of God and humanity.[200] Furthermore, in *On Religious Af-*

---

194. Wesley, "Sermon X," 117.
195. Smith, *Listening to God*, 37–38; Smith, *Voice of Jesus*, 44–46.
196. Wesley, "Sermon X," 115; cf. 117.
197. Wesley, "Sermon X," 115; cf. 113–14.
198. Wesley, "Sermon X," 117–22.
199. Edwards, *Religious Affections*, 10. Cf. Smith, *Voice of Jesus*, 48.
200. Edwards, *Distinguishing Marks*, 2:266–69.

fections (1746), Edwards identified twelve positive signs of an authentic experience of truly gracious and holy affections. These signs can be organized according to the origin, characteristics, and consequences of the affections.[201] True religious affections will originate from supernatural and divine things while being grounded in their excellent and lovely character and the mind's enlightenment. Furthermore, they will have the characteristics of the conviction of religious truths, evangelical humility, and a change of nature into Christlikeness. Finally, they will lead to a greater longing for spiritual things as well as the exercise and fruit of Christian practice.[202]

From this survey, one can see that a continuity exists between the writings of Puritans, Quakers, and Pietists; those of modern Roman Catholics; and older writings on the criteria of spiritual discernment. While definite differences were maintained among all of the various writers included in this survey, a certain consistency existed on the main criteria used for spiritual discernment. The criteria of Jesus Christ, the Holy Spirit, Scripture, and sanctification appear frequently and persistently throughout the history of spiritual discernment.

THE CRITERIA OF SPIRITUAL DISCERNMENT AND THE IMAGE OF GOD: A SUMMATIVE ANALYSIS AND CRITIQUE

Despite its many variances, the history of spiritual discernment reveals that certain doctrinal criteria consistently were held to and defended by theologians who wrote on spiritual discernment, revealing the centrality and necessity of doctrine within spiritual discernment and justifying its continued use for criteria of discernment. To a certain extent, throughout church history, talk of spiritual discernment criteria simply was talk of Christ, the Holy Spirit, Scripture, and sanctification (*telos*). As will be shown in the following analysis, the major criteria of spiritual

---

201. Howard, *Affirming the Touch*, 121. One wonders whether Edwards was working off of Richard Sibbes by how his twelve signs can be organized similar to Sibbes's organization. Edwards was familiar with Sibbes's work, even quoting him in a footnote when discussing the twelfth sign of an authentic experience of grace. See Edwards, *Religious Affections*, 316. Either way, a clear affinity exists between Edwards's work on spiritual discernment and previous Puritans.

202. Edwards, *Religious Affections*, 88–343. For a recent interpretation of Edwards's work on discernment, see McDermott, *Seeing God*.

discernment seen in the history of the church continue to find a place of prevalence in contemporary writings.

Still, as systematic theologians continue to develop doctrine, spiritual discernment also should continue adapting particular doctrines for use as criteria of discernment.[203] One doctrine particularly well suited for such an adaptation is the doctrine of the image of God. Conformity to the image of God is one *telos* of sanctification described in the New Testament, one product of the Holy Spirit's work, and one way to discuss conformity to Christ.[204] In other words, the criteria of Christ, Scripture, the Holy Spirit, and sanctification coalesce into the criterion of the image of God. Still, the use of the image of God as a criterion of discernment is a lacuna within the history of spiritual discernment. As such, to show how the image of God relates to the criteria of Scripture, Christ, the Holy Spirit, and sanctification, and how it is a legitimate and valuable doctrinal criterion to use in spiritual discernment, an analysis of each of the four major criteria in turn will be useful, showing how they are discussed in contemporary writings and how they connect to the image of God.

The Criterion of Scripture and the Image of God

Drawing from the wealth of historical works on spiritual discernment, contemporary authors organize the criteria of discernment in various ways, often emphasizing the criteria of doctrine, the fruit of the Spirit, the imitation of Christ, and growth in sanctification.[205] Contemporary

---

203. In 2013, Kees Waaijman noted that 280 studies on spiritual discernment had been published in the previous twenty years, most of which focused on the world of spirits, Ignatius and historical figures, or communal discernment. See Waaijman, "Discernment and Biblical Spirituality," 5–7. Doctrinal application has not been a major emphasis in recent works on spiritual discernment. As such, a continued need exists for the study of spiritual discernment to be shaped into contemporary applicable forms through the use of contemporary doctrine.

204. As Waaijman wrote, "Discernment perceives someone's ultimate destiny," which for every believer consists of perfect conformity to the image of God. See Waaijman, *Spirituality*, 513.

205. Beyond these major criteria, theologians also have put forward various other criteria, such as rational deliberation, the consideration of one's circumstances, the will of God for a universal community of love, the quality of one's dialogue with God, the reality that God is beyond one's control, the glory of God, and unity with the body of Christ. See Mumford, *Take Another Look*; Morris and Olsen, *Discerning God's Will*, 78–80; Hughes, "Ignatian Discernment," 435; Barry, "Theology of Discernment," 139; Barry and Connolly, *Practice of Spiritual Direction*, 101–14; Chan, *Spiritual Theology*, 203.

theologians continue to hold that authentic spiritual experiences will conform to Scripture.[206] One axiom of spiritual discernment, as Gordon T. Smith stated, is that "the inner witness of the Spirit will never contradict the written witness; indeed, to discern is to consider how the Scriptures are to be lived in a particular time and place, to discover how the Spirit applies the truth to a specific person or people."[207] In other words, the process of discernment simply is a process in which one applies Scripture and doctrine to one's life and spiritual experiences.

Multiple implications are contained within this criterion. First, conformity to Scripture also entails conformity to apostolic and catholic doctrine, or the understanding of Scripture from within the *regula fidei*.[208] One's spiritual experiences must be consistent with "what is historically and reliably known of the revealed God," and this knowledge has been handed down within a "body of beliefs held in common by the churches—that is, the teachings of Christ and of the prophets and apostles that are now incorporated in Holy Scripture as the foundational document of Christianity" and faithfully interpreted from within the economy of the church apostolic and catholic.[209] As Cassian explained, one must be able to identify when the coin is stamped with the effigy of an usurper, as when Scripture is twisted in the mouth of Satan or the unorthodox. So, conformity to Scripture also implies conformity to an orthodox understanding of Scripture.

Second, conformity to Scripture includes conformity to the realities of salvation history. Scripture contains "a vision of salvation history" that acts as "the backdrop for measuring what is spiritual and what is not."[210]

---

206. Howard, *Affirming the Touch*, 347; Morneau, "Principles of Discernment," 166; Dubay, *Authenticity*, 160–70; Oden, *Life in the Spirit*, 67; Spohn, "Reasoning Heart," 45; Farnham et al., *Listening Hearts*, 44.

207. Smith, "Discernment," 405. Smith also added, "And second, to know the witness of the Spirit, one must be in community. This does not mean that the witness of the Spirit is the same as the voice or will of the community; rather, it is a recognition that individuals who attend to the Spirit are resolved to live in mutual submission within the body of Christ." To a certain extent, community also could be considered a major criterion of spiritual discernment throughout history. Spiritual discernment never can take place in pure isolation. Interestingly, the image of God cannot be "imaged" in pure isolation either, especially given its relational aspect, as will be explained in the following chapter.

208. Cunningham, "*Extra arcam Noe*," 172. Cf. Dubay, *Authenticity*, 165–68. Dubay noted that sound doctrine will be "at odds with the prevailing spirit of the world."

209. Oden, *Life in the Spirit*, 67; Bockmuehl, *God Who Speaks*, 98.

210. Morneau, "Principles of Discernment," 167.

The foundation and apex of salvation history is Jesus Christ and his life, works, teachings, death, and resurrection. Discernment is a process that ties one's spiritual experiences to Christ, who is the source of Christian life and teaching.[211] Overall, the content of one's spiritual experiences, if they are authentic experiences, will align with Scripture and the traditions of the church; it also will communicate the God of Christianity and the particularities of Jesus Christ and salvation history as contained in Scripture.

To use Scripture as a criterion of discernment is to say that one's spiritual experiences must align with the realities revealed in Scripture, including the reality of God, God's acts, and the results of those acts, one of which is human beings made in the image of God, now fallen and yet restored by Christ and growing in conformity to that image. Scripture provides the Christian community with a clear picture of salvation history and growth in sanctification, connecting the Christian's life and beliefs to the death and resurrection of Jesus Christ and revealing the differences between what leads to life and what leads to death. Conformity to the image of God is one central and important way that Scripture describes the human person within the process of sanctification. As Robinson explained, "We engage in discernment within a very specific context—that of the Christian ideal. The incarnation, life, death and resurrection of Jesus makes clearer who God is and what humankind is called to be."[212] As Christians are called by Scripture to be growing in conformity to the image of God, spiritual experiences that align with Scripture and the realities revealed in Scripture will cohere with the particular reality of the image of God.

The Criterion of Christ and the Image of God

According to Jon Sobrino, the ultimate criterion of spiritual discernment is Jesus Christ.[213] All of Christian spirituality is concerned with shaping oneself into the likeness of Jesus Christ, both internally and externally.[214] Evan B. Howard explained, "By articulating those tendencies by which

---

211. Downey, *Understanding Christian Spirituality*, 108.
212. Robinson, "Encounter with God," 179.
213. Sobrino, *Christology at the Crossroads*, 129; cf. Morneau, "Principles of Discernment," 165–66; Downey, *Understanding Christian Spirituality*, 108.
214. Demarest, *Satisfy Your Soul*, 70–74.

God revealed in Jesus Christ is known, we also articulate important criteria by which the church recognizes the presence and action of God."[215] Discernment rests upon the person of Christ as the ultimate example and measurement of holy living. Scripture presents Christ as the example which Christians are to follow, with the goal of spiritual growth being for the Christian to become like Christ, united with Christ through the power of the Holy Spirit in his life, death, and resurrection.[216] Howard stated this criterion clearly: "If discernment is the evaluation of what is from God, then Jesus himself is the clearest sign of what 'from God' might look like."[217]

Furthermore, from its beginning to its final consummation, authentic Christian spirituality will be centered on Christ, beginning with conversion to Christ, continuing through growth into the likeness of Christ, and being consummated at the second coming of Christ with perfect union to Christ.[218] Many characteristics of authentic spiritual experiences are implied by the criterion of Christ. Spiritual experiences conforming to the criterion of Christ will be trinitarian, scriptural, creational (or incarnational), empowered by the Holy Spirit, self-sacrificial, both individual and corporate (seeking communion), and embracing of human personhood, to name only a few.[219] They will lead beyond the artificial imitation of the external aspects of Jesus's life toward a deep devotion to God and a passionate pursuit of proclaiming the kingdom of God.[220] Both orthodox doctrine and a kingdom praxis are necessarily entailed within this criterion.[221]

One difficulty with this criterion is seen in the impossibility of reducing the life of Christ to a list of characteristics. The complexities, intricacies, and nuances of Christ's life always will supersede any attempt at such reduction. William A. Barry was correct when he stated, "If we would be imitators of God, we can do nothing more helpful than to get to

---

215. Howard, *Affirming the Touch*, 376. Howard also interestingly stated, "Some of the most needed research in the area of the theology of discernment will surround the doctrines of Christology and theology proper."

216. Morneau, "Principles of Discernment," 166–67; Downey, *Understanding Christian Spirituality*, 108; Au and Au, *Discerning Heart*, 199.

217. Howard, *Brazos Introduction*, 376–77.

218. Demarest, *Satisfy Your Soul*, 71.

219. Demarest, *Satisfy Your Soul*, 71–72; Wolff, *Discernment*, 23–35.

220. Au and Au, *Discerning Heart*, 199.

221. Sobrino, "Following Jesus as Discernment," 18–21.

know Jesus better. He is the human image of God *par excellence*. In Jesus we find enfleshed the mind and heart of God. If we would be perfect as our heavenly Father is perfect, then we can do no better than to develop an intimate relationship with Jesus."[222] In other words, to understand this criterion more fully, one must know Christ personally, and one must flesh out this criterion based on the life of Christ as presented in the Gospels. If conformity to the image of Christ entails conformity to the image of God (see chapter 3), then the criterion of Christ directly entails and justifies the use of the criterion of the image of God. In order to fill in the image of God as a criterion of spiritual discernment with any content, the categories of the image of God must be tied intimately to the life of Christ as presented in the Gospels (see chapter 4).

The Criteria of the Holy Spirit, Sanctification, and the Image of God

Authentic spiritual experiences will produce the fruit of the Holy Spirit and conform to the nature of the Holy Spirit, as the Spirit is revealed in Scripture.[223] In this way, discernment looks to the consequences of spiritual experiences as signs for or against authentication, depending on whether those experiences lead to or away from the things of the Spirit.[224] In particular, the fruit of the Spirit pertains to the development of virtuous affections—affections that are internally and communally harmonious and oriented toward the things of God.[225] Where the Spirit is, there will be love, joy, peace, and so forth (Gal 5:22).[226] This criterion is basically Ignatian spirituality and, like Ignatius did, it must be nuanced depending on whether an individual is living in sin or actively pursuing holiness. Beyond internal affectivity, the fruit of the Holy Spirit is also the fruit of sanctification (Eph 5:8–10), inclusive of good and loving works.[227]

---

222. Barry, *Paying Attention to God*, 68.

223. Howard, *Affirming the Touch*, 347; Green, *Weeds Among Wheat*, 72; Bockmuehl, *God Who Speaks*, 65; Smith, *Voice of Jesus*, 58–60.

224. Morneau, "Principles of Discernment," 172; Howard, *Brazos Introduction*, 392; Morris and Olsen, *Discerning God's Will Together*, 78–80.

225. Buckley, "Discernment of Spirits," 277. See also Spohn, "Reasoning Heart," 30–52; Dubay, *Authenticity*, 147.

226. Dubay, *Authenticity*, 110; Bockmuehl, *God Who Speaks*, 98.

227. Larkin, *Silent Presence*, 20–24; cf. Farnham et al., *Listening Hearts*, 46–47; Dubay, *Authenticity*, 146–59; Sheets, "Profile of the Spirit," 370–75. Sheets claims that, in order to cohere with the nature of the Holy Spirit, spiritual experiences must be holy, spiritual, true, eschatological, communal, incarnational, fostering universal relations,

As such, the fruit of the Holy Spirit is both internal and external, corresponding to the nature of the works of the Holy Spirit.

The Holy Spirit has a variety of roles within the lives of Christians, including such works as assuring them of the love of God, convicting them of sin, leading them into all truth, guiding their decisions, and growing them in sanctification.[228] Experiences of the Holy Spirit will align with these roles. The assurance of the Holy Spirit leads one to be humble and to love as God has loved. The conviction of the Holy Spirit is a feeling of guilt that leads to humility, confession, and liberation.[229] This guilt is to be distinguished from the condemning guilt imposed upon one by the self or the devil.[230] So, the conviction of the Holy Spirit leads to forgiveness, and one can be sure that the forgiveness of sins is from God because only God forgives, regenerates, and reconciles individuals to himself.[231] The Spirit leads believers to the truth, and thus to the word of God, enabling and illuminating believers to understand and humbly submit to that word. As such, the Spirit will always guide believers to discern the authenticity of spiritual experiences based on the truth of Scripture. The Spirit, again like Ignatius said, will guide one's decision making through periods of consolation, desolation, and the rational acknowledgment of one's situation.[232]

Overall, the role of the Holy Spirit is to lead believers into growth in sanctification. As such, all thoughts (intellect), feelings (affect), and desires (volition) that move one toward sanctification are products of the Holy Spirit's work of sanctification.[233] What Christ achieved, the Spirit applies to believers; as Thomas Oden wrote, "God not only forgives sin through the Son but through the Spirit works to overturn the power of sin in actual daily interpersonal behavior and life in community. The gospel not only announces the death and resurrection of Christ but calls us to die to sin and live to God by the power of the Spirit."[234]

---

charismatic, adhering to God's will, liberating, of Christ, involving unity through variety, and leading to spiritual harmony.

228. Smith, *Listening to God*, 38–39; Smith, *Voice of Jesus*, 73.
229. Smith, *Voice of Jesus*, 88–96.
230. Smith, *Listening to God*, 39.
231. Rupnik, *Discernment*, 30.
232. Smith, *Voice of Jesus*, 110–26, 139–52.
233. Rupnik, *Discernment*, 26.
234. Oden, *Life in the Spirit*, 4; cf. 52–57.

In relation to sanctification and the image of God, the Holy Spirit is "the bond by which Christ effectually binds us to himself."[235] The Holy Spirit unites one to Christ and conforms one into the image of Christ, who is the image of God (2 Cor 3:17–18). Gordon T. Smith wrote, "To be a Christian is to walk in the Spirit, to be led by the Spirit, to respond to the Spirit, who transforms us into the image of Christ."[236] Therefore, the ministry of the Holy Spirit is Christocentric, glorifying and pointing to Christ while transforming believers into the image of Christ. Since Christ is also the perfect image of God, the fruit of the work of the Holy Spirit in sanctification can be described as conforming believers into the image of God. Therefore, the criteria of the Holy Spirit and sanctification provide justification for the use of the image of God as a criterion of spiritual discernment.

Ultimately, the criterion of the image of God inheres within and grows out of the criteria of Scripture, Christ, the Holy Spirit, and sanctification, grounding the use of the image of God as a criterion within these previously established criteria. Scripture reveals sanctification; Christ models and achieves sanctification; the Spirit applies sanctification; and conformity to the image of God is the goal of sanctification. As Kees Waaijman wrote, "Humans are created in God's image and called to mature into perfect likeness to him. This is the fundamental distinction in which . . . the articulation of the spiritual journey is delineated in all the great spiritual writers."[237]

DOCTRINE AND THE PLURALITY OF CHRISTIAN SPIRITUALITIES

So far in this chapter, the history of spiritual discernment and criteria has shown that doctrinal criteria—in particular, Scripture, Christ, the Holy Spirit, and sanctification—have held a central role within spiritual discernment, that these criteria often took on a teleological orientation in relation to sanctification and the *telos* of spirituality, and that the image of God is able to be used as such a criterion insofar as it inheres in and builds off of these established criteria and is one way in which the *telos* of spirituality is described. This history seems to indicate that the use of

---

235. Calvin, *Institutes*, 3.1.1.
236. Smith, *Voice of Jesus*, 16.
237. Waaijman, *Spirituality*, 511.

doctrinal criteria for spiritual discernment is both justified and necessary. Yet, as noted in the introduction, Christian scholars disagree on the specific relationship between theology and spiritual experience.

Some scholars hold that spirituality and theology are mutually interactive yet autonomous fields, in which spirituality flows beyond the boundaries set by theology or holds priority over theology. Others view theology as providing the criteria by which to interpret and judge spiritual experience. Still others say that doctrine must guide and control spirituality.[238] According to Kees Waaijman, the study and practice of spirituality have become detached from their doctrinal moorings, like ships on the high seas without a compass, and set adrift both in academia and society, oriented around a "mystical core" and embedded in globalization and inter-religious dialogue.[239] Nonetheless, Philip Sheldrake argues that the question of criteria, developed along theological lines, is essential for the study of spirituality, especially given the plurality of approaches in the field.[240] Overall, the relationship between doctrinal criteria of spiritual discernment and spiritual experience needs clarification. While some scholars may object to the use of doctrine to control and guide spirituality, doctrinal criteria are necessary authorities over spiritual experience if spirituality is to be kept from drifting into mere subjectivity, relativism, and individualism. Furthermore, doctrinal criteria are able to be developed in such a way that they avoid the construction of an overly rigid or narrow view of spirituality.

Christian Spirituality Without Doctrinal Criteria

Without clear doctrinal criteria, Christian spirituality becomes reduced to a natural spirituality of sorts. Yet a vast expanse exists between, on the one hand, the merely human pursuit of personal fulfillment or self-transcendence and, on the other hand, the human response to "God's revelation in Jesus Christ and the Scriptures, leading to self-surrender, worship, and service."[241] Spirituality without authoritative doctrinal boundaries easily can become eclectic, focused on self or miscellaneous social and

---

238. See Sheldrake, "Study of Spirituality," 166–67; Sheldrake, *Spirituality and Theology*, 85–87, 95.

239. Waaijman, "Discernment," 14–15.

240. Sheldrake, "Study of Spirituality," 170.

241. Demarest, *Satisfy Your Soul*, 65–66.

environmental issues, or a New Age and relativistic spiritualism in which works or quasi-religious lifestyles unlock personal transcendence and connection with some vague Ultimate Reality.[242] Christian spirituality is quite different from these spiritualities, focusing on the encounter between the human person and the divine person of Christ. The focal point of Christian spirituality, according to Mark McIntosh, is not "the states of inner transcendence experienced by the self, but rather the patterns, structures and images that embody the beckoning of the other and the response this invocation evokes."[243] In other words, authentic spirituality is not a self-centered pursuit of one's own goals or desires for self-transcendence but is a response to the call of the Other who is God as revealed in Jesus Christ and a recognition of one's place within the realities of God's works of creation and redemption.[244] As Eugene Peterson correctly cautioned, "Spirituality is always in danger of self-absorption, of becoming so intrigued with matters of soul that God is treated as a mere accessory to my experience."[245]

Explaining why spirituality often is looked upon with suspicion, Peterson wrote that "in actual practice spirituality very often develops into neurosis, degenerates into selfishness, becomes pretentious, turns violent."[246] The reason for this degeneration is that an overly subjective spirituality "lies open to the aberrations inherent in the human condition."[247] At this point, Evan B. Howard's work on experience is essential and quite enlightening. Without doctrinal criteria, spirituality is vulnerable to all of the previously mentioned corruptions within the operations, stages, and relationships of fallen human experience. Spirituality becomes a product of prejudice and personal ambition, defined by self-centeredness rather than God-centeredness, and liable to create subjective and individualistic divisions rather than healthy relationships of communion and unity. In particular, without the necessary doctrinal criteria, one's cognitive stages of Understanding and Judging will

---

242. Demarest, *Satisfy Your Soul*, 66–69.

243. McIntosh, *Mystical Theology*, 21–22.

244. Cf. McIntosh, *Mystical Theology*, 23. McIntosh argues that the anthropological approach to the study of spirituality, as seen in Sandra Schneider's work, leaves open the possibility of relegating spirituality "to a non-theological realm labeled, appropriately, 'private devotion.'"

245. Peterson, "Saint Mark," 338.

246. Peterson, "Saint Mark," 330.

247. Dubay, *Authenticity*, 92.

remain faulty and unreliable—a result of the lack of discernment—and will lead to flaws in the latter stages of Deciding, Acting, and Worldview Adjusting.[248]

Concerning subjectivity, when an experience is raised above doctrine as an unchallengeable authority, the intensity of an experience quickly can "[absolve] one from discretion, critical reflection, and the doctrinal content of Christian faith, . . . transferring the religious guidance of a single person or of an entire community to an unchallengeable subjectivity, to sentimentality or superstition or excited enthusiasms."[249] While the experiential is invaluable and must be accounted for within spiritual life, the experiential devoid of doctrinal grounding becomes reduced to an expression of human subjectivity, in which the role of the divine Other is replaced by an unchecked and overactive religious imagination.[250] If the validation of religion and religious experience is completely internal, located within one's consciousness, then religion becomes subjective and thus relative and individualistic.[251] The good becomes identified with that which feels good rather than that which is objectively good, and authentic religion becomes replaced with individualistic decadence.[252]

Unity in Diversity: The Balance of Doctrine and Experience

Plenty of examples can be drawn from Christian history when doctrine was either neglected or misused to create or enforce unhealthy spiritualities. On the one hand, instances can be brought up when doctrine was placed under other more authoritative criteria such as reason or experience, as in Enlightenment rationalism, which led to a secular subjectivism based on autonomous reason, or in the various forms of Illuminism—such as Montanism or Jansenism—that raised inner inspiration above external criteria and resulted in ecstatic extravagancies.[253]

On the other hand, historical instances exist when doctrine was misused to enforce an unhealthy spirituality. Some argue, for example, that the church hierarchy in the Middle Ages created particular doctrinal

---

248. Cf. Howard, *Brazos Introduction*, 160–63; Howard, *Affirming the Touch*, 344.
249. Buckley, "Discernment of Spirits," 274–75.
250. McIntosh, *Mystical Theology*, 9.
251. Dubay, *Authenticity*, 92.
252. Dubay, *Authenticity*, 85–87.
253. Anderson, "Free Spirits," 30; Dubay, *Authenticity*, 52–53.

rules of spiritual discernment in order to hold a greater clerical control over women, which may have contributed to late medieval and early modern witch hunts.[254] Even if this interpretation of medieval Roman Catholicism is a bit of a stretch, as disagreement exists among scholars as to the extent to which spiritual discernment was an issue of gender during that period, one can see how doctrinal criteria easily can become a means of either control or exclusion, resulting in an unhealthy spiritual echo chamber in which preestablished theology becomes unquestionable and unreformable.[255]

Theology is always in need of being reformed (*semper reformanda*) according to Scripture, and bad theology can lead to bad discernment. Flawed views of the nature of God can lead to flawed interpretations of one's experience—for example, an overly negative view of God impacting one's interpretation of one's experience of shame.[256] Martin Luther is an example of this phenomenon. Based on his understanding of the "righteousness of God" as a formal righteousness by which God punishes the unrighteous sinner, Luther wrote, "Though I lived as a monk without reproach, I felt that I was a sinner before God with an extremely disturbed conscience."[257] Upon his realization that the righteousness of God is that by which God justifies sinners, Luther's entire spiritual experience of his imperfections was changed, and he felt that he was "born again and had entered paradise itself through open gates."[258]

Furthermore, doctrine should not be used solely as a "trump card that ends the discussion" concerning spiritual discernment.[259] Nor should theology be used to dismiss the experiential aspects of salvation, turning sanctification into a mere ontological abstract rather than a concrete experience.[260] While doctrine must be kept as an authoritative criterion over experience, a dialogue between theology and personal experience must

254. See Hollywood, "Feminist Studies," 363–86.

255. Cf. Anderson, "Free Spirits," 7–12. Anderson engaged with this question of gender and spiritual discernment in dialogue with others who have written on the topic such as Rosalynn Voaden and Nancy Caciola. See Voaden, *God's Words, Women's Voices*; and Nancy Caciola, *Discerning Spirits*.

256. Lonsdale, *Music of the Spirit*, 152–53.

257. Luther, "Preface," 11.

258. Luther, "Preface," 11.

259. Liebert, *Soul of Discernment*, 110.

260. Zahl, *Holy Spirit*, 71. In much of this book, Zahl sought to critique a kind of "complacency with theological abstraction" and a lack of "practical recognizability" concerning sanctification and the work of the Holy Spirit.

be maintained that does not dismiss the experiential as unimportant or invalid.[261] Explaining the need to balance established doctrine with the unique ways in which the Spirit might move within an individual, Thomas Oden wrote, "God the Spirit is always meeting us in a new way, yet always in continuity with the ways in which the triune God has already become self-revealed in the histories of Israel, Jesus, and the church."[262] Insofar as Christian spirituality is based on the experience of God through Jesus Christ, there is only one Christian spirituality; but, insofar as a variety of complementary and legitimate expressions of this spirituality can exist in one's life, one can speak of multiple and diverse Christian spiritualities.[263] As such, Christian spirituality represents a unity within diversity—unity in that the spiritual experience will be of the one true God and diversity in the particularities of legitimate responses to that reality as well as the diverse ways in which that reality can be experienced and perceived.

The Image of God and the Balance of Particularity and Diversity

In conclusion, Christian discernment must uphold the particularities of Christian doctrine.[264] Remove the particularities of Christian doctrine, and one removes the criteria of spiritual discernment. The particularities and normativity of the revelation of God in Jesus Christ make clear who God is, who humanity is, and of what salvation and spiritual life consist.[265] The *telos* of Christian spirituality is not a general movement toward self-transcendence or from self-centeredness to Reality-centeredness; it is a movement toward union with God in Christ through the power of the Holy Spirit, which involves conformity to the image of God.

Additionally, Christian discernment also must recognize the diverse and individual means and experiences of spiritual growth that may result from differences between peoples' temperaments, personalities, life

---

261. Liebert, *Soul of Discernment*, 110; Cunningham, "*Extra arcam Noe*," 174.

262. Oden, *Life in the Spirit*, 67.

263. Chan, *Spiritual Theology*, 20–21; LaCugna and Downey, "Trinitarian Spirituality," 968.

264. McIntosh, *Mystical Theology*, 34; Zahl, *Holy Spirit*, 34; LaCugna and Downey, "Trinitarian Spirituality," 980; Lonsdale, *Music of the Spirit*, 45; Berthoud, "Discerning Spirituality," 52, 56; Downey, *Understanding Christian Spirituality*, 108; Dockery, "Paul's View," 348.

265. Robinson, "Encounter with God," 179. Cf. Bloesch, *Spirituality Old and New*, 29–30.

situations, learning styles, and so on, as well as the freedom of God to communicate and make himself known in pluriform ways, according to his wisdom and power.[266] One way to uphold this unity in diversity is to distinguish between the means and the ends of spiritual growth. For example, one end of spiritual growth is to be perfect in love and humility, but love and humility may be produced by a variety of means.[267] The value of criteria, then, to a great extent, lies in how they give believers ways of judging the direction in which a spiritual experience is moving them, whether toward or away from the *telos* of Christian spirituality. In particular, the criterion of the image of God guides believers in this way, providing a guiding *telos* without rigidly or exclusively defining one external expression of the path toward that *telos*. Therefore, the previously stated objections or concerns to the use of doctrinal criteria for spiritual discernment do not invalidate the use of the image of God as a criterion. The criterion of the image of God is able to balance the doctrinal and the experiential and to recognize the unity within diversity of Christian spirituality.

---

266. Au and Au, *Discerning Heart*, 74, 79–81, 94; Howard, *Brazos Introduction*, 390; Zahl, *Holy Spirit*, 53; cf. Catherine of Siena, *Dialogue*, 103.194–95.

267. Catherine of Siena, *Dialogue*, 103.196.

3

The Image of God as a Criterion for Discerning Authentic Spiritual Experiences

Due to the reality that Christian believers still, in part, deal with their fallen human natures and the resulting ambiguities and obscurities within spiritual experiences, the discernment of spiritual experiences is absolutely necessary. Doctrinal criteria—such as Christ, the Holy Spirit, Scripture, and the *telos* of sanctification—are necessary to identify the authenticity of a spiritual experience. The doctrine of the image of God can act as one such doctrinal criterion, based on how it inheres within and grows out of these other widely established criteria. These statements express my argument so far, and in this chapter I will substantiate further my claim that the image of God can act as a criterion of spiritual discernment.

To reiterate my main thesis, I am arguing that, as christological and teleological, the image of God is able to act as a criterion of spiritual discernment by identifying the specific ways in which conformity to the image of Christ takes on functional, relational, and structural aspects. As such, a spiritual experience must conform to or move one toward conformity with the image of God to be counted authentic.

In chapter 2, I showed that the criteria of Christ, the Holy Spirit, Scripture, and sanctification have all been used widely throughout history as criteria of spiritual discernment. I further made some initial claims about how the image of God inheres within these criteria and grows out of them, thus providing initial justification for my claim that the image of God is able to act as a criterion of spiritual discernment. In the first section of this chapter, I will substantiate that claim further by focusing on how Scripture depicts the image of God in relation to Christ and sanctification. If conformity to Christ and growth in sanctification are two established criteria of spiritual discernment, and the image of God is one way to describe those criteria, then Scripture shows the validity of the initial part of my main thesis, that the image of God can act as a criterion of spiritual discernment.

The second part of my thesis clarifies the way in which the image of God acts as a criterion—namely, by how it identifies the three aspects in which conformity to the image of Christ takes place and, thus, the material content of what a spiritual experience must conform to or move one toward conformity with in order to be considered authentic. This second claim assumes that the image of God is multifaceted. As such, in order to defend this claim, in the second and third sections of this chapter, I will explore the main systematic positions on the image of God and put forward a heuristic and multifaceted position that connects function, relation, and structure to the image of God without delineating a taxonomy between them, showing that the image of God, at least, either consists in or entails these three aspects. If the image of God consists in or entails these three aspects, then these aspects can act as the material measurement by which the authenticity of a spiritual experience is judged.

THE IMAGE OF GOD AS CREATIONAL, CHRISTOLOGICAL, AND TELEOLOGICAL: THE BIBLICAL DATA

Man and Woman: Created in the Image of God

The image of God appears infrequently in Scripture, and yet Scripture locates it at multiple places within the drama of salvation, securing its importance as a doctrine. Human beings are created in the image of God and later conformed to that image in salvation.[1] As such, humanity cannot be fully understood apart from the doctrine of the image of God. The first appearance in Scripture of the image of God is in Gen 1:26–28, when God created man and woman in the image (צֶלֶם) and likeness (דְּמוּת) of himself as the climax of creation. The occurrence of צֶלֶם and דְּמוּת in verse 26 is an example of Hebrew parallelism, indicating that these words

---

1. Casey, "*Suspensa expectatio*," 86; Berkouwer, *Man*, 67.

are used synonymously with each other.² Humans alone are described as made in the image of God in the world, indicating the uniqueness with which God made humanity.

In the context of the ancient Near East (ANE), the term צֶלֶם is an overtly physical term, referring to a cult image, or an idol or statue, which is corporeal and visible.³ Interestingly, Richard Middleton notes that the creation story in Gen 1 involves the creation of a cosmic sanctuary in which God dwells and reigns (cf. Isa 6:1–5; 66:1–2; Jer 23:24).⁴ Therefore, when God made human beings in his image, he made them as the representatives of his presence within his cosmic temple on the Earth. The representative nature of the image is strengthened by how kings in the ANE often were referred to as images of their god, given the divine task of protecting the citizens within their domain.⁵ More will be said about this context in the next section, but for now the important thing to note is that the creation account in Genesis democratizes this royal ideology, indicating that all of humanity, both male and female, are representative images of God.⁶

The implications of being created in the image of God are manifold. The image of God shows that humans have a creational holiness and sanctity that afford them a unique value and dignity within creation.⁷ Human beings are made according to the likeness of God and thus according to a dislikeness from all other creatures.⁸ In other words, humans are set apart by God to be unique and different from other creatures. Within the context of Gen 1 and 2, the uniqueness of human beings is immediately evident in their relationship with God and the function that God commands them to fulfill. Stephen J. Harper explained this unique relationship:

---

2. Bird, *Evangelical Theology*, 744; Cortez, *Theological Anthropology*, 16.

3. McConville, *Being Human*, 17; Middleton, *Liberating Image*, 25.

4. Middleton, *Liberating Image*, 81–84, 87. Middleton defends this view by pointing out the common occurrence of such an idea in the ANE, the prominence of sevens and its multiples in the creation story and as associated with the temple (1 Kg 8), as well as the parallels between the creation account and the construction of the tabernacle (Exod 25–31).

5. Levenson, *Creation*, 114.

6. Etzelmüller, *Gottes verkörpertes Ebenbild*, 278–80.

7. Harper, "Old Testament Spirituality," 315–16; Jewett, *Who We Are*, 55.

8. Watson, *Text and Truth*, 277.

Because we have been made "like God" we are equipped for relationship with God. In the act of creation, God demonstrated a desire for relationship beyond and outside of the Godhead. By creating human beings in the *imago dei*, God made possible both the desire and ability for every person to relate beyond himself/herself—to others, to every other part of creation, and ultimately to God.[9]

God created human beings in order to call them into relationship with him. Humans are called to participate in the life of God, and this relationship includes a partnership in his sacred rule and reign over this world.[10] God calls humanity to exercise dominion over the earth (Gen 1:26–28), stewarding, cultivating, and preserving it.[11]

The book of Genesis upholds the continued existence of the image of God in humanity, even after the fall. In Gen 5:1–3, the creation of humanity in the image of God is reiterated, and the transferral of this status from Adam to Seth is indicated. The genealogical transmission of the image of God is implied by how Seth is made in the image of Adam and by how the ANE viewed the image of a king as always passed down within his royal dynasty.[12] Genesis 9:6 also reiterates that all human beings—even after the fall—are made in the image of God, giving this explanation as the reason why murder is prohibited (cf. Jas 3:9).[13] In fact, nowhere does Scripture ever state that the image of God is corrupted or abolished. As Michael Bird explained, "There is no indication that the image—whatever it is—is marred, tarnished, diminished, or nullified. Humanity is in the image of God before the fall (Gen 1:26–27) and after the fall (Gen 5:1–2; 9:6; Jas 3:9–10)."[14]

---

9. Harper, "Old Testament Spirituality," 317.

10. McConville, *Being Human*, 27–28; Harper, "Old Testament Spirituality," 317; Etzelmüller, *Gottes verkörpertes Ebenbild*, 283–84.

11. Harper, "Old Testament Spirituality," 317; Etzelmüller, *Gottes verkörpertes Ebenbild*, 285–86.

12. Dempster, *Dominion and Dynasty*, 58; Blocher, *In the Beginning*, 89–90; Farris, *Theological Anthropology*, 82.

13. Van Huyssteen, *Alone in the World*, 120.

14. Bird, *Evangelical Theology*, 745.

Christ: The Image of God

The image of God in the New Testament is a christological and teleological concept.[15] Francis Watson went as far as saying, "It is impossible to explain how humankind is created in the image of God without explaining how the image of God is Christ."[16] His point was that a full understanding of the image of God must include both the texts from Genesis and their christological transformation in the New Testament.[17] At least three main texts bear directly on the christological reorientation of the image of God in the New Testament: 2 Cor 4:4, Col 1:15, and Heb 1:3.

Second Corinthians 4:4 states clearly that Christ "is the image of God."[18] Paul placed this reference to the image of God within the context of creation (2 Cor 4:6; 5:17; cf. Col 1:15; 3:9–11), indicating that he was applying to Christ the image of God from Gen 1, 5, and 9.[19] Just as the image of God in Genesis entails representing God's presence, Christ supremely represents God's presence by perfectly shining forth "the light of the knowledge of the glory of God" (2 Cor 4:6). In other words, as the image of God, Christ radiates the glory of God, making God known. Christ's glory simply is God's glory.[20]

The New Testament also calls Christ "the image of the invisible God" (Col 1:15) and the "exact representation of God's nature" (Heb 1:3). Ultimately, Christ is uniquely the one true and perfect image of God; and insofar as the image of God correlates with the divine presence of God, Christ alone is the image of God by nature, being the eternal Son of God and also God incarnate.[21] In Colossians, Christ is called the image of the invisible God, and F. F. Bruce argued that to "say that Christ is the image of God is to say that in him the nature and being of God have been perfectly revealed—that in him the invisible has become visible."[22]

---

15. Cortez, *Resourcing Theological Anthropology*, 99.
16. Watson, *Text and Truth*, 282.
17. Watson, *Text and Truth*, 282.
18. The Greek texts reads ἐςτιν εἰκὼν τοῦ θεοῦ. All translations of the New Testament, unless otherwise stated, are my own translations.
19. Watson, *Text and Truth*, 281–82.
20. Grenz, *Social God*, 211; McFarland, *Divine Image*, 51; Hughes, *True Image*, 24–26.
21. Cf. Cortez, *Resourcing Theological Anthropology*, 114–15.
22. Bruce, *Epistles*, 57–58.

Individuals who have seen Christ have seen the Father (John 14:9), for Christ perfectly reveals the Father.

Scholars are divided as to whether Christ is the image of God eternally or only as incarnate. Mark Cortez argues that Christ as the image of God refers to the humanity of the incarnate Son of God.[23] His argument is that "if we locate divine presence at the heart of what it means to be the image of God, then the full reality of the image simply is the incarnation: the fullness of God's presence in bodily form."[24] As such, Cortez argues that Christ, being the one instance of hypostatic union, is by nature the image of God.[25] While he admits that Col 1:15–20 and Heb 1:1–3 connect the image of God with the eternal Son of God, he argues that the eternal Son is the image of God only by virtue of God's eternal decree for the Son to become incarnate.[26]

Other scholars hold that the image of God also applies directly to Christ as the uncreated and eternal Son of God.[27] Focusing on Colossians, the argument is that Christ is eternally the image of God because of his relation to God as well as his role in creation and reconciliation (1:16–20). For Paul, Christ is the image of God because (ὅτι) all things were created by and through him; he exists before all things; he holds all things together; and all the fullness of God dwells in him and reconciles all things through him. Overall, Christ is the image of God by being consubstantial with God, by creating and sustaining the universe, and by being God's agent of reconciliation.[28] As such, Christ is the image of God as both the eternal son of God and as God incarnate.

Hebrews 1:3 likewise notes the uniqueness of Christ, stating that he is the radiance of God's glory and the exact representation of God's nature. Kathryn Tanner explained the import of this text:

> The image most properly speaking—the express or perfect image of God (Heb 1:3)—just is the second person of the trinity, the perfect manifestation of all that the first person is. When the Genesis verses talk about the image of God they are not, then,

---

23. Cortez, *Resourcing Theological Anthropology*, 101.
24. Cortez, *Resourcing Theological Anthropology*, 115.
25. Cortez, *Resourcing Theological Anthropology*, 116.
26. Cortez, *Resourcing Theological Anthropology*, 118–28.
27. Davison, *Participation in God*, 201, 268; Hughes, *True Image*, 17.
28. Hughes, *True Image*, 28–29; Kelsey, *Eccentric Existence*, 2:965. Cf. Bird, *Evangelical Theology*, 743–44.

referring in the first place to human beings but to an imaging relationship that occurs within the trinity itself.[29]

Because Christ is the image of God, to be created in the image of God is to be created in the image of Christ.[30]

A distinction must be made between Christ, who is the image of God, and humans, who are made in that image. Kathryn Tanner and Philip Edgcumbe Hughes both hold that Christ alone is the image of God, whereas humans are not the image of God. Hughes made this distinction: "Thus the Son, who *is* the Image, by becoming man became *in* the image, without however ceasing to *be* the Image. It is as consubstantial with God that he *is* the Image and as consubstantial with us that he identified himself with our human existence *in* the image."[31] Tanner similarly notes that only Christ is the perfect image of God. Furthermore, the humanity of Christ is in the image of God differently than other humans are in the image of God, given that Christ's humanity is perfectly united to the second person of the Trinity in the incarnation.[32] Tanner took this point so far as to say that "there is only one perfect or express image of God—the second person of the trinity—and that perfect image becomes the creature's own by way of a close relationship with it, the closer the better, a closeness consummated in Christ."[33]

Not all agree on this distinction. Richard Lints holds that Gen 1:26–28 states that humanity is the image of God, not that humanity is merely made in the image of God.[34] Caren Imes similarly argues that the preposition בְּ is flexible; when attached to *image* in the context of Gen 1:26–27, it refers to identity qua capacity rather than space, time, realm, or manner.[35] One difficulty with this position is that if humans are the image of God, then when humans are damaged and corrupted by sin, the image of God is damaged and corrupted by sin. Contrasting with Lints and Imes, Tanner holds that the preposition בְּ Gen 1:26–27 refers to how humans are made "in," "after," or "according to" the image of God.[36]

---

29. Tanner, *Christ the Key*, 6. Cf. Jewett, *Who We Are*, 56.
30. Bird, *Evangelical Theology*, 742.
31. Hughes, *True Image*, 29.
32. Tanner, *Christ the Key*, 13. Cf. Cortez, *Resourcing Theological Anthropology*, 115.
33. Tanner, *Christ the Key*, 14. Cf. Crisp, "Christological Model," 217.
34. Lints, *Identity and Idolatry*, 61. Cf. Levering, *Doctrine of Creation*, 166n78.
35. Imes, *Being God's Image*, 4–6.
36. Tanner, *Christ the Key*, 5.

The preposition בְּ is understood thus to denote that the image of God is a model or standard of measurement with which God made human beings.[37]

One complication comes in 1 Cor 11:7, where Paul stated that a man "is" (ὑπάρχων) the image and glory of God and woman is the glory of man. If one is to try to maintain the position that humans are made in the image of God and are not the image, two responses to this complication are possible. First, one could argue that Paul's use of ὑπάρχων is to be understood in the sense of "having" and "possessing," rather than "being."[38] As such, Paul is saying that man possesses the image of God. If Paul had wanted clearly to state that a man is the image of God, then he likely would have used a cognate of εἰμί, like he does when referring to the woman.

Second, even if this first response is incorrect, 1 Cor 11:7 creates a theological problem if one's interpretation of it implies that man is the image of God and woman is not. If both man and woman are in the image of God, then Paul must be applying *image* to man in a unique and particular sense in this passage. The context of this verse is headship and order within the church, surrounding head coverings (1 Cor 11:2–16). Paul seems to refer to the image in man solely to reiterate his point that just as Christ is the head of every man, men image God, in part, by being the head of their wives. As such, Paul is not using "image of God" in 1 Cor 11:7 in the full sense of the term, with all of its creational and christological meaning. Rather, he is making a point about the relationship between a man and his wife.[39] Therefore, this verse does not undercut the distinction between Christ, who is the image of God, and man, who is created in that image.

Christians: Conformed to the Image of God

While the New Testament focuses the image of God on Christ such that Christ alone is the one true image of God, the New Testament also maintains that all human beings still are made in the image of God (Jas 3:9). Furthermore, certain passages put forward the idea that humans are able to be conformed to the image of God, as Marc Cortez explained: "The

---

37. Brown, *Hebrew and English Lexicon*, 91.
38. Balz and Schneider, *Exegetical Dictionary*, 3:39.
39. Hughes, *True Image*, 22–23.

good news is that we can be 'transformed into his image' (2 Cor 3:18) as we 'put on the new self' that is being 'renewed in knowledge in the image of its Creator' (Col 3:10; cf. Eph 4:22–24)."[40] Some scholars take such passages to mean that "the image of God that has become perverted . . . is being set straight again."[41] In other words, the image of God was perverted, corrupted, twisted, or lost in the fall, and human beings united to Christ are having the image restored within them. However, the New Testament does not talk about the image being corrupted or twisted. Rather, human beings are the ones who have become corrupted and twisted.

The image of God is that to which human beings are being restored, not that which is being restored. Believers are being "conformed to the image of his Son" (Rom 8:29), "transformed into that same image from glory into glory" (2 Cor 3:18), and "renewed in knowledge according to the image of its creator" (Col 3:10). All of these passive verbs—conformed, transformed, renewed—not only indicate that this change is a work of God through the Holy Spirit but that it is a work that changes the human being, not the image of God. As the previous section showed, the image of God is Christ, and Christ did not become corrupted, twisted, or lost in the fall of humanity. Rather, human beings and human experience have become fallen and in need of restoration.

Because Christ is the image of God, to be conformed to the image of Christ is to be conformed to the image of God. Commenting on Rom 8:29, Anthony Hoekema made this point: "Since the Son . . . is the perfect image of God the Father, we will not do violence to the text if we interpret the expression 'image of his Son' as being equivalent to 'image of God.'"[42] Because the Son shares the same divine nature (or essence) as the Father, to be in the image of the Son is to be in the image of the Father.[43] Therefore, when Rom 8:29 states that God has predestined those whom he foreknew to be conformed to the image of his Son, conformity to the image of God becomes the predestined *telos* for the children of God.[44] Christ, then, is both the "primal archetype and eschatological prototype" of what it means to be made in the image of God.[45]

40. Cortez, *Resourcing Theological Anthropology*, 114.
41. Hoekema, *Created in God's Image*, 86.
42. Hoekema, *Created in God's Image*, 23.
43. Aquinas, *Summa Theologica* I, Q 93, A 5, ad 4; cf. Tanner, *Christ the Key*, 5.
44. Hoekema, *Created in God's Image*, 23.
45. Bird, *Evangelical Theology*, 741. Cf. Van Huyssteen, *Alone in the World*, 124; Hughes, *True Image*, 27.

Furthermore, the image of God is both the creational design and intended soteriological end (*telos*) of human beings. Salvation is a process of personal transformation into Christlikeness, and Christlikeness involves being conformed to the image of God, including within that conformity the various aspects of human experience.[46] Therefore, when 1 Cor 15:49 states that believers shall one day bear the image of the heavenly one, it is looking forward to the completion of Rom 8:29, when believers will be perfectly conformed to the image of God, having fully put on the new self, which is created after the likeness of God by the work of the Holy Spirit (Eph 4:22–24; cf. 2 Cor 3:18; 1 John 3:2).[47] Conformity to the image of God, seen in this way, is one way in which growth in sanctification—which is the work of the Holy Spirit—and conformity to Christ are described. Therefore, since conformity to Christ and growth in sanctification are two established criteria of spiritual discernment—as shown in chapter 2—and the image of God is one way to describe these criteria, the image of God can act as a criterion of spiritual discernment.

Excursus: The Image of God in Non-Christians

One potential difficulty with using the image of God as a criterion of spiritual discernment is the fact that all human beings are made in the image of God. The distinction that upholds the use of the image of God as a criterion of spiritual discernment is the distinction between being made in the image of God and being conformed to the image of God. The former is universal and static, while the latter is nonuniversal and degreed.

Theologians have expressed this dichotomy in a variety of ways. Paul K. Jewett explained the difficulty of this dichotomy: "The attempt to maintain a balanced theological position in one's approach to the question of the image as retained, yet lost and restored, has proved difficult to achieve."[48] Some theologians explain this dichotomy by describing the image as either lost or damaged in the fall and then restored in Christ. In the fall, the image became corrupted by sin or even completely lost. In

---

46. Dunn, *Theology of Paul*, 468. Francis Watson makes the point that conformity to the image of God is the antithesis of conformity to the world (Rom 12:2). See Watson, *Text and Truth*, 292.

47. Hughes, *True Image*, 27; Cortez, *Resourcing Theological Anthropology*, 115.

48. Jewett, *Who We Are*, 57.

Christ, the image is restored.[49] As one theologian explained, the image of God is like a mirror that has been covered by the dirt of sin and evil. Once God washes away this dirt, the mirror will reflect once again the glory of God.[50] The difficulty with positions such as these is that Scripture never talks about the image of God being corrupted or defiled or even dirtied by sin. People made in the image of God are the ones who are damaged and dirtied by sin.[51]

Other theologians have sought to explain how the image is retained by sinners and yet restored in salvation by defending a dual-aspect image as either generic and specific, formal and material, broad and narrow, or ontological and moral, and so on.[52] For example, the distinction between a broader and narrower image holds that humans remained human after the fall but lost their communion with God. In other words, the image of God in the broader sense refers to what makes humans human and, thus, what remains in humans after the fall. The image of God in the narrower sense refers to human communion with and conformity to God, which was lost after the fall and restored in Christ.[53] A recent example of a dual-aspect position is Kathryn Tanner, who argues that the image of God can be understood in both a weak and a strong sense. The weak sense refers to the imitation of God, and the strong sense refers to union with God. The strong image was lost in the fall, and the weak sense was distorted. Christ, on the other hand, reverses the effects of the fall and leads one to greater union with God.[54] At least two difficulties beset these types of positions. First, Scripture does not use a dualistic language in reference to the image of God, as if the image of God was both maintained and lost after the Fall. The language Scripture uses is image maintained and conformity lost. To reiterate, the image never is portrayed as damaged by

---

49. Hoekema, *Created in God's Image*, 23.
50. Harrison, *God's Many-Splendored Image*, 38–39.
51. Kilner, *Dignity and Destiny*, 233.
52. Jewett, *Who We Are*, 58.
53. Berkouwer, *Man*, 38–41.
54. Tanner, *Christ the Key*, 32–35. Meredith Kline held to a unique position that distinguishes between image and glory. For Kline, the image is stative and universal, while the glory of humanity's similarity to God comes in degrees. While this position is similar to the dual-aspect positions on the image of God, Kline did well to indicate that it is glory, and not the image, that comes in degrees. See Kline, *Images of the Spirit*, 30–31. Cf. Lossky, *In the Image*, 139.

sin, not even in part. Second, dual-aspect conceptions of the image are contrastingly dualistic and seemingly unable to be organically united.[55]

From the biblical survey in this chapter, a few parameters need to be observed surrounding this issue of the image of God. First, all people are made in the image of God and, as a result, hold dignity and value. Second, Christ is the image of God. Third, conformity to the image of God is one way to describe growth in sanctification and conformity to Christ. These three statements together indicate that the image of God, in itself, does not come in degrees. Neither is it damaged by sin. Furthermore, the status of being made in the image of God is neither degraded nor damaged by sin. What was damaged by sin and what does come in degrees in salvation is one's conformity to the image of God, who is Christ. The point of this clarification is to safeguard one's language about the image of God. As John Kilner wrote, "It is vital that people not think that God's image has been damaged by sin. Many things about people are badly damaged, but God's image and people's status as created in that image are not."[56]

Commenting on Kilner's view that Christ is the image of God and explaining how one can hold together the creational and soteriological texts on the image of God, John Hammett and Katie McCoy wrote,

> At the very least, Kilner is right to caution us as to how we use language. Those who affirm the image of God as completely lost in the fall are at odds with the fact that Scripture describes humans as still created in God's image after the fall (Gen 9:6 and Jas 3:9 particularly). Furthermore, to be precise in our language, if Christ is the image of God, then Kilner is right. Christ is not damaged by our fall. . . . Yet, it is in keeping with Scripture to say that the way humans manifest, or exhibit, or live out their status of being created *in* or *according to* the image of God has been impacted and damaged by the fall; not the image itself, but the way in which humans live it out has been damaged.[57]

Therefore, the image of God can be used as a criterion of spiritual discernment insofar as conformity to the image of God has been damaged by the fall and is being restored by virtue of union with Christ. When using the image of God as a criterion of discernment, I am not claiming that the image of God or the status of being created in the image of God comes in degrees. Every human is equally made in the image of God, but

---

55. Berkouwer, *Man*, 61.
56. Kilner, *Dignity and Destiny*, 159.
57. Hammett and McCoy, *Humanity*, 85.

Christians are uniquely growing in conformity to the image of God by the power of the Holy Spirit in sanctification. As such, one can use the image of God consistently as a criterion of spiritual discernment while also upholding the status of nonbelievers as being made in the image of God.

THE MAIN SYSTEMATIC POSITIONS ON THE IMAGE OF GOD

Scholars are divided on how all of the biblical data on the image of God hold together in one coherent and systematic position. At the level of systematics, Marc Cortez is correct when he notes that the image of God "is one of the most notoriously debated topics in theological anthropology."[58] Four main positions exist on the issue—structural (or substantive), functional, relational, and multifaceted.[59]

The Structural Image

The structural view has been the most widely held position in history on the image of God.[60] This position states that the image of God consists in a capacity or a set of capacities within human beings that sets them apart from other creatures or makes them similar to God. These capacities have been identified with such things as reason, self-determination, free will, moral agency, wisdom, love, and interpersonal communication.[61] Multiple arguments are used in defense of this position. First, only human beings are made in the image of God and so the image must consist of something unique to human beings, such as capacities that set humans

---

58. Cortez, *Resourcing Theological Anthropology*, 100.

59. Peppiatt, *Imago Dei*, 9; Blomberg, "True Righteousness and Holiness," 68. Beyond these four main positions, many nuanced and less widely held positions exist, such as viewing the image of God as creativity (MacQuarrie), an unbounded nature (Tanner), kinship or kind (McDowell), identity (Lints, Peterson), intended communal function (Baker), ecclesial-communal relation (Grenz), or epistemology only (McFarland). See MacQuarrie, *In Search of Humanity*, 24; Tanner, *Christ the Key*, 16, 53; McDowell, "Image of God," 30–35; Peterson, *Imago Dei*, 54, 77–78; Lints, *Identity and Idolatry*, 34–42; Imes, *Being God's Image*, 30–39; Baker, *Covenant and Community*; Grenz, *Social God*, 240; Kelsey, *Eccentric Existence*, 1008–51.

60. Cortez, *Theological Anthropology*, 18.

61. Farris, *Theological Anthropology*, 84–85; Bird, *Evangelical Theology*, 745; Cortez, *Theological Anthropology*, 19; Levering, *Doctrine of Creation*, 145.

apart from other animals and parallel the divine nature of God.⁶² This argument has come under heavy criticism within recent decades as disciplines such as biology and neuroscience have challenged previously held assumptions about human uniqueness, showing that many of the capacities that humans have are held by other creatures to various degrees.⁶³ Not all agree on this point though. Some scholars still hold that science upholds the uniqueness of human capacities, including flexible reasoning, social cognition, and the ability to adopt and follow moral norms.⁶⁴

A second argument for the structural image is the idea that since Christ is the image of God and is called the Word (or Logos), then the image of God should be associated with reason (Word).⁶⁵ Critics of the structural position have multiple objections as to why the image of God should be related to reason. Scripture never identifies a specific capacity at the core of the image of God, and doing so is to make the image of God too narrow.⁶⁶ Reason alone cannot capture the multidimensionality of human nature. The image of God refers to the whole of a human person and so must incorporate all the facets of human existence, including affectivity, volition, and relationality.⁶⁷ Furthermore, some scholars argue that to equate the image of God with reason both leads to a devaluation of the body and makes the image of God something that comes in degrees, leaving infants and the mentally disabled outside of the image of God and lacking dignity and value compared to others.⁶⁸

The proponent of the structural view does have further responses to these objections. Even though proponents of the structural view hold that the image of God relates to the human soul rather than body, they will argue that this relation does not devalue the body. The body is still valuable given the doctrine of creation, the incarnation of Christ, and the future resurrection. Also, one could argue that the image of God refers to the

---

62. Cortez, *Theological Anthropology*, 18; Farris, *Theological Anthropology*, 85.

63. Van Huyssteen, *Alone in the World*, 108; Cortez, *Theological Anthropology*, 20.

64. Farris, *Theological Anthropology*, 103–104; Visala, "Human Cognition," 91. For more on this debate, see Case-Winters, "Rethinking the Image," 813–26; Fisher, "Animals, Humans and X-Men," 291–314; and Ayala, "Human Nature," 31–48.

65. Levering, *Doctrine of Creation*, 153.

66. McFarland, *Difference and Identity*, 15.

67. Erickson, *Christian Theology*, 469; Chandler, *Christian Spiritual Formation*, 34; Bird, *Evangelical Theology*, 746.

68. Cortez, *Theological Anthropology*, 20–21; Van Huyssteen, *Alone in the World*, 134; Middleton, *Liberating Image*, 24; Bird, *Evangelical Theology*, 746; Kilner, *Dignity and Destiny*, 1.

soul, not the body, because God is immaterial.[69] Oliver Crisp made this point: "How can a corporeal body be said to be made in the image of an essentially immaterial agent, like God? This seems to be a straightforward category mistake."[70] Furthermore, in relegating the image of God to the human soul, the structural view has a unique response to the objection concerning infants and the mentally disabled. The image of God relates to capacities held by the soul. All human beings have such a soul, and so all human beings are made in the image of God. Even infants and the mentally disabled who are unable to actualize these capacities fully—due to the limitations of their bodies and brains—still possess these capacities within their souls and, thus, are made fully in the image of God.[71]

Joshua Farris is a recent example of a scholar who holds to the structural position. Farris argues that the image of God primarily has to do with human identity, as "captured within the Reformed emphasis on a holistic immaterial substantial ontology."[72] He rejects the functional and relational views as insufficient in themselves, given that relations and functions necessitate a particular kind of substance. Furthermore, since God is immaterial and Christ is essentially spiritual and only contingently embodied, for something to image God, it must be immaterial.[73] As such, for Farris, the image of God is neither a functional reality, a relational reality, or even a strict set of properties; it is simply an internal property of the soul that sums up the kind-nature of human beings.[74]

---

69. Farris, *Theological Anthropology*, 86. Cf. Jewett, *Who We Are*, 62–77, 384–94; Levering, *Doctrine of Creation*, 173, 187. Space does not permit exploring the intricacies of the debate on whether the image of God incorporates the body or not. See Van Huyssteen, *Alone in the World*, 145–47, 154; Peppiatt, *Imago Dei*, 90; Plantinga et al., *Introduction to Christian Theology*, 184; Tanner, *Christ the Key*, 52; McDowell, "Image of God," 31–32.

70. Crisp, "Christological Model," 220.

71. Visala, "Human Cognition," 95, 98–99; Jewett, *Who We Are*, 67; Levering, *Doctrine of Creation*, 180, 189–90.

72. Farris, *Theological Anthropology*, 79–80.

73. Farris, *Theological Anthropology*, 89–93.

74. Farris, *Theological Anthropology*, 104–5. By not narrowing the image of God to a specific capacity, such as reason, Farris avoids the objection that the structural position is too narrow.

The Functional Image

One of the biggest limitations of the structural position is its lack of exegetical support. Many Old Testament theologians, seeking to ground the doctrine of the image of God within an exegesis of Gen 1 and the context of the ancient Near East (ANE), argue that the image of God consists of representation and function.[75] The functionalist view is expressed in a diversity of ways, but the overarching theme of this position is that "humanity has a God-given role in creation that carries with it both an authority and a responsibility to mediate the rule, reign, and presence of God on earth while under God's rule themselves."[76]

The functional view has been expressed, among other things, as dominion, royal office, priestly presence, and stewardship. As dominion, being created in the image of God is expressed as representing God and participating in his rule and reign over creation. The image, then, is not so much what humans are as much as what they do. Humans are called to exercise God's authority and power over creation, underneath God's ultimate rule.[77] Furthermore, humans take on a royal office when they exercise the royal power of God, who is the King over all things. They also act as priests within creation, mediating God's divine blessings and presence to the world, insofar as creation acts as God's royal temple.[78] Ultimately, this role is one of wise stewardship, not destructive domination.

One argument for this position is that, in Gen 1:26–28, the creation of man and woman in the image of God is juxtaposed closely to the mandate to have dominion over and subdue the created world.[79] Image and likeness are thus understood as indicating the unique relationship that humans have to God as his vice-regents.[80] Both terms share a similar semantic context, implying a similative comparison between humanity and divinity.[81] Within the context of God's creative and sovereign power (Gen 1) and the mandate to rule over creation (Gen 1:26, 28), the similitude

---

75. Middleton, *Liberating Image*, 88; Farris, *Theological Anthropology*, 88–89.

76. Peppiatt, *Imago Dei*, 27. For early examples of this position, see von Rad, *Genesis*, 60; Clines, "Image of God," 53–103; Hehn, "Zum Terminus 'Bild Gottes,'" 36–52.

77. Garr, *Image and Likeness*, 163; Bird, *Evangelical Theology*, 749; Van Huyssteen, *Alone in the World*, 135.

78. Middleton, *Liberating Image*, 27, 88–90; Swann, *Imago Dei*, 183; Van Huyssteen, *Alone in the World*, 157.

79. Middleton, *Liberating Image*, 26.

80. Dempster, *Dominion and Dynasty*, 59.

81. Garr, *Image and Likeness*, 166.

indicated by image and likeness corresponds with God's wise rule and reign over creation. Scholars who reject this position argue that Gen 1:26–28 never equates image and dominion. Rather, dominion is a consequence of being made in the image of God.[82] Furthermore, one could argue that the image of God must be understood in light of more texts than just Gen 1, texts such as Gen 2; 5:1; 9:6 and New Testament texts about Christ and the image of God.[83] When one considers these other texts, the concept of function does not capture adequately the depth of meaning that Scripture applies to the image of God. One response to this objection is that Christ is the perfect representation of God, perfectly ruling, mediating divine blessing to the world, and stewarding creation, all of which sum up the functional view of the image of God.

Another argument for the functional position looks to extrabiblical evidence from the ANE. In the ANE, kings such as Ptolemy V Epiphanes, Amunhotep III, and Thutmosis IV all were called images of God and seen as cultic intermediaries and representatives of their gods.[84] The author of Genesis would have been familiar with this royal ideology and so uses the term *image of God* in order to democratize this royal ideology, viewing all human beings as created in the image of God.[85] Another common occurrence in the ANE was for a suzerain to place physical images of himself throughout his land to remind his subjects of his sovereignty, and so humans are the images of God that the Creator placed within his land as a reminder of his presence and power.[86] The biggest critique of this argument is that it relies more on extrabiblical sources than on intrabiblical passages, in particular New Testament passages.[87]

Furthermore, just as one critique of the structural position concerned infants and the mentally disabled, a similar critique could be made of the functional position. By making the image of God about exercising dominion, the image of God is not democratized. Government leaders and the powerful are able to exercise this function to a much greater degree than infants, the mentally disabled, or even the vast majority of the

---

82. Watson, *Text and Truth*, 293; McConville, *Being Human*, 20–22; Blomberg, "True Righteousness and Holiness," 73.

83. Cortez, *Theological Anthropology*, 23.

84. Levenson, *Creation*, 114; Middleton, *Liberating Image*, 110, 117–21; cf. Bird, "Male and Female," 129–59.

85. Middleton, *Liberating Image*, 145, 207.

86. Fee, *Pauline Christology*, 487; Garr, *Image and Likeness*, 163.

87. Cortez, *Theological Anthropology*, 22–23.

population.[88] Additionally, the function of dominion relies upon and assumes a specific cognitive structure that enables humans to rule over the creation. One potential response to these objections is to say that being made in the image of God is similar to holding a royal title or identity. Whether or not one actively exercises that title or identity, one still has it and all the rights and responsibilities attached to it. This response is similar to how the structural position distinguishes between having a rational soul and having a body that permits the exercise of rationality. Therefore, on the functional account, to be made in the image of God could mean that one has the right, responsibility, and authority to exercise wise dominion, even if one never does so to a great extent.

The Relational Image

Some theologians, unsatisfied with either of these first two positions on the image of God, have sought a third option, viewing the image of God in relational terms. For them, being made in the image of God means that humans are fundamentally relational beings, reflecting God within their relationships with God, each other, and creation.[89] This position has been expressed in a variety of ways, explaining the image of God as the capacity for relationship with God, the actual relationship that humans have with God, or as the human being in relation with God. Additionally, some scholars include human relationships with each other and creation.[90] As Robert Jenson explained, "In Genesis, the specific relation to God is *as such* the peculiarity attributed to humanity. If we are to seek in the human creature some feature to be called the image of God, this can only be our location in this relation. As the relation is the occurrence of a personal address, our location in it must be the fact of our reply."[91] In other words, what makes human beings unique is that they are called into a unique relationship with God, and, as G. C. Berkouwer points out, this relationship with God is what unites all the aspects of human nature.[92]

---

88. Levering, *Doctrine of Creation*, 171.

89. Hammett and McCoy, *Humanity*, 100; Cortez, *Theological Anthropology*, 24. Cf. Jenson, *Systematic Theology*, 2:55–58.

90. Hammett and McCoy, *Humanity*, 114.

91. Jenson, *Systematic Theology*, 2:58.

92. Berkouwer, *Man*, 34–35. For earlier sources on this position, see Brunner, *Man in Revolt*, 91–113, 499–515; Brunner, *Christian Doctrine*, 55–61; Barth, *Church Dogmatics*, 3.1.182–206.

A common argument used to defend this position is that the Trinity is inherently relational. God is an eternal intra-Trinitarian relationship, and so humans image God by also being made in relationship with God and with each other as male and female (Gen 1:27).[93] This position also is supported textually by how Gen 2 is all about the human relationship with God.[94] Furthermore, Christ models this relationality in the New Testament, with his perfect relationship with God and with his emphasis on community.[95] Basically, God is essentially personal, and he made human beings for relationship with him.[96]

Scholars raise multiple objections against the relational view. First, Gen 1 seems to be contextually independent from Gen 2, and so understanding Gen 1 in light of Gen 2 is not widely accepted.[97] Second, human relationality is different from intra-Trinitarian relationships, unless one posits a social Trinity.[98] These two initial objections seem relatively weak, given that exegetical support for the relational position is found in Gen 1:27 and given that any comparison between humanity and God must be understood analogically, in light of God's divine simplicity.

Third, just like the functional view, the relational view depends upon a structure that grounds relationality. Finally, just like the other positions, this position also must deal with infants and the mentally disabled. In response to these last two objections, John Hammett and Katie McCoy put forward a relational view of the image of God that seems to avoid these two objections. They view the image of God as a creational capacity that all people possess within their spirit, which is similar to the response from the structural position.[99] Furthermore, they do not associate this capacity with reason, will, or conscience, leaving open the possibility—based on recent research on disability—that relationship with God could be experienced on another level than that afforded by rational capacities.[100]

---

93. Cortez, *Theological Anthropology*, 24–27; Van Huyssteen, *Alone in the World*, 137.

94. Cortez, *Theological Anthropology*, 25.

95. Cortez, *Theological Anthropology*, 27.

96. Hughes, *True Image*, 5–6; Hammett and McCoy, *Humanity*, 114.

97. Cortez, *Theological Anthropology*, 27.

98. Crisp, "Christological Model," 221–22.

99. Hammett and McCoy, *Humanity*, 114, 118.

100. Hammett and McCoy, *Humanity*, 117.

The Multifaceted Image

In response to the perceived inadequacy of any one position to describe fully the meaning of being made in the image of God, some scholars have turned to multifaceted positions, seeking to incorporate all three positions into one comprehensive position. Scholars who argue for this position hold that no one position is sufficient. Since the image of God is something that Scripture applies to the whole person, the meaning of the image of God must be complex.[101] Furthermore, the arguments and evidence used to support the structural, functional, and relational positions can be used together to support a multifaceted position. One need not assume that structure, function, and relation conflict with one another.[102]

Multiple recent theologians have opted for a form of the multifaceted approach. For example, Marc Cortez's multifaceted position joins the relational and functional aspects together through the concept of "divine presence." Building on the ANE context of images, Cortez holds that the essence of an image is to be a manifestation of someone's presence and authority. Functionally, being the image of someone carries the authority and dominion of that individual. Relationally, to image a personal God involves personal and covenantal relationship with God and other humans. His position does not include the structural aspect, seeing it as overly problematic.[103] Similar to Cortez, Michael Bird defends a relational and functional position but does so through the category of royal status rather than divine presence. For Bird, the image of God is a royal status, giving people a special standing with God (relationship) and a unique vocation as God's vice-regents (function).[104]

In contrast to Cortez and Bird, Millard Erickson holds that the structural aspect of the image of God is the primary aspect, whereas function and relation are either secondary aspects or consequences of the image of God.[105] A third contrasting example comes from Anthony Hoekema, who defined the image of God as having structural and functional aspects, with relationships being the way in which the functional

---

101. Howard, *Brazos Introduction*, 153; Cortez, *Theological Anthropology*, 28.

102. Turner, "Temple Theology," 105; Kidwell, "Elucidating the Image," 42.

103. Cortez, *Theological Anthropology*, 31–37; Cortez, *Resourcing Theological Anthropology*, 99, 109–13. Cortez does acknowledge that function and relation necessitate various capacities, but those capacities themselves are not a part of the image of God. Cf. Harper, "Old Testament Spirituality," 311–27.

104. Bird, *Evangelical Theology*, 749–52.

105. Erickson, *Christian Theology*, 469–71.

aspect is exercised.[106] Contrasting with Hoekema, W. Ross Hastings argues that "the structural and functional take their cue from and act as subsets of the relational and are dependent for their optimal functionality or imaging upon the relation."[107] Finally, one scholar who argues that one need not identify one aspect as more primary than the others is Jonathan King. Similar to the three aspects mentioned above, King argues that the image of God consists of three aspects: the official (kingly and priestly offices), the constitutional (human ontology), and the ethical-relational (relationships that involve responsibility).[108]

Multifaceted positions are not without their weaknesses. By incorporating the three previous positions into one position, multifaceted positions also must overcome the challenges and weaknesses of those positions while at the same time showing that the three positions are related organically in a way that justifies the multifaceted position over against one of the other three positions.[109] Additionally, as is evident from comparing various multifaceted positions, theologians do not agree on how structure, function, and relation correspond with each other within a multifaceted position or whether one or two aspects are more primary than another.

THE MULTIFACETED IMAGE: A HEURISTIC DEFINITION

For the purpose of applying the image of God to the study of spiritual discernment, I will not answer all of the questions and debates on the image of God. The complexities surrounding this highly debated topic are too numerous. Instead, a heuristic definition of the image of God that fills in the concept with content while leaving certain questions unanswered will be enough for my current purposes. One idea upon which many of the positions on the image of God agree is that the image of God is, to various degrees, related to structural, functional, and relational aspects. Whether as constitutive of the image of God, as primary and secondary aspects of the image of God, or as the consequences or prerequisites of the image of God, these three aspects are connected frequently to the image of God.

---

106. Hoekema, *Created in God's Image*, 86.
107. Hastings, *Theological Ethics*, 102.
108. King, *Beauty of the Lord*, 113–24.
109. Cortez, *Theological Anthropology*, 30.

To explain, both function and relation necessitate structure. J. P. Moreland explained this relationship:

> As image-bearers, human beings have all those endowments necessary to re-present and be representative of God, and to accomplish the tasks placed before them and exhibit the relationality into which they were meant to live, such as endowments of reason, self-determination, moral action, personality and relational formation. . . . Thus, even the functional, relational aspects of the image of God have ontological implications.[110]

Additionally, structure also entails function and relation. The purpose for which God gave human beings their unique structure is for them to exercise dominion over creation and to have personal relationships with God and each other. The being of a creature always manifests itself within that creature's acts, such that structure in absentia of function and relation is a mere caricature.[111] Just as structure is related organically to function and relation, function and relation are related organically to one another. The function of exercising dominion as God's vice-regents over creation is itself a specific kind of relationship with God, with other humans, and with the created world.[112] Furthermore, in relational terms, God personally calls and entrusts humans to function as his vice-regents over the Earth.[113] In other words, function can be expressed in relational terms, and relation can be expressed in functional terms.

The heuristic approach to the image of God notes that the functional approach entails structure and relation; the relational approach entails structure and function; and the structural approach entails relation and function. The three aspects are all related organically with one another such that if one is present, the other two are at least consequentially present. Much of the debate surrounding the image of God concerns the distinction between the essence of the image of God versus the prerequisites and consequences of the image of God. While this debate is both valid and valuable, one need not debate over such distinctions in order to make the weaker claim that the image of God either consists in or entails structure, function, and relation. This weaker formulation of the multifaceted approach correlates function, relation, and structure with the image of

---

110. Moreland, *Recalcitrant*, 4. Cf. Visala, "Human Cognition," 97; Turner, "Temple Theology," 106; Levering, *Doctrine of Creation*, 155.

111. Davison, *Participation in God*, 108.

112. Van Huyssteen, *Alone in the World*, 121; Dempster, *Dominion and Dynasty*, 59.

113. Hammett and McCoy, *Humanity*, 99.

God without delineating a taxonomy between them or clarifying which aspects are primary, secondary, or consequential.

In one way or another, structure, function, and relation are closely related to the image of God such that growth in conformity to the image of God will consist of growth in structure, function, and relation. Growth in structure—intellect, affectivity, and will—will result in growth in function and relation; growth in function—dominion and stewardship—will likewise produce growth in structure and relation; and growth in relation—with God, other humans, and creation—will lead to growth in structure and function.

Given this heuristic definition of the image of God, the aspects of structure, function, and relation can act as the content by which growth in conformity to the image of God is measured and, thus, as the various ways in which the authenticity of a spiritual experience is judged. Based on its relation to Christ and sanctification, the image of God is able to act as a criterion of spiritual discernment, and it does so by enumerating what growth in conformity to the image of God entails, namely growth in structure, function, and relation.

CONCLUSION: CHRIST, THE IMAGE OF GOD AND THE TELOS OF CHRISTIAN SPIRITUALITY

In chapter 2, criteria of spiritual discernment were seen to be drawn often from the general maxim that authentic spiritual experiences will move one closer to God and the things of God. This maxim is why Christ, the Holy Spirit, Scripture, and sanctification are all widely accepted criteria of spiritual discernment. In particular, authentic spiritual experiences—as produced by the Holy Spirit and in alignment with doctrinal truth—will help one grow in sanctification and in Christlikeness. In the current chapter, I explained that one way Scripture describes this growth is conformity to the image of Christ, who is the image of God. All people are made in the image of God, but growth in conformity to the image of God is something unique to individuals being sanctified.

Conformity to the image of God is the *telos* of Christian spirituality; it is the end toward which the Holy Spirit always will move someone. Therefore, one can have assurance that one's spiritual experiences are authentic when they move one toward conformity to the image of God. Given that the image of God consists of or entails structural, functional, and relational aspects, authentic spiritual experiences will either conform to or lead one to grow in conformity with these three aspects. Furthermore, given that Christ is the perfect image of God, one can assume that Christ perfectly exemplified the three aspects of the image of God during his earthly ministry. Accordingly, the image of God as revealed perfectly in Christ and in his life can act as a criterion of discernment, insofar as it provides guiding principles with which to measure whether a spiritual experience is leading or has led one to grow in conformity to the three aspects of the image of God. The concrete ways in which growth in structure, function, and relation are observed remains to be seen, and the best way to explore this question is to turn to the life of Christ, in which one sees the perfect image of God exemplified.

4

Principles for Spiritual Discernment
The Three Aspects of the Image of God in the Life of Christ

IN *THE HOLY SPIRIT and Christian Experience*, Simeon Zahl distinguished between talking about salvation and sanctification as a "purely ontological reality" versus a "concrete and historical 'realm of human consciousness.'"[1] He explained, "Instead of talking, as the New Testament so often does, about the effects of the Spirit's work on real bodies in time, theologians revert instead to ontological language about union with Christ, about salvific participation in the Godhead, or about deification and theosis."[2] While such ontological language is valuable to theological understanding, it does not exhaust what can be said about salvation and sanctification. When talking about the image of God as a criterion of spiritual discernment, in an attempt to be as concrete as possible, the material content of what growth in conformity to the image of God entails can be found in the person and life of Christ.

So far, I have explained how fallen human experience necessitates spiritual discernment, how doctrine is a necessary criterion of spiritual discernment, and how the image of God is able to act as a criterion of discernment. The purpose of this chapter is to take the three aspects of the image of God and show how Christ exemplifies them, how believers grow in conformity to Christ's example, and how the great traditions of

---

1. Zahl, *Holy Spirit*, 71.
2. Zahl, *Holy Spirit*, 71.

Christian spirituality compare and contrast with Christ's example. The value of incorporating the spiritual traditions into this discussion on the three aspects of the image of God is that they help reveal some of the various ways in which the effects of authentic and inauthentic spiritual experiences have manifested concretely in the life of the church over time. Conformity to the image of God takes on a variety of shapes within the various spiritual traditions, highlighting the beautiful unity within diversity of Christian spirituality. To use Simeon Zahl's language, the spiritual traditions help elucidate "the effects of the Spirit's work on real bodies in time," including the Spirit's work of drawing believers into conformity with the three aspects of the image of God.[3]

The main goal of this chapter is to identify general principles that correspond to each aspect of the image of God in order to describe how each aspect relates to authentic spiritual experiences by correlating each principle of discernment to the life and teachings of Christ, to the life of the believer, and to the life of the church within its spiritual traditions. These principles summarize how authentic spiritual experiences, based on the criterion of the image of God, lead to the gradual restoration of conformity to the image of God within a believer, as evidenced by a believer's imitation of Christ along the three aspects of the image of God.

Based on the image of God as a criterion of spiritual discernment, authentic spiritual experiences will conform to or lead one to grow in conformity with (1) Christ's cognition, affectivity, and volition; (2) Christ's participation in the love of God as it is expressed relationally toward God, other humans, oneself, and creation; and (3) Christ's threefold office of prophet, priest, and king. Each main section of the chapter is organized around an aspect of the image of God and its corresponding general principle of discernment. The point of general principles is to have specificity without rigidity. Manifestations of authentic spiritual experiences will not be universally uniform, yet they always will lead toward conformity to the image of God. The exemplarity of Christ cannot be fully reduced to such things as a set of principles or a chapter in a book. As such, the general principles will be broad, acting as guides to spiritual discernment in how they locate perspectives from which to view spiritual experiences in light of the person of Christ—the perfect image of God.[4]

---

3. I will be engaging mostly with the spiritual traditions as described by Richard Foster. See Foster, *Streams of Living Water*. I will give Foster's definition of each tradition in the footnotes when first discussing that tradition.

4. Focusing on general principles, this chapter will not present a comprehensive

THE STRUCTURAL ASPECT OF THE IMAGE OF GOD

Principle (1): Christ's Cognition, Affectivity, and Volition

The structural aspect of the image of God within the life of Christ corresponds with Christ's intellect (cognition), feelings and emotions (affectivity), and will (volition). Given that Scripture never identifies a particular structure or capacity within human beings as that which is the structural aspect of the image of God and given that—similar to the multiple aspects of the image of God—cognition, affectivity, and volition are interrelated, one can hold that the structural aspect of the image of God, at least, either consists in or entails the three aspects of cognition, affectivity, and volition.[5] In other words, conformity to the image of God must entail formation in thinking, feeling, and acting.[6]

According to the criterion of the image of God, authentic spiritual experiences will lead to changes within the depth dimensions of cognition, affectivity, and volition that mirror Christ's cognition, affectivity, and volition. In other words, authentic spiritual experiences will conform Christians closer to Christ's thoughts, beliefs, worldview, feelings, emotions, nuclear concerns, choices, habits, and lifestyle.[7] The principle of authenticity that the structural aspect of the image of God entails, then, is as follows. Principle (1): Authentic spiritual experiences will conform to or lead to growth in conformity with Christ's cognition, affectivity, and volition.

Authentic Spiritual Experiences and Cognition

Cognition and the Life of Christ

By leading a believer's intellect to conform to Christ's intellect, authentic spiritual experiences will lead believers more and more to view God, creation, themselves, and their place in creation through the lens of how

---

collection of examples from Christ's life, a believer's life, or the spiritual traditions. In order to demonstrate the validity of the three principles of discernment drawn from the criterion of the image of God, being comprehensive is not necessary. The examples given will be sufficient to show the fruit of using the three aspects of the image of God to discern spiritual experiences.

5. Hastings, *Theological Ethics*, 84; Howard, *Brazos Introduction*, 153.
6. Howard, *Christian Spiritual Formation*, 47.
7. Howard, *Brazos Introduction*, 47.

Christ views such things. Cognitive Christlikeness is having the mind (φρην, νους) of Christ (Phil 2:5; 1 Cor 2:16), with not just its beliefs but also its habitual attitudes, dispositions, and interests.[8] Christ not only held accurate beliefs about God and the world; he also developed cognitive habits and dispositions that filled his mind with God and the things of God.[9]

In general, cognitive Christlikeness can be summarized by sketching the outlines of such things as Christ's self-identity, Christ's view of God, and the worldview and cognitive virtues implied by both. Summarizing Christ's self-identity, Stephen Wellum wrote,

> Jesus understood that he came as the promised Christ and the eternal Son of the Father. He did not see himself and his role in redemptive history apart from all that the triune God had been doing in the world from its original creation. Jesus knew, rather, that he came as the one sent by his Father to accomplish the entire divine plan for the vice-regent rule of a righteous humanity over a "very good" creation. And Jesus understood that in him all of the promises maintained throughout all of the covenantal hostility between God and man would be fulfilled so that the Creator–Covenant Lord himself could dwell with man in covenantal peace. Jesus knew that he would bring the promised kingdom of God and that as the Son of God he would redeem a people for that kingdom. In sum, the New Testament gives us Jesus's own witness that he came as both God and man. More specifically, Jesus understood that he came as the Christ who is God the Son who has become incarnate according to the Scriptures, thus fulfilling God's eternal plan.[10]

A specific view of God and the world, pertaining to the creation of the world, the fall of humanity, and the redemption of humanity, emerges out of Christ's self-understanding. In the Gospels, Christ reveals himself to be the only begotten and eternally begotten Son of God, one with the Father, not created like the rest of humanity (Matt 3:17; John 1:1–5, 14; 10:30). Christ is God the Son. As such, he has intimate knowledge of both God and the acts of God, including "God's way of relating in and through what Jesus does and undergoes to draw all that is not God to

---

8. Vanhoozer, "Putting on Christ," 147–48; 160–61. Cf. Schmidt, "Scheidung der Geister," 24–25.

9. Cf. Vanhoozer, "Putting on Christ," 161.

10. Wellum, *God the Son Incarnate*, 148. For a scriptural defense of the various aspects of this quote, see Wellum, *God the Son Incarnate*, 149–65.

eschatological consummation."[11] Through such knowledge, Christ saw the world as good, as permeated by the presence and activity of a good and loving God, and as radically dependent upon God's providential care (Matt 6:25–34).[12]

Stories with Christ such as the man born blind (John 9), the woman at the well (John 4:1–42), the rebuke of Peter (Matt 8:33), and the wilderness temptation (Matt 4:1–11) are all examples of how Christ knew the workings of God, knew Scripture, had a specific self-understanding, and viewed the world through those realities. This knowledge is also evident in his theological debates with the Pharisees and Sadducees. In Matt 22:23–33, the Sadducees tried to trap Jesus with the story of the woman married seven times, seeking to manipulate Jesus into either denying the resurrection, admitting that polygamy exists in heaven, or arbitrarily restricting the woman's marriage in the resurrection to only one brother. Christ's response is striking. First, he undercut their argument by stating that there is no marriage in the resurrection. Then, going further, he rebutted their rejection of the resurrection by quoting a source in support of the resurrection that they would hold as authoritative—namely, the writings of Moses, rather than those of Daniel.[13] In Matt 22:34–40, the Pharisees tested Jesus by asking what commandment in the Law was the greatest. Jesus's response went beyond their initial question, summarizing the entire Old Testament law with the commandments to love God and love neighbor, thus, revealing his extensive knowledge of Scripture and his awareness of what matters most to God.[14]

Christ's self-understanding and knowledge of God and the world were articulated also in his teachings on the kingdom of God. Christ saw himself and his acts as fulfillments of Old Testament prophecy, viewing his life as the culmination of redemption history (Matt 15:3–4, 17; John 10:35; Luke 4:21). Sent by the Father, Christ took on human nature in order to proclaim the kingdom of God (Mark 1:15) and redeem humanity (John 3:16; Matt 20:28), acting as "God's agent in bringing in the kingdom."[15] He proclaimed the kingdom of God as God's sovereign rule brought about by and through his actions and seen in the miracles and

---

11. Kelsey, *Eccentric Existence*, 1028–29; Moreland, *Love Your God*, 50.
12. Willard, *Divine Conspiracy*, 61–64; Vanhoozer, "Putting on Christ," 162.
13. Moreland, *Love Your God*, 50–51; cf. 113.
14. Moreland, *Love Your God*, 50.
15. Burridge and Gould, *Jesus Now and Then*, 106.

teachings of his ministry (Luke 4:14–21; 7:18–23; cf. Isa 61:1–2).[16] Christ taught that the only way into the eternal life of the kingdom of God was through him and his sacrificial and substitutionary death (John 14:6), and he called his followers to shape their thinking according to God's kingdom (Matt 6:25–33).

Cognitive Christlikeness in the Life of the Believer

For the Christian, then, insofar as they pertain to cognition, authentic spiritual experiences will lead believers to leave behind thoughts and beliefs that do not cohere with Christ's cognition. They will show and further reveal God as good and as active in the world rather than as absent and unloving, and they will replace flawed images and ideas about God and the world with those that filled the mind of Jesus (Col 1:6, 9, 10; 3:10).[17] Authentic spiritual experiences will enlighten the mind by revealing "the truth of the Christian worldview in the midst of a diverse religious and philosophical culture" and by upholding the particularities of Jesus's identity and role in salvation history.[18]

By leading believers to take on the mind of Christ, authentic spiritual experiences will lead believers to have "a thought life centered on God in his goodness and greatness, and therefore on truth."[19] They will lead believers to spend more and more time filling their minds with God and the things of God (Phil 4:8) or, as J. I. Packer explained, to grow in a "permanent pervasive awareness of the inescapable reality, heart searching-presence, and saving love of our holy sovereign God, with a sense that we ought to pray to him, live to him, and seek to please him in all that we do, and at every turn of the road."[20] This growth may manifest as new

---

16. Burridge and Gould, *Jesus Now and Then*, 42.

17. Willard, *Renovation of the Heart*, 101; cf. Marshall, "Being Human," 63; Hammett and McCoy, *Humanity*, 127.

18. Howard, *Brazos Introduction*, 416; cf. Howard, *Christian Spiritual Formation*, 178–80.

19. Willard, *Renovation of the Heart*, 141.

20. Packer, "Ministry of the Spirit," 98; cf. Wilkins, *In His Image*, 116; Dubay, *Authenticity*, 70; Willard, *Renovation of the Heart*, 112, 218. Packer highlighted how cognitive Christlikeness also leads to affective and volitional Christlikeness. Packer also did well in highlighting how this growth is ultimately the role of the Holy Spirit. See Packer, "Ministry of the Spirit," 97–98. Among other things, the role of the Spirit is to reveal truth, illuminate the mind, convict one of sin, and confirm the truths of Scripture. Cf. Howard, *Christian Spiritual Formation*, 72.

insights into biblical truths about God or as a restless pursuit of truth and an uneasiness about or distaste for false knowledge, illusion, deception, or cognitive vices.[21] Furthermore, authentic spiritual experiences will lead to the cognitive virtues of the kingdom of God, such as intellectual humility, honesty, and charity. This growth will work against prejudice, unfounded bias, pride, ignorance, overconfidence, over-reliance on impulse, and the conception that thinking is opposed to faith.[22]

This cognitive Christlikeness not only occurs within the various depths of cognition but also within the various stages of the cognitive process, leading one both to understand and then to act on that understanding as one seeks to inhabit the kingdom of God and its virtues. The stage of Being Aware deepens to allow new possible realms of Experiencing, especially in regard to experiences of God and spiritual realities. Understanding and Judging grow in reliance on the logic of faith, and Deciding and Acting become more focused on God's wisdom and standards.[23] As Evan B. Howard explained, "The restoration of human experience intended by Christ aims at all of [the cognitive] stages: opening our Awareness of God, enlightening our Understanding of God, and so on."[24]

Cognitive Christlikeness in the Spiritual Traditions

Cognitive Christlikeness can manifest in a plurality of ways, as the traditions of Christian spirituality reveal. For example, in the Evangelical Tradition, cognitive Christlikeness often manifests as biblical fidelity and the daily study of Scripture.[25] Holding to the inerrancy of Scripture, evangelicals prioritize knowing God through knowing Scripture. In the Incarnational Tradition, on the other hand, cognitive Christlikeness takes on more of a world-oriented shape in which one grows in the knowledge of God by seeing God present and active throughout the material world

---

21. McIntosh, *Discernment and Truth*, 99.

22. Willard, *Renovation of the Heart*, 105; Howard, *Brazos Introduction*, 187, 256–57.

23. Howard, *Brazos Introduction*, 187; cf. 416–17.

24. Howard, *Brazos Introduction*, 416.

25. Foster, *Streams of Living Water*, 227. Foster defined the Evangelical Tradition as emphasizing "the faithful proclamation of the gospel," "the centrality of Scripture as a faithful repository of the gospel," and "the confessional witness of the early Christian community as a faithful interpretation of the gospel." See Foster, *Streams of Living Water*, 219.

and daily life.²⁶ Rejecting the duality between nature and the supernatural, Hans Boersma wrote, "The purpose of all of matter . . . is to lead us into God's heavenly presence, to bring about communion with God, participation in the divine life. . . . The entire cosmos is meant to serve as a sacrament: a material gift from God in and through which we enter into the joy of his heavenly presence."²⁷ In the contemplative Tradition, conformity to the cognitive aspect of the image of God occurs through unceasing contemplative prayer—the constant filling of the mind with God and the things of God.²⁸

Inauthentic spiritual experiences that compromise cognitive Christlikeness also have manifested in a variety of ways within Christian spiritual traditions. For example, at times within the Contemplative Tradition, spiritual experiences have led individuals away from a biblical Creator-creature distinction toward belief in a mystical union without distinction between God and humanity, or even toward belief in a mystical union between all things, including God, humanity, and creation.²⁹ Commenting on the compromised Christlikeness that can occur within the Charismatic Tradition, Richard Lovelace wrote, "The charismatic renewal continues to express the mystical spirituality of the Puritan and awakening eras, but often without the rational and theological checks against error and credulity maintained by evangelicals. . . . The charismatic garden has a luxuriant overgrowth of theological weeds, including the health-and-wealth gospel."³⁰ The examples of how authentic and inauthentic spiritual experiences manifest in regard to conformity to

---

26. Foster, *Streams of Living Water*, 269–71. Foster defined the Incarnational Tradition as concerning itself "with the relationship between spirit and matter," such that it sees God "manifest to us through material means."

27. Boersma, *Heavenly Participation*, 9.

28. Foster, *Streams of Living Water*, 52. Foster defined the Contemplative Tradition as consisting of a prayer-filled life in which there is a "steady gaze of the soul upon the God who loves us." See Foster, *Streams of Living Water*, 49.

29. See Eckhart, *Complete Mystical*, 330; Eckhart, *Teacher and Preacher*, 300–1; Rohr, *Universal Christ*, 12, 16, 20, 134, 137. For more on Eckhart's view of union without distinction, see Shuler, "Conscious of Christ," 155–69.

30. Lovelace, "Evangelical Spirituality," 222–23. David Lonsdale described this situation as "antinomian charismaticism," which is "the impulse to place uncritical trust in enthusiasm," based on "the power of intoxication of certain religious experiences as self-evidently the voice of the Spirit of God." See Lonsdale, "Church as Context," 245. Foster defined the Charismatic Tradition as the Spirit-empowered life, expressed through a yearning for the immediate presence of God within the *charismata* and the power of the Holy Spirit. See Foster, *Streams of Living Water*, 125–28.

Christ's cognition are not exhaustive but rather show that growth toward or away from conformity to the image of God is not uniform but manifests in a variety of ways.

Authentic Spiritual Experiences and Affectivity

Affectivity and the Life of Christ

In the Gospels, Jesus expressed a myriad of human affections and emotions, such as joy, compassion, love, anger, frustration, amazement, sorrow, and peace. He shows that human emotions and feelings, even in great degree, can be healthy and holy.[31] Stephen Voorwinde counted at least sixty explicit instances in the Gospels when Jesus's emotions are recorded. In Matthew, Jesus is astonished (8:10), stern (9:30), compassionate (9:36; 14:14; 15:32; 20:32), and sorrowful and troubled (26:37–38; 27:46). In Mark, Jesus is amazed (6:6), stern (1:43), compassionate (1:41; 6:34; 8:2; 9:22), grief stricken (14:33; 15:34), angry and distressed (3:5), deeply sighing (7:34; 8:12), indignant (10:14), and loving (10:21). In Luke, Jesus is amazed (7:9), compassionate (7:13), full of joy (10:21), distressed (12:50; 22:44), and sad (19:41). Finally, in John, Jesus's love is referred to at least eighteen times, and he also is described multiple times as feeling troubled (11:33; 12:27; 13:21), deeply moved (11:33, 38), rejoicing (11:15), shedding tears (11:35), joyous (15:11; 17:13), and zealous (2:17).[32]

In relation to growth in conformity to Christ the image of God, certain distinctions and qualifications must be made when referring to affective Christlikeness. Affective Christlikeness cannot be "some facile correspondence between Jesus's emotional life and ours today."[33] Voorwinde makes the argument that, as the Messiah, Jesus's emotions most often took place within the contexts of miracles and his anticipated passion.[34] Furthermore, he asserts that the Gospels are descriptive most of the time rather than prescriptive when referring to Jesus's emotions. As such, he holds that Christians must look to prescriptive passages in the Epistles or the teachings of Jesus in order to develop affective

---

31. Wilkins, *In His Image*, 45. He also expressed these emotions in a balanced and symmetrical manner. See Borgman, *Feelings and Faith*, 164–66.

32. Voorwinde, *Jesus' Emotions*, 9, 59–60, 119–20, 151.

33. Spencer, *Passions of the Christ*, 263.

34. Voorwinde, *Jesus' Emotions*, 216–17.

Christlikeness. Therefore, disciples of Christ are to love the Lord their God with all their heart, soul, mind, and strength (Matt 22:37); to love their neighbors as themselves (Matt 22:39); "to 'rejoice with those who rejoice' and to 'mourn with those who mourn' (Rom 12.15); to 'love one another deeply from the heart' (1 Pet 1.22); and to 'clothe themselves with compassion' (Col 3.12)."[35]

However, Voorwinde goes too far in dismissing the exemplarity of descriptive passages on Jesus's emotions. While the unique contexts of Jesus's life and ministry should be accounted for, the emotions that Jesus displayed signal the deep concerns, desires, and passions that drove and catalyzed such emotions and that should do the same for a believer's emotions.[36] In other words, even descriptive passages of Jesus's emotions can elucidate affective Christlikeness by how they are either based upon a reality that is still relevant to Christians today—such as God's love for his children—or based upon a more foundational principle, concern, or desire that Christians share with Christ—such as a love for God or being a child of God.

The foundational disposition out of which Jesus's emotions flow is "filial delight toward the loving Fatherhood of God," which is "the infused disposition that the indwelling Spirit brings about" in believers.[37] As adopted children of God, Christians can imitate the affectivity of Christ insofar as that affectivity models Christ's filial relationship with the Father. Rather than interpreting Christ's affectivity solely within the contexts of miracles and his passion, one also can approach his affectivity through the context of his love for the Father. As Diane Chandler explained, "The major movements of Jesus's emotions were chiefly predicated on his attachment to and love for the Father, readily evidenced when God's will was interrupted or compromised in others' lives."[38] For Jesus, his love for the Father was the epicenter around which all of his affections were organized, including his self-sacrificial love, compassion for others, and anger when God's love was opposed. Given that God is love (1 John 4:8), love is the only fitting foundation for Jesus's affectivity.

---

35. Voorwinde, *Jesus' Emotions*, 217.
36. Spencer, *Passions of the Christ*, 262.
37. Yeo, "Emotional Formation," 40, 36.
38. Chandler, *Christian Spiritual Formation*, 85–7. Chandler cited Jesus's anger and indignation toward the Pharisees (Mark 3:5) and during the temple cleansing (John 2:13–17) as examples of Jesus's anger born out of love. See also Spencer, *Passions of the Christ*, 70, 92.

Jesus's love was demonstrated in his obedience to the Father (John 14:31; cf. 1 John 3:16), his compassion toward the people around him (Matt 9:36; cf. Heb 4:15; Col 3:12), his teachings on life within the kingdom of God (Matt 5:45–48), as well as his joy and peace.[39] In obeying the will of his Father, Jesus experienced delight and joy (Isa 11:2–3). If King David found a fullness of joy in the presence of God (Ps 16:11), assumably such joy was one reason why Jesus frequently sought time alone with his Father.[40] Furthermore, Jesus had a great sense of peace, knowing that his Father is sovereign over all things (Matt 6:25–34) and that he (Christ himself) had overcome the world (John 16:31–33).[41]

Overall, then, affective Christlikeness involves conformity to Jesus's love for the Father and Jesus's ability to ground all of his affections within that love. The Gospels show that Jesus's concerns and emotions were oriented around the reality of God rather than self.[42] He held his affective operations within the framework of his love for his Father, allowing that love to guide and shape them.[43] At root was the ability to appraise and evaluate the significance of situations according to the love of God rather than the love of self.[44]

Affective Christlikeness in the Life of the Believer

For believers, conformity to Jesus's affectivity involves an increasing felt reception of the love of God and an overcoming of emotional bondage and dysfunction.[45] Authentic spiritual experiences will help believers "to actually feel more love for God and love for neighbor," which involves a softening of the heart and a lessened love for the world.[46] Rather than longing for the things of the world and being swept away by worldly emotions, believers will grow in the love of God and the things of God.[47]

---

39. Willard, *Renovation of the Heart*, 131–32; Borgman, *Feelings and Faith*, 157–63; Willard, *Divine Conspiracy*, 130.

40. Borgman, *Feelings and Faith*, 149–56. See also Luke 10:21; Heb 1:9; 12:2.

41. Willard, *Renovation of the Heart*, 133–35.

42. Howard, *Brazos Introduction*, 187.

43. Cf. Howard, *Christian Spiritual Formation*, 183–84.

44. Howard, *Affirming the Touch*, 222–23.

45. Chandler, *Christian Spiritual Formation*, 89.

46. Elliott, "Emotions," 425; Howard, *Brazos Introduction*, 256; Dubay, *Authenticity*, 159.

47. Willard, *Renovation of the Heart*, 119; Plantinga, *Not the Way*, 34.

Authentic spiritual experiences will not deny or repress the believers' feelings, desires, and passions, as much as gradually purify them, resulting in an increase "in the love and service of God."[48]

Central to affective Christlikeness are the felt acceptance and belonging that a child of God has in the presence of God and a growing delight in God and the things of God. First, explaining this filial disposition, Diane Chandler wrote, "When fully loved and accepted, we feel joy, happiness and delight, and are able to function with greater confidence, knowing that we are cared for and that our lives matter."[49] Authentic spiritual experiences will either be filled with or lead to growth in feelings associated with love and being a child of God, namely, joy, peace, delight, and holy sorrow and anguish.[50]

Second, just as Christ's affections were filled with the fruit of the Holy Spirit, so also will affective Christlikeness be filled with such fruit. As such, authentic experiences of the Holy Spirit will lead to more delight in God and the things of God. As Simeon Zahl explained,

> [This delight] is delight in the goodness of God and his ways as they are experienced in concrete lives in the world and a dismay over the reality of sin in the context of its particular instantiations that we experience. It is a delight that manifests as love for particular people and particular features of creation that we encounter, and which is most clearly visible in God's "incongruous" love for sinners, "without regard to worth," in Jesus Christ. And it is an experience of "well-being" that is matched to the creature's deepest purpose and vocation, deriving as it does from "the one in whom they have their being."[51]

Zahl does well to pair delight in the goodness of God with a love for one's neighbor and a dismay over the reality of sin. As Christ exemplified a balanced symmetry between love and such things as anger and sorrow, a beautiful symmetry also will be evident within authentic spiritual

---

48. Willard, *Renovation of the Heart*, 123; Demarest, "Human Personhood," 75; Mouroux, *Christian Experience*, 259.

49. Chandler, *Christian Spiritual Formation*, 83.

50. Willard, *Renovation of the Heart*, 133. Christ has promised his followers joy and peace (John 14:27; 15:11; 16:24; 17:13) as gifts of the Holy Spirit in the kingdom of God (Rom 14:17).

51. Zahl, *Holy Spirit*, 208.

experiences—holy hope balanced by holy fear, joy and comfort balanced with sorrow and sadness.[52]

Affective Christlikeness in the Spiritual Traditions

Affective Christlikeness can be seen in the emphasis of the Contemplative Tradition on love and the emphasis of the Social Justice Tradition on compassion. For contemplatives, prayer is affective, a turning of their loving gazes upon God in rapt attention. The more they contemplate God and the things of God, the more their emotions and desires become shaped toward God. Their delight in the presence of God is balanced by an emptiness felt toward that which is not God.[53] For example, describing his practice of prayer, Brother Lawrence wrote,

> I make it my business only to persevere in His holy presence, wherein I keep myself by a simple attention, and a general fond regard to God . . . or, to speak better, an habitual, silent, and secret conversation of the soul with God, which often causes me joys and raptures inwardly, and sometimes also outwardly, so great that I am forced to use means to moderate them and prevent their appearance to others.[54]

Other contemplatives, such as John of the Cross, viewed progress in spirituality along the lines of a love poem, reminiscent of the Song of Solomon, in which growth in spirituality leads to a loving union with God.[55]

In the Social Justice Tradition, love often is expressed through compassionate action, in which the affections are stripped of selfish and worldly concerns and centered on the love of God and the needs of others.[56] Describing his experience of the slave trade in Newport, John Woolman wrote,

---

52. Chan, *Spiritual Theology*, 208.
53. Foster, *Streams of Living Water*, 48–50.
54. Brother Lawrence, *Practice of the Presence*, 42.
55. John of the Cross, *Dark Night*, 295–96.
56. Foster, *Streams of Living Water*, 167–69. Foster defined the Social Justice Tradition as consisting of loving action within a virtuous life that works toward justice, compassion, and peace in relationship with people, social structures, and creation. Foster, *Streams of Living Water*, 166–67.

> Understanding that a large number of slaves had been imported from Africa into that town, and were then on sale by a member of our Society, my appetite failed, and I grew outwardly weak, and had a feeling of the condition of Habakkuk, as thus expressed, "When I heard, my belly trembled, my lips quivered, I trembled in myself, that I might rest in the day of trouble." I had many cogitations, and was sorely distressed.[57]

Such holy affections mirror Christ's holy anguish and sorrow.

Inauthentic spiritual experiences, leading away from conformity to affective Christlikeness, can manifest, among other things, as either the neglect or the blind trust of affections. Jonathan Edwards's *Treatise Concerning Religious Affections* is a great example of a theologian trying to chart a *via media* between these two extremes. Writing in 1746, in the aftermath of the First Great Awakening and in a culture of rationalism, Edwards sought to defend the centrality of religious affections and the necessity of guiding criteria for discerning true religious affections. Ignatius of Loyola's *Spiritual Exercises* is another example of a work that was written during a time when the role of affections within the spiritual life were at times either neglected—as in some of the writing of the scholastics—or blindly trusted—as in some of the spiritual movements that swept across Europe in the late medieval periods and after.[58]

From the Contemplative and Social Justice Traditions to the writings of Edwards and Ignatius, authentic and inauthentic spiritual experiences, as measured by affective conformity to the image of God, can manifest and have manifested in the life of the church in a plurality of ways. The comparison of Christian spiritual traditions with affective Christlikeness reveals that Christian spiritual traditions recognize the importance of Christlike affectivity within spirituality and the variety of ways in which the effects of authentic experiences of the Spirit concretely manifest within the affectivity of believers.

Authentic Spiritual Experiences and Volition

Volition and the Life of Christ

All of Christ's deliberations, decisions, and actions, and every aspect of his will, as seen in the Gospels, were oriented around responding to God

---

57. Woolman, *Journal*, 163.
58. Schreiner, *Are You Alone Wise*, 270.

in faith and obedience. Explaining what faith entailed for Christ, David Kelsey defined faith as "a combination of trust in God's hospitable generosity in relating creatively to all that is not God, and loyalty to God's creative project, which is expressed in a basic attitude of reverent and awed doxological gratitude for both his proximate and ultimate contexts."[59] The perfect faith of Christ is seen in the perfection and exemplarity of how he submits his will to the will of the Father. Every decision made and action done by Christ were directed to the Father, in submission to the Father's will and for the Father's glory (John 12:49–50; 14:31; 15:10; 17:1).[60]

Jesus obeyed the will of the Father perfectly (John 5:30: 6:38) and called others to do the same (Matt 12:49–50).[61] The testing of Jesus's will is seen at multiple times throughout the Gospels, such as in the wilderness temptation (Matt 4:1–11) and in the garden of Gethsemane (Matt 26:36–46). As Satan tempted Jesus to stray from the Father's will, Jesus responded with the word of God, showing how he lives not by bread alone but by the word of God.[62] This obedience to the will and words of the Father requires entrusting oneself entirely to the Father, as Marko Rupnik explained: "In Gethsemani, Christ entrusted his entire being to the will of the Father, thus surrendering himself to the Father's will."[63]

By surrendering to the Father's will, Christ also surrendered to the Father's mission for him. From the beginning of his ministry, Jesus proclaimed the arrival of the kingdom of God, with himself as the one through whom the kingdom was breaking into the world.[64] Christ lived each moment in his earthly ministry as an opportunity to make all things new and to teach and model what such newness looked like.[65] In the Sermon on the Mount, Jesus taught what a pure will, and thus volitional Christlikeness, looks like within the kingdom of God.[66] As such, volitional Christlikeness incorporates a certain set of virtues, namely the virtues of the kingdom of God, which include such things as dependence on God, humility, integrity, unity, righteousness, and faithfulness, each

---

59. Kelsey, *Eccentric Existence*, 1027.
60. Aumann, *Spiritual Theology*, 55, 60; Porter, "Will/Heart/Spirit," 83.
61. Wilkins, *In His Image*, 116.
62. Wilkins, *In His Image*, 45.
63. Rupnik, *Discernment*, 182; cf. Porter, "Will/Heart/Spirit," 85–86.
64. Morgan and McLendon, "Trajectory of Spirituality," 45.
65. Nouwen, *Spiritual Formation*, 9.
66. Willard, *Divine Conspiracy*, 97.

of which is marked by faith, hope, and love.[67] A "kingdom-minded" will exudes holiness and righteousness marked by Jesus's example of service, patience, endurance, suffering, gentleness, humility, obedience, unconditional love, compassion, meekness, reliance upon God, purity, peace, forgiveness, and other such things.[68] One way to summarize this volitional Christlikeness is found in Matt 6:33, when Christ states to seek first the kingdom and righteousness of God.

Volitional Christlikeness in the Life of the Believer

For believers, just as Christ was entirely devoted to the will and work of the Father, so also will authentic spiritual experiences conform to or lead to greater conformity with the will and work of the Father, the Son, and the Holy Spirit. As followers of Christ, Christians are called to take on the same kind of faith that Christ had, the faith that made him able to act in trust and faithful obedience to God's will.[69] Growth in volitional Christlikeness is growth in the habit of doing everything "in the name of the Lord Jesus" (Col 3:17), acting for him and as if he were acting through us.[70] Imitating how Jesus embraced the mission of God, volitional Christlikeness embraces the still ongoing mission of the kingdom of God, with Jesus as one's king. Christopher Morgan and Justin McLendon wrote, "As his disciples, we follow Jesus, 'the present-in-history king,' and we come under him, walk alongside him, believe his teachings, embrace his way of life, and participate in his mission (Matt 4:17–19)."[71]

Authentic spiritual experiences, then, will lead believers to move gradually from a self-oriented will to a will submitted to God. Over time such experiences will encourage a single-minded devotion to God and a character developed out of habitual acts of loving God and neighbor.[72] Both taking up one's cross and dying to oneself (Matt 16:24) will be

---

67. Morgan and McLendon, "Trajectory of Spirituality," 45–49.

68. Quarles, "New Creation," 94–98; Wilkins, *In His Image*, 45–47.

69. Plantinga et al., *Introduction to Christian Theology*, 191; Willard, *Great Omission*, 24–28; Willard, *Renovation of the Heart*, 68; Kelsey, *Eccentric Existence*, 1027; Porter, "Will/Heart/Spirit," 87.

70. Willard, *Divine Conspiracy*, 273.

71. Morgan and McLendon, "Trajectory of Spirituality," 45. Cf. Willard, *Renovation of the Heart*, 151–52.

72. Howard, *Brazos Introduction*, 187; Willard, *Renovation of the Heart*, 143, 150–51.

aspects of this conformity to volitional Christlikeness, in which reliance upon the Holy Spirit reorders one's intentions and decisions toward God-oriented, ethical acts.[73] The result of this transformation of the will is what Paul Moser calls "volitional attunement," in which believers' knowledge of God becomes volitionally conformed to their filial relationship with God, such that they know God as authoritative and trustworthy in such a way that they entrust themselves to God as his obedient children.[74]

Corresponding to growth in submission to God's will, authentic spiritual experiences also will lead to growth in the virtues of the kingdom of God. J. P. Moreland explained this reality: "As a disciple grows, he or she learns to see, feel, think, desire, believe, and behave the way Jesus does in a manner fitting to the kingdom of God and the disciple's own station in life. With God's help, I seek to live as Jesus would if He were me."[75] Just as affective Christlikeness is centered on love, this affective love acts outward through the volitional operations, leading to patience, kindness, humility, generosity, forgiveness, and all the virtues of the kingdom of God expressed as acts and habits produced by the will.[76] Overall, then, authentic spiritual experiences will lead the will to grow in habitual attunement to God, to be governed by the pull of the good over the bad, and to grow in freedom from sin and evil influences.[77]

Volitional Christlikeness in the Spiritual Traditions

Growth in volitional Christlikeness is expressed in all the various traditions of Christian spirituality that have been discussed so far. To a great extent, each tradition is an expression of the virtues of the kingdom, insofar as each tradition affords ways to submit to the will of God. One tradition in particular, the Holiness Tradition, places volitional Christlikeness at the forefront of spiritual growth. According to Richard Foster, the Holiness Tradition emphasizes "the inward re-formation of the heart and the development of 'holy habits,'" which "make our lives function

---

73. Wilkins, *In His Image*, 71; Willard, *Renovation of the Heart*, 71; Wolff, *Discernment*, 25; Demarest, "Human Personhood," 75.

74. Moser, *Elusive God*, 57–59, 90–97, 126.

75. Moreland, *Love Your God*, 174.

76. Dubay, *Authenticity*, 150; Howard, *Christian Spiritual Formation*, 185.

77. Howard, *Christian Spiritual Formation*, 189; Willard, *Renovation of the Heart*, 219, 227; Demarest, "Human Personhood," 75.

appropriately and . . . bring forth substantial character formation."[78] Inauthentic spiritual experiences in this tradition can manifest as legalism, Pelagianism, or a perfectionism focused on external standards of behavior.[79] Additionally, authentic spiritual experiences in this tradition can be evident in a variety of ways, seen in the works of John Wesley and Dietrich Bonhoeffer.

Wesley is well known for his writings on Christian perfection. Whether or not one agrees with his definition of perfection as sinless perfection, much about his emphasis on progress in sanctification is still commendable. Wesley avoided Pelagianism by consistently viewing grace as the source of salvation and faith as the condition of salvation.[80] Commenting on how justification leads to sanctification and participation in God, he wrote,

> By salvation, I mean, not barely (according to the vulgar notion) deliverance from hell, or going to heaven, but a present deliverance from sin, a restoration of the soul to its primitive health, its original purity; a recovery of the divine nature; the renewal of our souls after the image of God in righteousness and true holiness, in justice, mercy, and truth.[81]

This present deliverance from sin—this volitional Christlikeness—entails "loving God with all our heart, mind, soul, and strength," which "implies that no wrong temper, none contrary to love, remains in the soul and that all the thoughts, words, and actions are governed by pure love."[82]

While Wesley emphasized growth in conformity to the image of God as an overcoming of sin through perfect love, Bonhoeffer's view of "costly grace" led him in the 1930s and 1940s to grow in volitional Christlikeness by working against the compromises of the pro-Nazi German church, seeking the downfall of Hitler, and, in general, sharing "in God's suffering at the hands of a godless world."[83] For Bonhoeffer, "cheap grace" is "grace without discipleship, grace without the cross, grace without the living, incarnate Jesus Christ."[84] Costly grace, on the other hand, is like

---

78. Foster, *Streams of Living Water*, 61.
79. Foster, *Streams of Living Water*, 91–94.
80. Wesley, "Sermon I," 8; cf. Wesley, *Farther Appeal*, 4.
81. Welsey, *Farther Appeal*, 2. See also O'Brien, "John Wesley," 50.
82. Wesley, *Plain Account*, 62.
83. Bonhoeffer, *Letters and Papers from Prison*, 480.
84. Bonhoeffer, *Discipleship*, 44.

a treasure in a field or a costly pearl that is worth selling everything else in order to possess it; it is costly because it requires individuals to give up their lives, and it is grace because it calls them to new life in Christ.[85]

Wesley and Bonhoeffer present two examples of how volitional Christlikeness can be evident in a believer's life. Authentic spiritual experiences leading to conformity to Christ's volition can lead to an overcoming of sin, a suffering for the sake of the gospel, or a growth in the virtues of the kingdom of God. The traditions of Christian spirituality show the plurality of forms that conformity to Christ's volition can take. These forms are the concrete ways in which growth in conformity to the image of God and, thus, the effects of authentic spiritual experiences are evident. These spiritual traditions also indicate the effects by which inauthentic spiritual experiences are known. In relation to the volition, those effects would include legalism, Pelagianism, and perfectionism. Overall, the comparison of the spiritual traditions to the structural aspect of the image of God has indicated that authentic spiritual experiences lead to cognitive, affective, and volitional Christlikeness in many ways, upholding and elucidating the unity within diversity of Christian spirituality.

THE RELATIONAL ASPECT OF THE IMAGE OF GOD

Principle (2): Christ's Love for God Relationally Expressed

When Christ took on human nature in the incarnation, he also took on human relationality. However, the incarnation was not the beginning of relationality for Christ. As the second person of the Trinity, Christ existed from eternity past within the intra-Trinitarian life of the Godhead, which is characterized by divine love and mutual indwelling (perichoresis).[86] The mutual love shared between the Father, the Son, and the Holy Spirit is seen throughout the life and teachings of Christ, flowing out from the inner life of God toward creation and human beings in the mission of the Son (John 3:16). Since Christ is the perfect image of God, the perfect love of God is central to what conformity to the image of God means.[87] This love is expressed relationally in Jesus's commandments to love God

---

85. Bonhoeffer, *Discipleship*, 44–45.

86. Hall, *Relational Spirituality*, 58–59.

87. Hoekema, *Created in God's Image*, 22, 63. Hoekema wrote, "If it is true that Christ perfectly images God, then the heart of the image of God must be love. For no man ever loved as Christ loved."

with all of one's heart, soul, and mind and to love one's neighbor as oneself (Matt 22:37-39). Therefore, conformity to the image of God places love at the center of a Christian's web of relationships. In other words, conformity to the image of God is participation in the divine love of the Trinity such that all of a believer's relationships are based on love.[88] The relational aspect of the image of God thus entails the following principle of authenticity. Principle (2): Authentic spiritual experiences will conform to or lead one to grow in conformity with Christ's participation in the love of God as it is expressed relationally toward God, other humans, oneself, and creation. In other words, such experiences will lead disciples of Christ to grow relationally in love toward God, others, themselves, and creation as they take the love of Christ as their own within these various relationships. This relational love is concretely evident throughout the life and teachings of Christ, a study of which will reveal the nature of relational Christlikeness for believers.

Authentic Spiritual Experiences and Relationship with God

Christ's Relationship with God

The Gospels show Christ in relationship with God, other humans, himself, and creation. Christ's relation to creation will be examined in the next section on the functional aspect of the image. In relation to God, Jesus lived in intimate union and perfect communion with his Father (John 17:11, 21).[89] This intimacy is seen in multiple ways in his life and ministry. As the incarnate Son, he lived in perfect, sinless reliance upon his Father, being filled with the Holy Spirit and following everywhere the Spirit led (Luke 4:1-14). He consistently waited upon and listened for his Father, speaking only what he heard from his Father (John 8:26, 28; 12:49-50). By waiting and listening, Jesus modeled dependence on God rather than human autonomy. He showed that true freedom is not independence from God but rather a freedom from sin through dependence on God, acknowledging the authority of the Father and submitting to his will (Luke 22:42).[90]

---

88. Gunton, *Triune Creator*, 208-11.
89. Wilkins, *In His Image*, 44, 116.
90. Bockmuehl, *God Who Speaks*, 48-53.

As John 5:30 makes clear, he could do nothing on his own, such that all that he did was done while relying upon and being united with his Father. He did not seek his own will but sought the will of his Father in submission to his Father. This submission both flowed from and maintained the unity between the Father and the Son for, as Steven Porter wrote, "When we do the will of others because we trust and love those persons, the doing of their will brings with it a relational union or oneness."[91] Porter is correct when he identifies trust as an element of Christlike submission. Even though Christ experienced great pain, sorrow, and suffering, he trustingly obeyed the Father's will for the joy that was set before him (Heb 12:2).[92] Furthermore, such submission is seen in how Christ resisted temptation in the wilderness (Matt 4:1–11) and in how he sought the Father's will over his own in Gethsemane (Matt 26:36–46). Finally, an account of Christ's intimate fellowship with his Father would be incomplete without mention of his prayer life. Christ's intimate trust, steadfast reliance, and submission all were bolstered by his consistency in prayer (Luke 5:16), and Jesus prayed to his "Abba" with "an awareness of a very natural and personal relationship with his Father."[93]

The Believer's Relationship with God

Authentic spiritual experiences will conform to or lead to growth in conformity with Christ's loving relationship with God. Just as for Christ, such a relationship for the believer will consist of such things as love, trust, obedience, submission, thanksgiving, and prayer. Growing in conformity to the image of God will totally reorient believers' lives toward God, including their cognition, affectivity, and volition, as they grow in loving God with all of their heart, soul, mind, and strength (Mark 12:30).[94]

Explaining how Jesus's harmony with the Father is exemplary for believers, Steven Porter wrote, "Just as Jesus listened to the words of his Father (his Father's commandments) and remained in his Father's loving care, so we, too, listen to the words of Jesus (his commandments) and remain in his loving care."[95] Believers stay in loving union with God by

---

91. Porter, "Will/Heart/Spirit," 85; cf. Mulholland, *Invitation to a Journey*, 100.

92. Wilkins, *In His Image*, 189.

93. Burridge and Gould, *Jesus Now and Then*, 106–7; Wilkins, *In His Image*, 44–45.

94. Howard, *Brazos Introduction*, 188–89, 232, 258; Howard, *Christian Spiritual Formation*, 47; Hoekema, *Created in God's Image*, 76, 87.

95. Porter, "Heart/Will/Spirit," 87.

entrusting themselves to God through listening to and submitting to the commands of Jesus. This trusting love manifests as a dependence upon God in all things and a prioritization of God's direction in life.[96] As Christ developed a filial attitude of trust and reliance upon his Father, so also will growth in conformity to the image of God consist of cultivating a believer's childlike disposition toward the Father.[97]

Finally, just as Christ's relationship with his Father was grounded in his robust and constant time in prayer, authentic spiritual experiences will lead to growth in a Christian's prayer life. Concerning the location of prayer within the spiritual life, Evan B. Howard wrote, "Prayer is by definition the relational meeting place of God and God's people. Even though our relationship with God extends into all kinds of other areas (in fact, it must spill over), it is centrally located in the midst of our prayerful communication with God."[98] Prayer by definition is interpersonal relationship with God, as it is the main form of how believers intimately communicate with God.[99] Jesus modeled this centrality of prayer, and relational Christlikeness will do the same. Corresponding to a robust prayer life as well as dependence on and submission to God is a profound awareness of living life *coram Deo*.[100]

Relationship with God in the Spiritual Traditions

Similar to how all the traditions of Christian spirituality are various expressions of volitional Christlikeness, so also, these traditions each manifest different ways in which believers are able to grow in relationship with God. Whether through the stillness of contemplative prayer, the purity of

---

96. Willard, *Renovation of the Heart*, 197.

97. Aumann, *Spiritual Theology*, 54–55.

98. Howard, *Christian Spiritual Formation*, 128. One area in which relationship with God "spills over" is the arena of spiritual warfare. Implied in Jesus's relationship with the Father is a relationship set against evil spirits. In his life, death, and resurrection, Christ resisted the devil's temptations, cast out many demons, and triumphed over all the forces of darkness (Col 2:15; Heb 2:14–15; Jude 1:6; Rev 12:9). Christ has victory over all evil forces. Likewise, in the already-not-yet tension of salvation, followers of Christ share in his victory (Luke 10:19; Jas 4:7; 1 John 4:4). Authentic spiritual experiences, then, will either conform to or lead one to grow in conformity with victory in spiritual warfare, whether that involves detecting the lies of the devil, withstanding temptation, or rejecting evil influence. See Howard, *Christian Spiritual Formation*, 188–89.

99. Howard, *Christian Spiritual Formation*, 137–43.

100. Lovelace, *Dynamics of Spiritual Life*, 130–31.

heart in the Holiness Tradition, the love of neighbor in pursuit of social justice, the material living of the Incarnational Tradition, or the passionate desire for the immediate and powerful presence of the Holy Spirit within the Charismatic Tradition, authentic spiritual experiences can lead to growth in conformity to Christ's relationship with God in many ways.

A simple comparison between the Contemplative Tradition and the Charismatic Tradition will show that a believer's relationship with God can grow in vastly different ways. The contemplative John of the Cross wrote that union with God is achieved through a "dark night of the soul." This dark night involves a purgative contemplation of God, in which one's spiritual, sensual, and affective faculties are darkened, yet purified. Progress within the dark night is signified by a cessation of pleasure or consolation in the things of God and created things combined with a strengthened spirit and a mind centered upon God.[101]

For the Charismatic Tradition, progress in relationship with God comes about more often through the powerful presence of the Holy Spirit than the still darkness of purgative contemplation. The overwhelming presence of the Holy Spirit fills the believer with an overflowing love of God that brings with it "great power including at times signs and wonders of the Spirit's supernatural victory over sin and the powers of darkness."[102] As Ralph Macchia explained, "The Spirit falls on us ever anew to provoke a deeper drinking and a richer overflowing [of love].... [The] fullness of the Spirit is experienced when we overflow with love toward God in worship and with love for sinners in empowered witness."[103] Overall, the traditions of Christian spirituality reveal different ways that authentic spiritual experiences can lead to growth in conformity to Christ's relationship with God.

Authentic Spiritual Experiences and Relationships with Others

Christ's Relationship with Others

Not only did Christ have a loving and intimate relationship with the Father and the Spirit; he also emphasized loving interpersonal relationships

---

101. John of the Cross, *Dark Night*, 311–15.
102. Macchia, *Tongues of Fire*, 306.
103. Macchia, *Tongues of Fire*, 307.

within his earthly ministry, and he commissioned his followers to live in fellowship with one another as his body (Matt 28:18–20; cf. 1 Cor 12:12–31).[104] Voorwinde summarized the "basic emotional tenor" of Jesus's life and ministry with John 13:1, "Having loved his own who were in the world, he loved them to the end."[105] Christ's ministry was wholly directed toward the people around him, as Anthony Hoekema explained: "When people came to him in need, whether that need was for healing, food, or forgiveness, he was always ready to help them."[106] Although tired and hungry, he forgot his own weariness when ministering to a Samaritan woman at a well (John 4). Settling an argument between his disciples about who would be great among his followers, Jesus remarked that the Son of Man came to serve, not to be served (Mark 10:45). Exemplifying the greatest form of love, Christ laid down his life for his friends (John 15:13).[107]

The image of Christ is "the image of One who gave himself totally, completely, absolutely, unconditionally for others."[108] Through his death, Christ embodied God's unconditional love for all, showing that true love for others involves bringing them into God's intended purpose for their lives.[109] This love of Jesus went out toward all people, irrespective of their situation, including the lost, the sinful, the sick, the sorrowful, and the outcast.[110] Richard Burridge and Graham Gould clarified this love of Jesus: "In accepting the poor, the weak, women, Gentiles, lepers and other people considered unimportant by the religious authorities, Jesus was accepting people back into the culture of the people of God without requiring them to go to the temple and make sacrifices."[111] Wherever Jesus appeared, people and groups that society excluded and suppressed were freed from their isolation and invited into a new family, a spiritual family.[112]

---

104. Cortez, *Theological Anthropology*, 26.

105. Voorwinde, *Jesus' Emotions*, 217.

106. Hoekema, *Created in God's Image*, 74.

107. Hoekema, *Created in God's Image*, 74. In his sacrificial death, Christ inseparably joined together the love of God with the love of others. See Mulholland, *Invitation to a Journey*, 42–43.

108. Mulholland, *Invitation to a Journey*, 41.

109. Dyrness, "Life and Death," 58; Wilkins, *In His Image*, 170.

110. Wilkins, *In His Image*, 116.

111. Burridge and Gould, *Jesus Now and Then*, 107.

112. Schmidt, "Scheidung der Geister," 21–22.

The priority of family is upheld in the New Testament through Jesus's birth into a nuclear family, obedience to his earthly parents, and filial orientation toward his eternal Father. Furthermore, Jesus held both marriage and children in high esteem (Matt 19:6; Mark 10:14).[113] Beyond the biological family, Christ invited all people into a spiritual family—the church—in union with him as children of God, namely what is described as the body and bride of Christ (Matt 9:15; 1 Cor 12:12–31; Eph 5:25–32; Rev 19:7).[114] Overall, Jesus's life was directed toward others. He met them in their sorrows and sicknesses, inviting outcasts into relation with him. He lived in community with his disciples, whom he viewed as family (Matt 12:46–50).[115] He also commanded his followers to love others in the same way he loves them (John 13:34–35), sending them out into the world to love their neighbors unconditionally and to invite all people into the spiritual family of God.

The Believer's Relationship with Others

Growth in conformity to the image of God thus entails growth in an outward-oriented life of neighborly love. As authentic spiritual experiences move believers to love God as Jesus loves God, believers also will be moved to love their neighbors and live in community in the body of Christ as Jesus modeled and taught.[116] By leading to closer union with Christ, authentic spiritual experiences will either conform to or lead to greater conformity with the love that Jesus has for others. Christians growing in conformity to the image of God will mediate God's love in their friendships, families, communities, and all the various arenas of relationship.[117] Their relationships will become filled with self-sacrificial love and service rather than pride, conceit, and selfishness.[118] As they grow in love, they will become more and more eager to use their abilities and resources to help and heal the people around them, sharing the

---

113. Chandler, *Christian Spiritual Formation*, 110.

114. Hastings, *Theological Ethics*, 98.

115. Wilkins, *In His Image*, 46.

116. Boa, *Conformed to His Image*, 43; Willard, *Renovation of the Heart*, 132; Morgan and McLendon, "Trajectory of Spirituality," 36.

117. Hall, *Relational Spirituality*, 67; cf. Willard, *Renovation of the Heart*, 182–83.

118. Dyrness, "Life and Death," 58; Moser, *Understanding Religious Experience*, 269; Willard, *Great Omission*, 62.

burdens and joys of their neighbors and accepting them into a loving community of belonging.[119]

Relational Christlikeness, in relation to other human beings, is characterized by "warmth, loving, caring, acceptance, responsiveness, empathy, genuineness, attentiveness, concern, support [and] understanding."[120] Toxic traits such as deception, assault, withdrawal and isolation, oppression, injustice, defensiveness, self-justification, and manipulation do not have a place within relational Christlikeness.[121] Rather, conformity to Christ's relational love for others consists of forming righteous relationships filled with love, forgiveness, compassion, justice, and all of the characteristics of the kingdom of God.[122] Within relational Christlikeness, marriages image the relationship between Christ and the church (Eph 5:15–27), and friendships mirror Christ's self-sacrificial love.[123]

By leading to conformity with the relational aspect of the image of God, authentic spiritual experiences will incorporate believers more deeply into relationship with a local church community.[124] Darrell Bock made a similar point: "God does not bring us into fellowship with him and make us a part of his people to function in isolation."[125] Implied is the reality that separation from the church often shows separation from the Holy Spirit. Relational Christlikeness directly entails participation in the body of Christ and fellowship with other Christians in mutual love and edification.[126] Drawing together the image of God and participation in the body of Christ, Todd Hall stated,

---

119. Hoekema, *Created in God's Image*, 78.

120. Perlman, *Relationship*, 29.

121. Willard, *Renovation of the Heart*, 190, 194–96, 220; cf. Morgan and McLendon, "Trajectory of Spirituality," 38.

122. Howard, *Brazos Introduction*, 188–89, 258; Howard, *Christian Spiritual Formation*, 72; Hoekema, *Created in God's Image*, 87.

123. Hastings, *Theological Ethics*, 95; cf. Chandler, *Christian Spiritual Formation*, 111, 114–15. Relational Christlikeness does not necessitate that one be married, given that Christ was never married. See Hoekema, *Created in God's Image*, 76.

124. Ashley, "Turn to Spirituality," 161.

125. Bock, "New Testament Community," 103; cf. Groeschel, *Spiritual Passages*, 53.

126. Hoekema, *Created in God's Image*, 89. That the Holy Spirit leads Christ followers to participate in the body of Christ does not mean that they never are to leave a local church community for another. Such transitions can be healthy if their current church community is not fostering their relational Christlikeness due to the presence of toxic traits or an unwillingness to develop authentic community. The main point is that the Holy Spirit never will lead them to disengage completely from participating physically within the body of Christ and thus within the local church.

> Believers are to love each other in the same way God loves us, thereby manifesting the image of God. This happens through a Spirit-empowered, relational process in which we find our identity by being "in Christ," which means participating in the love among the Trinity. Yet, we do this not in an individually focused way but by participating in the body of Christ, thereby sharing together in the dynamic of God's love. The ecclesial self-in-community images God in this rich, multifaceted love for one another in the new family of God, and by extension, for all humanity.[127]

In other words, growth in conformity to the image of God, in reflecting relational Christlikeness, always will be centrifugal, pushing outward toward relationship with others, whether expressed in marriage, family, friendships, or the body of Christ.

Relationship with Others in the Spiritual Traditions

As Christ exemplified love in his relationships with other human beings, authentic spiritual experiences also will manifest such love in a Christian's relationships. This love takes on different shapes within the spiritual traditions, highlighting the unity in diversity of Christian spirituality as well as the specificity without rigidity of the image of God as a criterion of discernment. In the Azusa Street Revival of early twentieth-century Pentecostalism, the love of neighbor tore down walls of segregation, and huge crowds of both black- and white-skinned believers worshiped in united community.[128] Within the Incarnational Tradition, the love of neighbor is carried out in valuing the spiritual worth of relationships within family, work, society, and marriage.[129] For example, in *Spiritual Friendship*, Aelred of Rievaulx argued that friendship was instituted by God within creation as something that leads to an experience of Christ and friendship with God.[130]

Concerning relationships with others, inauthentic spiritual experiences often manifest as relationships of selfishness. Aelred drew this point out through his examination of the various kinds of relationships. Carnal friendships are based on a mutual pursuit of sensual pleasure and

---

127. Hall, *Relational Spirituality*, 63.
128. Foster, *Streams of Living Water*, 117.
129. Foster, *Streams of Living Water*, 263–66.
130. Aelred of Rievaulx, *Spiritual Friendship*, 51–68.

vice. Worldly friendships are based on mutual, selfish, and worldly gain. Spiritual friendships, in contrast to carnal and worldly friendships, are based on morality and the pursuit of justice, grounded in benevolence and love.[131]

At other times, inauthentic spiritual experiences can manifest as isolation from the local church. One's thoughts might go to the stereotypical hermit or to those Christians who sought the solace of the desert as an escape from worldly living in the early church, yet even hermits like St. Anthony or desert fathers like Abba Moses often lived in community with other believers as a localized expression of the body of Christ.[132] A modern example of true isolation from the church would be those individuals who, for various reasons, have become disenchanted with the "established" church, preferring to express their spirituality privately in the comfort of their homes and outside the shepherding of the people ordained to teach and lead within Christ's church. The spirit of Christ never will lead a believer to forsake the body of Christ. Nonetheless, the Spirit might lead a believer to reform an expression of the church. For example, Bonhoeffer's dissatisfaction with and disgust at the pro-Nazi German church did not lead him to walk away from the established church and take on a privatized form of religion. Rather, he pursued a purification of the church, leading him to take on a role of leadership in the Confessing Church.[133]

Authentic Spiritual Experiences and Relationship with Oneself

Christ's Self-Identity

Many scholars do not mention relationship with oneself as part of the image of God. Nonetheless, the fourth degree of love, according to Bernard of Clairvaux, is to love self for God's sake.[134] He explained this love as follows: "As God himself willed that everything should be for himself, so we, too, will that nothing, not even ourselves, may be or have been except for him, that is according to his will, not ours."[135] For Bernard,

---

131. Aelred of Rievaulx, *Spiritual Friendship*, 60–61.
132. See Athanasius, *Life of St. Anthony*; Cassian, *Conferences*.
133. Foster, *Streams of Living Water*, 74.
134. Bernard of Clairvaux, "On Loving God," 195.
135. Bernard of Clairvaux, "On Loving God," 195–96. While Bernard argued that this fourth degree of love is possible only in eternity, given that to love in this way is

this love is the fourth degree of love, in which the love of God includes a believer's will for God to be all in all (1 Cor 15:28). Relationship with oneself is included within one's loving relationship with God and is part of the relational aspect of the image of God insofar as the love of God demands the development of a particular love of self. This love for self, as an extension of the love of God, encapsulates the submission of self to God through the ways discussed previously under the structural aspect of the image of God. Beyond love of self, relationship with oneself also relates to self-identity and whether that self-identity is, in itself, submitted to God.

Jesus Christ perfectly knew and lived out his self-identity. Despite being "criticized, rejected, slandered, misunderstood, plotted against, betrayed, denied, and abused by his family and friends, his disciples, the Jewish religious leaders, and the Romans," Jesus unfailingly "derived his identity from his relationship with his Father and not from the opinions of his family and peers."[136] He never doubted his identity as the Son of God or the Son of Man, and his identity was verified by the resurrection, which acted as God's divine stamp of approval on Jesus's life and teachings.[137] The particularities of Christ's self-identity already have been discussed in the section on "Christ and Cognition," and they will not all be repeated here. The point is that Jesus knew who he was based on his relationship with God and not based on the negative pressures of the world. He knew that the Father had given all things to him, that he had come from the Father, and that he was going back to the Father (John 13:3); and he consistently lived out this identity in his life and teachings.[138]

The Believer's Self-Identity

Likewise, every human being has the option to derive a self-identity based either on his or her relationship with God or on the opinions of other human beings. When believers grow in conformity to the relational aspect of the image of God as a result of having authentic spiritual experiences that inform their self-perception, they will grow in understanding

---

to become like God, the already-not-yet reality of a believer's regeneration means that, if nothing else, some sort of progress toward this love is possible in this life, such that believers are able to love themselves for the sake of God in various degrees, if not in perfection.

136. Boa, *Conformed to His Image*, 44–45.
137. Habermas, *Risen Jesus*, 108–10.
138. Boa, *Conformed to His Image*, 44.

their God-given identities as children of God, entering deeper into God's love and into a God-glorifying love of self.[139]

This aspect of growth in conformity to the image of God takes place in light of God's revealed truth in Scripture.[140] Kenneth Boa cited over forty passages of Scripture that—applied to the life of a follower of Christ—elucidate the various parts of a believer's God-given identity. To name a few, as a child of God, one is justified, redeemed, a friend of Jesus, no longer a slave to sin, set free from the law of sin and death, a co-heir with Christ, a saint, a partaker in Christ's righteousness and sanctification, indwelled by the Holy Spirit, made alive in Christ, a member of Christ's body, chosen by God, holy and beloved, and so much more.[141]

Self-Identity in the Spiritual Traditions

Authentic spiritual experiences, conforming to relational Christlikeness, will conform to or lead to growth in conformity with one's self-identity as a child of God. In the Contemplative Tradition, for example, this growth occurs through the practice of solitude, in which believers are confronted by the presence and truths of God, without distraction from the voices of the world, so that their wills and ways become aligned with God's will and ways. Contemplative solitude is not to be a time for narcissistic introspection or obsession, which would be the effects of inauthentic spiritual experiences. Rather, as Bernard of Clairvaux stated, love of self for God's sake requires "human affection to dissolve in some ineffable way, and be poured into the will of God."[142] Conformity to Christ within one's self-identity, then, is a process of purgation and purified affections, not self-obsession.[143]

A second example is found in the emphasis of the Charismatic Tradition on the power of the Holy Spirit. Through emphasizing the real presence of the Holy Spirit in the lives of believers, the Charismatic Tradition also rightly emphasizes how believers are given a new identity and made new, being regenerated and empowered by the Holy Spirit to live

---

139. Wilkins, *In His Image*, 79–83; Willard, *Renovation of the Heart*, 194.
140. Howard, *Brazos Introduction*, 258.
141. Boa, *Conformed to His Image*, 36–41.
142. Bernard of Clairvaux, "On Loving God," 196.
143. Bernard of Clairvaux, "On Loving God," 196.

out their identities as children of God freed from sin and the forces of darkness.[144]

The examples above from the spiritual traditions do not exhaust the ways in which relational conformity to the image of God can take place. Rather, they show that growth in conformity to the image of God, as the outcome of authentic spiritual experiences, can develop in many ways.

THE FUNCTIONAL ASPECT OF THE IMAGE OF GOD

Principle (3): Christ's Threefold Office of Prophet, Priest, and King

The functional aspect of the image of God holds that humans are called by God to exercise a royal and priestly dominion of caring stewardship over creation as God's representatives. Much of the work on the functional image of God focuses on the Old Testament context of the ancient Near East. Nevertheless, when applied to the New Testament and to Christ, the functional image of God takes on a particular shape, oriented around the offices of Christ. Adam was given a divine vocation, the cultural mandate, to have dominion over the earth and subdue and develop it (Gen 1:26–28). While Adam failed to fulfill this divinely given vocation, the incarnate Christ perfectly fulfilled it and enabled his followers to participate in his continuing ministry of dominion on earth, through the power of the Holy Spirit.

During his earthly ministry, Christ exercised his dominion through a threefold office (*munus triplex*) of prophet, priest, and king.[145] As king, Christ is the risen and reigning Lord over the world and the Son of God. He defends and sustains his people within redemption, restraining and conquering all of his enemies and subduing and rescuing human beings to himself through the atonement of his sacrificial death and resurrection. He governs through his word and by the power of the Holy Spirit, as head of the church and Lord of the kingdom of God. As priest, Christ reconciles sinners to God, making intercession and atonement for them through his substitutionary sacrifice, working to purify and cleanse them

---

144. Macchia, *Tongues of Fire*, 301–307.

145. In the structural image of God, volitional Christlikeness focuses on submitting to the will of God. In the functional image of God, while submission to the will of God is still a central facet of this aspect of the image of God, the functional image of God is set apart from volitional Christlikeness in how it takes on a more vocational emphasis, centered on God's call to Adam in Gen 1:26–28.

from sin and to mediate between God and humanity. As prophet, Christ is the revealer of God's divine will concerning salvation. He proclaims the words of God and is the word of God.[146]

Summarizing the *munus triplex* of Christ, Thomas Oden wrote, "He is at the same time the teacher of true religion, expiator of sin, and bearer of legitimate authority to guide and judge future history."[147] Christ inhabits these offices "at the same time," and as such, each office coheres inseparably within each other in the work of Christ. Christ's kingship is understood through his priestly atonement, and his kingship provides the authority that upholds his prophetic and priestly offices. Furthermore, Christ's priesthood is revealed and defined by his prophetic teaching on the kingdom of God, and his priestly atonement reveals the love and grace and justice of God and is thus prophetic. Finally, Christ's prophetic office reveals him as both king and priest.[148] As a result of this coinherence, talk of Christ's royal dominion (kingly office) or priestly stewardship (priestly office)—common ways to define the functional aspect of the image of God within its Old Testament context—is also talk of Christ in his prophetic office and, consequently, Christ in his *munus triplex*.

Insofar as Christ calls and invites his followers to participate in his work, he invites them to function vocationally within his *munus triplex*, continuing his work in this world as the body of Christ.[149] Therefore, one can talk of conformity to the functional aspect of the image of God through the categories of the *munus triplex*. This point leads to the third general principle of discernment drawn from the criterion of the image of God. Principle (3): Authentic spiritual experiences will either conform to or lead to growth in conformity with Christ's threefold office of prophet, priest, and king.

---

146. Peters, *God*, 349–50, 391; Letham, *Work of Christ*, 22; Rodrigues, "Scriptural Christology of Hebrews," 42; Otto, "Baptism," 217; Oden, *Word of Life*, 280–85.

147. Oden, *Word of Life*, 285.

148. Oden, *Word of Life*, 285.

149. Wilkins, *In His Image*, 46; Howard, "Vocational Formation," 167, 170. By *vocation* or *vocational calling*, I am not talking solely about vocational ministry in the sense of a full-time job within the church, Christian academia, or other similar institutions. Rather, I am focusing on how Christ "calls" (*vocat*) all believers to participate in his ongoing ministry. One's vocation as a Christian is to participate in Christ's work in every realm of one's life, including work, family, church, and the public square.

Authentic Spiritual Experiences and the Office of King

Christ's Kingly Office

Christ mediates the reign and presence of God on earth through his royal representation of God as God the Son incarnate (John 10:38; Col 2:9).[150] As the creator of and sovereign over all of creation, Christ is the high king who has all authority (Matt 28:18) to rule over human beings, nature, the spiritual realm, and all created things.[151] Christ rules over all human beings as their sovereign Savior and judge, and all will bend the knee and acknowledge his Lordship one day (Phil 2:10–11). He also rules over nature, as seen in the many miracles he performed—stilling the sea, walking on water, turning water into wine, multiplying food, healing diseases, and raising the dead.[152] Christ knew how to subdue nature and shape it after his Father's will. Christ also had victory and power over the kingdom and forces of darkness. His ministry was a spiritual battle, destroying the power of sin, darkness, and demons, and giving captives freedom from sin and victory over evil. He resisted the temptations of the devil, cast out demons, and conquered death in the resurrection.[153] As the image of God, all things were created through him and for him, and all things hold together in him, including all thrones, dominions, rulers, and authorities. In everything, Christ is preeminent (Col 1:15–20).

Christ exercised his royal dominion, during his earthly ministry, to inaugurate and establish the kingdom of God on earth, a kingdom in which the presence and values of God are manifest.[154] He used his royal authority and power through the avenues of self-sacrifice and servanthood (Matt 20:25–28), setting the example for Christians to follow.[155] Christ's power is antithetical to the kind of power exercised by selfish and prideful earthly rulers but not antithetical to washing his disciples' feet.[156] Over every aspect of the created order, Christ continues to exercise his royal dominion to establish the ways of God among human beings, thus fulfilling the human vocation in which Adam failed. By inaugurating the

---

150. Cortez, *Theological Anthropology*, 32.
151. Letham, *Work of Christ*, 198–202.
152. Hoekema, *Created in God's Image*, 74.
153. Lovelace, *Dynamics of Spiritual Life*, 72.
154. Kilner, *Dignity and Destiny*, 76.
155. Plantinga et al., *Introduction to Christian Theology*, 193.
156. Jastram, "Man as Male," 24; Peppiatt, *Imago Dei*, 35.

kingdom of God on earth, Christ fulfilled the cultural mandate of Gen 1:26–28, for the kingdom of God works to subdue and develop God's creation in God-glorifying ways. Jesus did not simply go along with the culture of the time, but with "wisdom and tact," he "broke tacit assumptions that countered kingdom values."[157] He engaged with the unclean and the outcast. He worked against the established structures of the religious elite. He called for peaceful living under one's magistrates. Ultimately, he beckoned "a lost world to God and to kingdom living."[158]

The Believer's Royal Vocation

Jesus Christ also calls and authorizes his followers to continue his royal dominion on earth as God's representatives. As Lucy Peppiatt explained,

> Jesus Christ is not only the second Adam who himself models perfect obedience and submission to God the Father, but he also confers authority upon those who are submitted to himself to carry out the will of God on earth. This authority . . . is to be characterized by humbling oneself under God, engaging in self-sacrifice, and preferring others. In imitation of the Savior Christ, whom Christians follow, serving as God's representatives on earth is meant to be submissive, self-denying, meek, and nonviolent.[159]

As such, believers are called to imitate Christ's royal office through being representatives of God on earth, as children of God and co-heirs with Christ (Rom 8:17; cf. Eph 2:6). This functional Christlikeness is accomplished through the cultural mandate, which is the royal vocation given to children of God, who are to mediate God's rule on earth and extend the kingdom of God.[160]

Similar to Christ, this human vocation not only entails the development of culture; it also entails authority over the powers of darkness and growth in spiritual giftings as the means to work toward God's kingdom. Humans are not given authority over all things like Christ, but they are given authority to develop the innate possibilities of the physical world

---

157. Chandler, *Christian Spiritual Formation*, 124.
158. Chandler, *Christian Spiritual Formation*, 124.
159. Peppiatt, *Imago Dei*, 35.
160. LaCugna, "Practical Trinity," 280–81; Sutanto, "Cultural Mandate," 593; Sands, "Imago Dei," 38.

and to develop culture and civilization.[161] Bolstering this dominion is the God-given authority that believers have over sin and the forces of darkness, sharing in Christ's resurrection life and being gifted with the power of the Holy Spirit.[162] Overall, a Christian's vocation is to love and serve God by reflecting God's glory in all of life. By being a child of God, Christians inhabit a royal office as God's representatives in which they continue the work of the cultural mandate, proliferating God's kingdom of faith, hope, and love.[163]

Growth in conformity to the kingly office of functional Christlikeness will entail at least three things, and accordingly, these three things never will be contradicted by authentic spiritual experiences. First, such growth will involve developing and practicing a *creatio ex naturam* that is analogous to and characteristic of Christ's loving creation of all things ex nihilo. A believer's creative habits—whether they be in agriculture, economics, the arts, or anything that contributes to human flourishing—will become progressively more and more oriented around the upholding of human dignity and God's glory.[164]

Second, in consequence, such growth will entail a reoriented approach to work. Rather than approaching work as an opportunity for self-aggrandizement, selfish gain, or growth in earthly power and wealth, believers will approach work as an aspect of their royal vocation and thus as an opportunity to provide for the needs of others and validate their dignity, to develop God's creation toward its intended end, and to glorify God through the pursuit of a kingdom-minded culture.[165]

Third, in connection with the pursuit of a kingdom-minded culture, growth in conformity to the royal office of functional Christlikeness will involve growth in what Eugene Peterson called "vocational holiness," which is the representation of the kingdom of God in a culture devoted to the kingdom of self.[166] Christ modeled vocational holiness in how he

---

161. Bavinck, *Beginning and the End*, 29–30.

162. Lovelace, *Dynamics of Spiritual Life*, 136; Chandler, *Christian Spiritual Formation*, 172.

163. Chandler, *Christian Spiritual Formation*, 152; Dyrness, "Life and Death," 59; Wilkins, *In His Image*, 151; Hastings, *Theological Ethics*, 83.

164. Edgar, *Created and Creating*, 168; Sutanto, "Cultural Mandate," 594.

165. Hastings, *Theological Ethics*, 88; Volf, *Work in the Spirit*, 79; Hoekema, *Created in God's Image*, 79, 88; Dyrness, "Life and Death," 63.

166. Peterson, *Under the Unpredictable Plant*, 50.

overcame the worldly temptations of power, prestige, and compromise.[167] Rather than conceding to cultural demands, authentic spiritual experiences will lead believers to grow in the prioritization of God's glory and goodness in work, just as Christ did, by submitting to the will and word of God.[168]

Royal Vocation in the Spiritual Traditions

Given how humans are called to exercise a royal dominion as the children of God over many different aspects of life, conformity to this aspect of the image of God has manifested in the traditions of Christian spirituality in a plethora of ways. All of the great traditions of Christian spirituality, at least in part, work toward a Christlike exercise of human dominion in the various realms of life. The Incarnational and Social Justice traditions, in particular, stress the importance of a Christian's royal vocation. For the Incarnational Tradition, dominion occurs through a reclamation of the dignity and sacredness of work as believers seek to work in the ways that Jesus would if he were them. Sacramental living even extends into family life as well as cultural, political, and institutional life.[169]

Examples of this dominion, or vocational holiness, can be seen in the Benedictine view of the sacredness of manual labor or in how Franciscans served the poor.[170] In the Protestant Reformation, dominion was expressed through the "protestant work ethic" and Luther's priesthood of all believers, both of which called all Christians to fulfill God's vocational call on their lives by serving as God's representatives within the world.[171] Christlike dominion also is found in the call of the Social Justice Tradition to establish the kingdom of God presently on earth. Seen in the writings of Walter Rauschenbusch, the church is called to work for the salvation of both individuals and societies and to repent from both individual and collective sins, taking the burden of social reform seriously and believing in the present import of the kingdom of God.[172]

---

167. Chandler, *Christian Spiritual Formation*, 174.
168. Sutanto, "Cultural Mandate," 601–2.
169. Foster, *Streams of Living Water*, 263–65.
170. Foster, *Streams of Living Water*, 270.
171. McGrath, *Reformation Thought*, 277–79.
172. Rauschenbusch, *Social Gospel*, 1–22.

Authentic Spiritual Experiences and the Office of Priest

Christ's Priestly Office

Enumerating the various aspects of Christ's priestly office, Thomas Oden wrote, "The priestly office of the Son functions in three ways: (1) he makes perfect satisfaction to God the Father, through his suffering and death on the cross; (2) he intercedes with the Father for the contrite in heart, in order to (3) bring the blessing of redemption to humanity."[173] First, Christ was sent into the world in order to redeem humanity, reconciling them to God through his sacrificial death. Second, Christ is the eternal priest of the new covenant, interceding on behalf of believers before the Father. Third, Christ brings reconciliation and redemption to human beings, making them new and giving them eternal life.[174]

Christ did many priestly acts during his earthly ministry. He healed the unclean and declared them clean. He cared for the stewardship of the created world and how that stewardship impacted human relationships and the powerless, working against sin, sickness, hunger, and death and calling others to a selfless stewardship of their resources.[175] As a priest, Christ ministered to physically and spiritually sick individuals and societies. As Richard Lovelace explained,

> In the New Testament, Jesus comes bringing not only forgiveness to the faithful but healing for the sick, bread for the hungry, sight for the blind and hearing for the deaf. We might be inclined to spiritualize all of these matters, but we have seen Christians within history bringing them to literal fulfillment! We would do better to broaden their meaning to include the healing of sick societies.[176]

Furthermore, Christ cleansed the temple and declared his body to be the temple (John 2:19–21), showing his concern for the purity of holy places and for the accessibility of the presence of God. As the atoner of and interceder for human beings, Christ sought to bring people to God and remove barriers that obstructed their unity. Additionally, his teachings often focused on matters of priestly concern, such as peoples' relationship

---

173. Oden, *Word of Life*, 303–4.
174. Aumann, *Spiritual Theology*, 228.
175. Dyrness, "Life and Death," 56.
176. Lovelace, *Dynamics of Spiritual Life*, 388.

to God, the temple and the presence of God, obedience to the Law, and purification and forgiveness.

The Believer's Priestly Vocation

Christ incorporates his followers into his priestly work, forming them into a priesthood of believers (John 17:17–20; 1 Pet 2:9).[177] Believers are called to a self-sacrificial service of others that draws people to God and removes barriers between God and humanity. As priests, believers are to be concerned with such things as holiness, purity, and obedience to the commands of God. In priestly terms, believers are anointed by the Holy Spirit, consecrated in likeness to Jesus, and called to intercede self-sacrificially for their neighbors by caring for them, by working to meet their needs, and by mediating the presence and love of God to them (1 John 2:20; 3:2–3, 16–24).[178] In order to mediate the blessings of God to their neighbors, Christians also are called to be priests over creation, stewarding the created realm as an expression of God's beauty and goodness and working toward harmonious relationships with nature and human beings. Believers are to serve, not consume creation, participating in God's care of creation and seeking the renewal of creation (Rom 8:18–24).[179] By such stewardship, culture is purified and oriented around mutual service rather than selfishness, upholding both the dignity of human beings and the beauty and glory of God.

If a spiritual experience is authentically from the Holy Spirit, that experience will not lead Christians away from living out their priestly vocations. Rather, authentic spiritual experiences will encourage believers toward a greater self-sacrificial and priestly care for the spiritual, physical, emotional, and relational needs of their neighbor as well as a care for the preservation of God's creation.

Priestly Vocation in the Spiritual Traditions

Concerning the priestly office of Christ, inauthentic spiritual experiences have manifested in the traditions of Christian spirituality as a narrowing of the gospel that presents salvation as an escape from the world and

---

177. Swann, *Imago Dei*, 167–68.
178. Swann, *Imago Dei*, 168.
179. Hastings, *Theological Ethics*, 88, 100.

worldly responsibility, excluding from salvation much of Christ's priestly office. Richard Foster identified two ways a limited view of salvation can occur within the Evangelical Tradition: first, as an overemphasis on getting to heaven that eclipses the meaning of present life and, second, as an individualism that "neglects social responsibility and prophetic insight."[180] Nevertheless, Christ's priestly office is evidenced adequately in the Evangelical Tradition when, for example, salvation is fleshed out in connection to a Christian worldview, as in the writings of Al Wolters. Wolters takes a priestly stance toward creation and current life through the articulation of a biblical worldview applied to "every sector of human life."[181] Wolters defends a cosmic view of redemption, viewing sanctification as "the process whereby the Holy Spirit, in and through the people of God, purifies creation from sin."[182] In other words, Christians are called to be priests within the world, working to sanctify individuals, societies, and all of creation.[183]

To a great extent, all of the spiritual traditions are priestly insofar as they invite people to heal from their trials and tribulations in communion with Christ, yet traditions manifest the priestly stewardship of creation in different ways. In the Incarnational Tradition, sacramental living is a rejection of a Gnostic dualism that claims the material creation is bad. Approaching creation as a good, this tradition seeks to take care of and cultivate the world because it is a gift from God, and this approach leads to an ecological sensitivity of sorts.[184]

In the Social Justice tradition, on the other hand, the stewardship of creation is a means to provide for the poor and the helpless. This work manifests as a fight against cultures of selfish consumption and a development of cultures of cooperation.[185] Many individual Christians could be named as models of this aspect of conformity to Christ's priestly office. Taking care of the poor, the hungry, the powerless, and the destitute, Christians such as William Wilberforce, David Livingstone, Mother Teresa, Martin Luther King Jr., and others instantiated conformity to this aspect of the image of God in different ways.[186]

180. Foster, *Streams of Living Water*, 230.
181. Wolters, *Creation Regained*, 58, cf. 74.
182. Wolters, *Creation Regained*, 74, cf. 59.
183. Wolters, *Creation Regained*, 75–76.
184. Foster, *Streams of Living Water*, 266–67.
185. Rauschenbusch, *Social Gospel*, 45–56.
186. Foster, *Streams of Living Water*, 136.

Authentic Spiritual Experiences and the Office of Prophet

Christ's Prophetic Office

Meeting one night with Jesus, a man of the Pharisees named Nicodemus stated, "Rabbi, we know that you have come from God, a teacher" (John 3:2). Responding to Jesus's teachings, the crowds were amazed, for he taught as one having authority (Matt 7:28–29). When Jesus entered Jerusalem on his way to cleanse the temple, the crowds were saying to one another, "This is the prophet Jesus" (Matt 21:11). The Old Testament spoke of a prophet like Moses who was to come (Deut 18:15), and the New Testament identifies this prophet with Christ (John 6:14; 7:40; Acts 3:20–22).[187] As a prophet, Christ came proclaiming the good news of the kingdom of God, teaching the way of salvation, and inviting people to live out the ethic of the kingdom of God. Revealing the truths of God, he came to seek and to save the lost (Luke 19:10).[188]

In the Old Testament, prophets were the messengers of the Lord, proclaiming the words of God. In the New Testament, Christ both proclaims the word of God and is the word of God, perfectly revealing the Father and the way to salvation (John 1:1; 14:9).[189] Thomas Oden summarized Christ's prophetic office: "The prophetic office of Christ refers to the work of Christ in revealing fully the divine truth to humanity, proclaiming the divine plan of redemption, and calling all to accept the salvation offered."[190] Christ fulfilled this office during his earthly ministry. He also appointed apostles after him, who continued that ministry; and through the inspiration of the Holy Spirit, Christ continues to speak today through Scripture.[191]

The Believer's Prophetic Vocation

All Christians are called to participate in Christ's ongoing prophetic work, being commissioned to make disciples and teach them the truths

---

187. Rodrigues, "Scriptural Christology of Hebrews," 44; Quarles, "New Creation," 83–84. Cf. Burridge and Gould, *Jesus Now and Then*, 63.

188. Wilkins, *In His Image*, 45; Letham, *Work of Christ*, 91–102; Peters, *God*, 357; Nugent, *Fourfold Office of Christ*, 62.

189. Rodrigues, "Scriptural Christology of Hebrews," 43. Rodrigues makes the point that teaching God's Word is an aspect of both Christ's prophetic and priestly offices.

190. Oden, *Word of Life*, 286.

191. Letham, *Work of Christ*, 223.

and commands of God (Matt 28:18–20). The vocation of functional Christlikeness includes the call to proclaim the word of God and the truth of salvation in Christ to a dark and dying world. According to the image of God as a criterion of spiritual discernment, authentic spiritual experiences will conform to or lead to growth in conformity with the prophetic office of the functional aspect of the image of God. They will support a believer's calling to testify to the truths of Christ and proclaim Christ as the one way to salvation. If spiritual experiences lead a believer away from this calling, they are not authentic. The Holy Spirit never will lead believers to share the gospel less or to encourage other believers to forsake holy living.

Prophetic Vocation in the Spiritual Traditions

One primary way in which conformity to Christ's prophetic office has occurred within the spiritual traditions of the church is simply through the practice of evangelism, as seen in the Evangelical Tradition. Preachers such as Charles Spurgeon, Dwight L. Moody, and Billy Graham are well known for their vigorous passions for proclaiming the gospel and calling people to repentance and faith in Christ. The mission works of individuals such as William Carey, Hudson Taylor, and Adoniram Judson are also examples of conformity to Christ's prophetic office. Beyond preaching and missionary efforts, the proclamation of the gospel also can be seen in the apologetic efforts of individuals such as Francis Schaeffer or Norman Geisler. Still further, this prophetic office is found in all who simply share the good news of Christ with their friends, family, and neighbors. All of these examples count as possible instantiations of conformity to the prophetic office of Christ and thus as effects of authentic spiritual experiences.

Beyond evangelistic efforts, the prophetic office of Christ can take on the form of powerfully proclaiming the truths and promises of God over someone's life. With its emphasis on the gifts of the Holy Spirit, the Charismatic Tradition holds prophecy as central to the church's conformity to Christ.[192] At this point, though, a distinction must be made between foretelling and forthtelling. Forthtelling is a form of "expository

---

192. Macchia, "Prophetic Jesus," 26–30. Macchia argues that prophecy is not as much an individual gift as a performed act by the church. Elsewhere, Macchia talks about the church as a "prophethood of believers." See Macchia, *Spirit-Baptized Church*, 53.

and hortatory discourse," whereas foretelling is a form of "predictive discourse."[193] On the one hand, prophetic forthtelling is a sign of conformity to the prophetic office of Christ because it is a call, based on truths within Scripture, for people to repent, change their lives, trust in God, and live out the truths of the gospel. Prophetic foretelling, on the other hand, is itself a matter of discernment that hearkens back to the discussion in chapter 2 on the Old Testament approach to ascertaining whether someone was a true or false prophet. While a prophecy that meets the criteria for authenticity, as seen in the Old Testament, may be a sign that a spiritual experience was authentic and in conformity to the image of God, the actual act of proclaiming a foretelling does not count as an instance of authenticity without such verification.

False prophecies obviously would count as examples of inauthentic spiritual experiences, and history is rankled with false prophets. Another way in which inauthentic spiritual experiences have manifested within the life of the church, in relation to the prophetic office of Christ, is through redefinitions of the gospel. At times, for example, in the Social Justice Tradition, the gospel has been so redefined that it radically strays from the teachings of Christ and the apostles in the New Testament.[194] Authentic spiritual experiences, in conformity to the image of God, never will lead a believer to forsake the importance of the historical resurrection of Christ or to orient the message of salvation around the salvation of society in such a way that the sacrifice of Jesus is no longer proclaimed as salvation from personal sin and hell.

Overall, as with the other aspects of conformity to the image of God, the spiritual traditions show that, for functional Christlikeness, many ways exist for the effects of authentic spiritual experiences to manifest in the life of believers. The spiritual traditions are filled with a plethora of concrete examples of how believers grow in their conformity to the image of God as a result of having authentic spiritual experiences. Christian spirituality truly is a beautiful tapestry formed by the work of the Holy Spirit in which many different threads come together to present a unified image and design. That image and design is Christ, the perfect image of God.

---

193. Chisholm, "When Prophecy Appears," 562.
194. For example, see Rauschenbusch, *Social Gospel*, 38–44, 240–79.

CONCLUSION

In this chapter, to be as concrete as possible, I drew out three principles of discernment from the criterion of the image of God.[195] These principles apply the three aspects of the image of God to Jesus Christ to clarify further what growth in conformity to the image of God entails. Furthermore, these principles clarify the nature and effects of authentic spiritual experiences by indicating exactly what authentic spiritual experiences conform to and lead toward. These three principles were expounded through an examination of Christ's life and teachings as well as an application of Christ's example to the lives of believers and the spiritual traditions of the church. Christ's exemplification of being the image of God is that by which growth in conformity to the image of God is measured and that by which the effects of authentic spiritual experiences are identified, whether in the lives of believers or in the spiritual traditions. As was evident throughout the chapter, the effects of authentic spiritual experiences can manifest in many ways. The comparison of the spiritual traditions with the criterion of the image of God made this fact particularly evident. Through the three principles of discernment, the criterion of the image of God provides a specificity without rigidity that is able to account for the unity within diversity of Christian spirituality.

Principle (1) states that, based on the image of God as a criterion of spiritual discernment, authentic spiritual experiences will either conform to or lead to growth in conformity with Christ's cognition, affectivity, and volition. In other words, growth in conformity to the image of God structurally will involve formation in a believer's thinking, feeling, and acting within the various levels of depth and stages of cognition of human experience. Cognitively, believers will come to view God and all of creation more and more through the lens of how Christ viewed them, based on Christ's self-identity and view of God as well as his understanding of the

---

195. These principles can act as either positive or negative indicators—positive when a spiritual experience effects growth toward them and negative when a spiritual experience effects lack of conformity to or growth away from them. That a spiritual experience does not lead to growth in conformity to the image of God does not necessarily indicate that the experience was not authentic. The possibility always exists that a spiritual experience is authentic but that a believer is hard-hearted and hard-headed, dismissing it and not permitting it to be effective. However, if a spiritual experience leads against growth in conformity to the image of God, then that effect shows the experience is not authentic, for the Holy Spirit never would lead against conformity to the image of God. Furthermore, if a spiritual experience leads toward conformity to the image of God, then it is authentic, for only the Holy Spirit can produce such growth.

kingdom of God. True experiences of the Holy Spirit will neither support nor lead to thoughts or beliefs that do not cohere with Christ's worldview. Furthermore, authentic spiritual experiences will lead believers to center their thought lives on God and the things of God and to grow in the knowledge of God and the cognitive virtues of the kingdom of God.

Concerning the affectivity of the structural aspect of the image of God, Jesus Christ exemplifies how believers can and should express a full range of emotions in a godly way. The central disposition in which Jesus's emotions were based—and in which believers can imitate Jesus—was that of filial delight and love toward his loving Father. He delighted in obeying and living in the presence of his Father, and he anguished when people opposed God's love. Growth in conformity to affective Christlikeness involves growth in orienting one's emotions around the reality of God rather than self. This growth involves an increasing felt awareness of God's love and an overcoming of emotional bondage and dysfunction based on a believer's identity as a child of God and leading to a greater delight in God and a greater anguish when God's love is opposed.

Christ's volitional exemplarity is seen in his perfect and constant submission to the will and mission of the Father. He proclaimed the kingdom of God and modeled what virtue is in that kingdom. For Christ's followers, volitional Christlikeness will be an imitation of Christ's faithful submission to the Father's will and mission and Christ's practice of kingdom virtues. This growth in conformity to the image of God will look like believers taking up their crosses, dying to themselves, and growing in virtuous living in submission to God.

In the life of the church, conformity to Christ's cognition, affectivity, and volition has appeared in many ways within the Contemplative, Holiness, Charismatic, Social Justice, Evangelical, and Incarnational Traditions of Christian spirituality. For example, cognitive Christlikeness can manifest as biblical fidelity or as seeing God present in the world. Affective Christlikeness can involve affective contemplation, loving progress toward union with God, or compassionate action. Volitional Christlikeness can entail the overcoming of sin or the giving up of one's life for God. All of these examples consist of the effects of authentic spiritual experiences. In contrast, inauthentic spiritual experiences can involve such things as a disregard for the Creator-creature distinction, an antinomianism, neglected affections, blind trust in affections, legalism, and Pelagianism. All of these examples of how authentic and inauthentic experiences have been evident in the life of the church show that conformity to the image of God can take on a variety of concrete forms, and no spiritual tradition is completely safe from the possibility of inauthentic spiritual experiences.

Principle (2) holds that authentic spiritual experiences will conform to or lead to growth in conformity with Christ's participation in the love of God as it is expressed relationally toward God, other humans, oneself, and creation. The relational aspect of the image of God is seen in the life and teachings of Jesus Christ as the love of God flowing out into all of his relationships. Conformity to this aspect of the image of God places love at the center of a believer's relationships, in imitation of Christ.

Christ lived in intimate union and loving communion with his Father, relying upon and trusting in his Father. For believers, authentic spiritual experiences leading to growth in conformity to Christ's relationality will either conform to or lead to growth in intimacy with God, in loving trust, obedience, submission, and prayer. Christ also lived out loving relationships with the people around him, serving and meeting the needs of others, laying down his life for his friends, and inviting all people into a new spiritual family. Authentic spiritual experiences will lead Christ-followers to become more self-sacrificially oriented toward their neighbors in love and toward community in the body of Christ through righteous relationships. In relation to himself, Christ perfectly loved himself for the sake of God—in other words, submitted himself fully to God out of his love for God—and he both knew and lived out his self-identity as God the Son incarnate, despite the backlash he received. Likewise, authentic spiritual experiences will lead disciples of Christ to grow into and accept their identities as children of God based on scriptural truths such as their justification, redemption, and freedom from sin.

In the life of the church, relational Christlikeness can look like contemplative stillness in the presence of God, a pure heart directed to God, a dark night of the soul, the desire for the powerful presence of God, a love-filled destruction of segregation, just and benevolent friendships, the love of self for God's sake, the proclamation of God's truth over a believer's life, and so much more. Inauthentic spiritual experiences, indicated by their lack of conformity to relational Christlikeness, can lead to relationships of selfishness or worldly gain, isolation from the local church, or a self-identity based on worldly voices.

Principle (3) states that authentic spiritual experiences will either conform to or lead to growth in conformity with Christ's threefold office of prophet, priest, and king. The functional aspect of the image of God holds that humans have a God-given vocation as God representatives to exercise a royal and priestly dominion of caring stewardship over creation. In the New Testament, Christ fulfills this vocation and the cultural mandate associated with it through his threefold office. Furthermore, Christ gives his followers the Holy Spirit to enable them to participate in his ongoing ministry and to grow in conformity with his threefold office.

First, in his kingly office, Christ is the royal representative of God as God the Son incarnate—creator of and ruler over all things and inaugurator of the kingdom of God. His miracles revealed his power over nature and the spiritual realm, and his resurrection revealed his victory over sin, death, and the realm of darkness. Authentic spiritual experiences will either conform to or lead to growth in conformity with Christ's kingly office. As children of God, believers conform to Christ's example by representing God on earth and living out their God-given vocation as his children, in humility, self-sacrifice, and humble service to others.

Second, in his priestly office, Christ redeems and reconciles human beings to God and intercedes on their behalf before the Father. He ministers both to sick individuals and to sick societies, caring for the spiritual and physical health and purity of humans and the world. Christ invites his followers to imitate his priestly office by forming them into a royal priesthood. As such, authentic spiritual experiences will lead believers deeper into their priestly vocation of interceding self-sacrificially for their neighbors in holiness and purity, leading them to mediate the presence and love of God to others and to steward the created order in service of others and God's glory.

Third, in his prophetic office, Christ proclaimed the good news of the kingdom of God and the way of salvation. He perfectly revealed divine truth to humanity and called all to accept salvation through his death and resurrection. Conforming to or leading to growth in conformity with Christ's prophetic office, authentic spiritual experiences never will lead Christians away from evangelism and disciple making. Rather, they will encourage Christians to share the gospel with the lost and to testify of Christ and his love.

In the life of the church, just as in the other aspects of the image of God, conformity to the offices of Christ has taken on many forms. This conformity can look like sacramental living, a renewed theology of work, working to establish the present kingdom of God in the world, ecological sensitivity, developing cultures of cooperation, serving the poor and powerless, the preaching of the gospel, evangelistic mission efforts, interpersonal evangelism, prophetic proclamation, and more. Disconformity to volitional Christlikeness as an indication of inauthentic spiritual experiences also can manifest in many forms, such as a limited view of salvation, false prophecy, or the redefinition of the gospel.

In conclusion, discernment criteria are never to be defined so narrowly that they become procrustean beds that create artificial models of sanctification and stifle the creative activities of the Holy Spirit. Nevertheless, spiritual experiences necessitate discernment, and discernment requires doctrinal criteria. The image of God is a doctrinal criterion of discernment that acknowledges the unity within diversity of Christian spirituality. The three principles drawn from the criterion of the image of God are valuable, not because they reduce discernment down into three simple statements, but because they afford unique perspectives on how authentic spiritual experiences conform to or lead to growth in conformity with the various aspects of the life of Jesus Christ.

Conclusion

IN THIS WORK, I have argued that the image of God is able to act as a criterion of spiritual discernment by identifying how authentic spiritual experiences conform to or lead believers to grow in conformity with the structural, functional, and relational aspects of the image of God. In chapter 1, I showed why spiritual experiences necessitate discernment. Human experience consists of cognitive, affective, and volitional operations that occur in various levels of significance (depth) within the cognitive process and a web of relationships. Due to sin, human experience is fallen, and the operations and cognitive process of human experience cannot always be trusted to perceive the true meaning and origin of a spiritual experience. Additionally, influence from the world or evil spirits can mislead and deceive. The result is that the meaning and origin of a spiritual experience can be ambiguous and obscure even to believers, necessitating spiritual discernment.

In chapter 2, I defended the necessity of doctrinal criteria for spiritual discernment and the legitimacy of the image of God as a criterion of discernment. Throughout Christian history, the criteria of Jesus Christ, the Holy Spirit, Scripture, and sanctification (*telos*) were upheld consistently as crucial to spiritual discernment. The criterion of the image of God inheres within and grows out of these four criteria, legitimizing its use as a criterion of spiritual discernment. Doctrinal criteria are necessary to safeguard the particularities of Christianity, and yet they also must recognize the unity within diversity of Christian spirituality. The criterion of the image of God is able to do just that by providing a specificity without rigidity to discernment.

In chapter 3, I further substantiated how the image of God acts as a criterion of discernment by outlining how Scripture depicts the image of God and by putting forward a heuristic and multifaceted account of the image of God. Scripture states that humans are made in the image of God, Jesus Christ is the image of God, and sanctification involves growth in conformity to the image of God. Since conformity to Christ and growth in sanctification are two established criteria of discernment, the image of God's relation to Christ and sanctification entails that it also is a criterion of discernment. The four main systematic positions on the image of God include structural, functional, relational, and multifaceted positions. While distinct, the three aspects of structure, function, and relation cannot be fully separated from one another. As such, the image of God either consists in or entails the three aspects of structure, function, and relation. Therefore, authentic spiritual experiences will conform to or lead to growth in conformity with the three aspects of the image of God.

In chapter 4, I identified three general principles of discernment that clarify how authentic spiritual experiences conform to or lead to growth in conformity with the image of God. These principles apply the three aspects of the image of God to the life of Christ, concretely identifying what growth in conformity to the image of God entails. Principle (1) states that authentic spiritual experiences will conform to or lead to growth in conformity with Christ's cognition, affectivity, and volition. Principle (2) states that authentic spiritual experiences will conform to or lead to growth in conformity with Christ's participation in the love of God as it is expressed relationally toward God, other humans, oneself, and creation. Principle (3) states that authentic spiritual experiences will either conform to or lead to growth in conformity with Christ's threefold office of prophet, priest, and king. When applied to the lives of believers and the traditions of Christian spirituality, these three principles reveal that authentic spiritual experiences produce many different and varied effects in the lives of believers, indicating that growth in conformity to the image of God occurs in a variety of ways and is not a universally uniform phenomenon.

Many opportunities for further research are evident at this point. While my research question focused solely on the spiritual experiences of Christians, further study could pursue the implications that the criterion of the image of God holds for the discernment of authentic spiritual experiences in the lives of non-Christians. One complicated issue with this topic is that some non-Christians are antagonistic toward Christianity, while others are friendly toward or progressing closer to Christianity. These different possible stances toward Christianity are variables that would need to be accounted for.

Further research could explore how the criterion of the image of God applies to corporate spiritual discernment. Spiritual discernment is not a task solely for individuals; it also takes place within corporate or communal settings. Another question concerns how a corporate body can grow in conformity to the image of God in relation to corporate spiritual experiences.

As mentioned in the introduction, the *telos* of Christian spirituality has been described in a variety of ways, including glorification, union with God, the beatific vision, and theosis. Each of these descriptions of the *telos* of Christian spirituality has the potential of being considered a criterion of spiritual discernment. More study could examine how each of these *teloi* illuminate unique aspects of spiritual discernment and authentic spiritual experiences. Another criterion worth additional study is the kingdom of God. At times, the criterion of the image of God incorporated insights from the kingdom of God, but more could be said.

More research also could explore the question of a comprehensive criteriology. The criterion of the image of God, though it is multifaceted, does not present a comprehensive criteriology. Such a criteriology would need to account for objective and subjective criteria as well as criteria of adequacy and appropriateness and other potential categories of criteria.[1] Some scholars such as Thomas Dubay and Mark McIntosh have put forward intricate criteriologies.[2] A comparison of historical and contemporary criteriologies could prove useful in the pursuit of a comprehensive criteriology and the identification of categories of criteria.

Further study could delve also into a more detailed history of spiritual discernment literature. In particular, the study of spiritual discernment within the various post-Reformation Protestant movements is not as researched as Roman Catholic sources have been. The works of Jonathan Edwards and John Wesley are the exceptions, and much more could be learned about spiritual discernment from the Puritans, Pietists, and many other Protestant movements.

---

1. Rakoczy, "Structures of Discernment Processes," 153; Sheldrake, *Spirituality and Theology*, 88–93; cf. Libanio, *Spiritual Discernment and Politics*, 106–22. External criteria relate to doctrine, internal criteria to the affections, criteria of adequacy to secular knowledge, and criteria of appropriateness to Christian understanding. Libanio distinguishes between subjective and objective criteria. For specific examples of criteria of appropriateness, see Smith, "Discernment," 404–6; Tracy, *Blessed Rage for Order*, 64–71; Berthoud, "Discerning Spirituality," 50–62; Lane, *Experience of God*, 26; Principe, "Pluralism in Christian Spirituality," 54–61.

2. Dubay, *Authenticity*, 144–81; McIntosh, *Discernment and Truth*, 93–107.

Additional research also could focus on a more in-depth and comprehensive description of the three aspects of the image of God as criteria of discernment in the life of Christ, believers, and the church, as chapter 4 began to do but did not do in a comprehensive manner. Chapter 4 provided enough data from specific examples to show that growth in conformity to the image of God can occur in many ways, but the chapter did not pursue an accounting of all those many ways. Each aspect of conformity to the image of God could be researched further along historical, theological, and anthropological lines.

Henry Scougal once wrote that individuals who are acquainted with true religion will "disdain all those shadows and false imitations of it. They know by experience, that true religion is an union of the soul with God, a real participation of the divine nature, the very image of God drawn upon the soul; or, in the Apostle's phrase, it is Christ formed within us."[3] Individuals who are acquainted with authentic spiritual experiences will know that those experiences shape them in many glorious and wonderful ways into the image of Christ. Christ is the believer's exemplar, and it is his image—the perfect image of God—to which believers are predestined to be conformed, for the glory of God the Father, through the redemption achieved by God the Son, and by the power of the Holy Spirit to sanctify all who place their faith in Christ. While spiritual experiences can be inauthentic, the image of God is a trustworthy criterion of spiritual discernment, identifying the many ways in which the Holy Spirit leads believers into conformity with the image of Christ.

---

3. Scougal, *Life of God*, 6–7.

Bibliography

Aelred of Rievaulx. *Spiritual Friendship*. Translated by Mary Eugenia Laker. Cistercian Fathers. Kalamazoo, MI: Cistercian Publications, 1977.

Agnew, Una, et al., eds. *"With Wisdom Seeking God": The Academic Study of Spirituality*. Leuven: Peeters, 2008.

Ailly, Pierre d'. *De falsis prophetis*. In *Joannes Gersonii Opera Omnia*, edited by Louis Ellies du Pin, 1:489–603. Antwerp: Sumptibus Societatis, 1706.

Aizawa, Ken. "What Is This Cognition That Is Supposed to Be Embodied?" *Philosophical Psychology* 28 (2015) 755–75.

Allen, Diogenes. *Spiritual Theology: The Theology of Yesterday for Spiritual Help Today*. Lanham, MD: Cowley Publications, 1997.

Alston, William P. *Perceiving God: The Epistemology of Religious Experience*. Ithaca, NY: Cornell University Press, 1991.

Anderson, Douglas R. *Strands of System: The Philosophy of Charles Peirce*. West Lafayette, IN: Purdue University Press, 1995.

Anderson, Hannah. *All That's Good: Recovering the Lost Art of Discernment*. Chicago: Moody Publishers, 2018.

Anderson, Wendy Love. "Free Spirits, Presumptuous Women, and False Prophets: The Discernment of Spirits in the Late Middle Ages." PhD diss., University of Chicago Divinity School, 2002.

Anthony, Dick, et al., eds. *Spiritual Choices: The Problem of Recognizing Authentic Paths to Inner Transformation*. New York: Paragon House, 1987.

Aquinas, Thomas. *Summa Theologica*. Translated by the Fathers of the English Dominican Province. London: Burns, Oates, & Washbourne, 1941.

Aristotle. *On the Soul*. Translated by W. S. Hett. Loeb Classical Library 288. Cambridge, MA: Harvard University Press, 2000.

Ashley, J. Matthew. "The Turn to Spirituality? The Relationship Between Theology and Spirituality." In *Minding the Spirit*, edited by Elizabeth A. Dreyer and Mark S. Burrows, 159–70. Baltimore: Johns Hopkins University Press, 2005.

Athanasius. *Life of Antony*. In *The Nicene and Post-Nicene Fathers*, edited by Philip Schaff and Henry Wace, translated by H. Ellershaw, 4:195–221. Buffalo, NY: Christian Literature, 1892.

Au, Wilkie, and Noreen Cannon Au. *The Discerning Heart: Exploring the Christian Path*. Mahwah, NJ: Paulist, 2006.

Augustine. *De Genesi ad litteram libri duodecim*. Corpus Scriptorum Ecclesiasticorum Latinorum, edited by Pragae F. Tempsky et al. 28. Vienna: Academiae Litterarum Caesareae, 1884.

Augustine, Daniela C. *The Spirit and the Common Good: Shared Flourishing in the Image of God*. Grand Rapids: Eerdmans, 2019.

Aumann, Jordan. *Spiritual Theology*. New York: Continuum, 2006.

Ayala, Francisco J. "Human Nature: One Evolutionist's View." In *Whatever Happened to the Soul? Scientific and Theological Portraits of Human Nature*, edited by Warren S. Brown, et al., 31–48. Philadelphia: Fortress, 1998.

Azadegan, Ebrahim. "Divine Hiddenness and Human Sin: The Noetic Effect of Sin." *Journal of Reformed Theology* 7 (2013) 69–90.

Baker, Doug P. *Covenant and Community: Our Role as the Image of God*. Eugene, OR: Wipf & Stock, 2008.

Balz, Horst, and Gerhard Schneider, eds. *The Exegetical Dictionary of the New Testament*. Vol. 3. Grand Rapids: Eerdmans, 1990.

Barbour, Hugh. *The Quakers in Puritan England*. New Haven: Yale University Press, 1964.

Barclay, Robert. *The Anarchy of the Ranters*. London: T. Sowle, 1717.

———. *An Apology for the True Christian Divinity: Being an Explanation and Vindication of the Principles and Doctrines of the People Called Quakers*. London: T. Sowle, 1703.

Barry, William A. *Paying Attention to God: Discernment in Prayer*. Notre Dame, IN: Ave Maria Press, 1990.

———. *Spiritual Direction and the Encounter with God: A Theological Inquiry*. Mahwah, NJ: Paulist, 1992.

———. "Toward a Theology of Discernment." *The Way Supplement* 64 (1989) 129–40.

Barry, William A., and William J. Connolly. *The Practice of Spiritual Direction*. New York: Seabury, 1982.

Barth, Karl. *Church Dogmatics*. Edited by G. T. Thomson et al. Edinburgh: T&T Clark, 1958.

Bavinck, J. H. *Between the Beginning and the End: A Radical Kingdom Vision*. Translated by Bert Hielema. Grand Rapids: Eerdmans, 2014.

Baxter, Richard. *The Practical Works of the Rev. Richard Baxter*. Edited by William Orme. 23 vols. London: James Duncan, 1830.

Belloso, Joseph M. Rovira. "Who Is Capable of Discerning?" In *Discernment of the Spirit and of Spirits*, edited by Casiano Floristan and Christian DuQuoc, 84–94. New York: Seabury, 1979.

Benner, David. *Desiring God's Will: Aligning Our Hearts with the Heart of God*. Downers Grove, IL: InterVarsity, 2005.

Berkouwer, G. C. *Man: The Image of God*. Grand Rapids: Eerdmans, 1962.

Berling, Judith A. "Christian Spirituality: Intrinsically Interdisciplinary." In *Exploring Christian Spirituality: Essays in Honor of Sandra M. Schneiders*, edited by Bruce H. Lescher and Elizabeth Liebert, 35–52. New York: Paulist, 2006.

Bernard, Charles Andre. "The Nature of Spiritual Theology." In *Exploring Christian Spirituality: An Ecumenical Reader*, edited by Kenneth J. Collins, 229–41. Grand Rapids: Baker, 2000.

Bernard of Clairvaux. *Monastic Sermons*. Translated by Daniel Griggs. Collegeville, MN: Liturgical Press, 2016.

———. "On Loving God." In *Bernard of Clairvaux: Selected Works*, translated by G. R. Evans, 173–206. Classics of Western Spirituality. New York: Paulist, 1987.

Bernardino of Siena. *De inspirationibus*. In *Sancti Bernardini Senensis, Ordinis Seraphici Minorum*, 3:130–67. Lugduni: Ioannis Antonii Huguetan and Marci Antonii Rauaud, 1650.

Berthoud, Pierre. "Discerning Spirituality: Biblical and Reformed Perspectives." *European Journal of Theology* 19 (2010) 50–62.

Bill, J. Brent. *Sacred Compass: The Way of Spiritual Discernment*. Brewster, MA: Paraclete Press, 2008.

Bird, Michael F. *Evangelical Theology: A Biblical and Systematic Introduction*. Grand Rapids: Zondervan, 2020.

Bird, Phyllis. "Male and Female He Created Them, Gen. 1:27b in the Context of the Priestly Account of Creation." *Harvard Theological Review* 74 (1981) 129–59.

Birgitta of Sweden. *Revelaciones, Book IV*. Edited by Hans Aili. Stockholm: Almquist & Wiksell, 1992.

Blocher, Henri. *In the Beginning: The Opening Chapters of Genesis*. Downers Grove, IL: InterVarsity, 1984.

———. *Original Sin: Illuminating the Riddle*. Grand Rapids: Eerdmans, 1997.

Bloesch, Donald D. *Spirituality Old and New: Recovering Authentic Spiritual Life*. Downers Grove, IL: InterVarsity, 2007.

Blomberg, Craig L. "True Righteousness and Holiness." In *The Image of God in an Image Driven Age*, edited by Beth Felker Jones and Jeffery W. Barbeau, 66–90. Downers Grove, IL: InterVarsity, 2016.

Boa, Kenneth. *Conformed to His Image: Biblical and Practical Approaches to Christian Formation*. Grand Rapids: Zondervan, 2001.

Bock, Darrell L. "New Testament Community and Spiritual Formation." In *Foundations of Spiritual Formation: A Community Approach to Becoming Like Christ*, edited by Paul Pettit, 102–20. Grand Rapids: Kregel, 2008.

Bockmuehl, Klaus. *Listening to the God Who Speaks: Reflections on God's Guidance from Scripture and the Lives of God's People*. Colorado Springs: Helmers and Howard, 1990.

Boersma, Hans. *Heavenly Participation: The Weaving of a Sacramental Tapestry*. Grand Rapids: Eerdmans, 2011.

Bona, Giovanni. *Tractatus de discretione spirituum liber unus: Principia regulasque tradens ad varia discernenda genera spirituum*. Paris: Mellier Fratres, Bibliop.- Editores, 1847.

Bonhoeffer, Dietrich. *Discipleship*. Philadelphia: Fortress, 2003.

———. *Letters and Papers from Prison*. Edited by John W. de Gruchy. Translated by Isabel Best et al. Philadelphia: Fortress, 2010.

Borgman, Brian. *Feelings and Faith: Cultivating Godly Emotions in the Christian Life*. Wheaton, IL: Crossway, 2009.

Brackley, Dean. *The Call to Discernment in Troubled Times: New Perspectives on the Transformative Wisdom of Ignatius of Loyola*. New York: Crossroad, 2004.

Brother Lawrence. *The Practice of the Presence of God*. Uhrichsville, OH: Barbour, 1993.

Brown, F. et al. *The Brown-Driver-Briggs Hebrew and English Lexicon*. Peabody, MA: Hendrickson, 2003.

Browning, Don S. *Religious Thought and the Modern Psychologies: A Critical Conversation in the Theology of Culture*. Philadelphia: Fortress, 1987.

Bruce, F. F. *The Epistles to the Colossians, to Philemon, and to the Ephesians.* New International Commentary on the New Testament. Grand Rapids: Eerdmans, 1984.

Brunner, Emil. *The Christian Doctrine of Creation and Redemption.* Translated by Olive Wyon. Philadelphia: Westminster, 1953.

———. *Man in Revolt: A Christian Anthropology.* Translated by Olive Wyon. New York: Scribner's Sons, 1939.

Buckley, Michael. "Discernment of Spirits." In *The New Dictionary of Catholic Spirituality*, edited by Michael Downey, 274–80. Collegeville, MN: Liturgical Press, 1993.

———. "The Structure of the Rules for Discernment of Spirits." *The Way Supplement* 20 (1973) 19–37.

Burke, Dan. *Spiritual Warfare and the Discerning of Spirits.* Nashua, NH: Sophia Institute, 2020.

Burridge, Richard A., and Graham Gould. *Jesus Now and Then.* Grand Rapids: Eerdmans, 2004.

Burton-Christie, Douglas. "Introduction: Beginnings." In *Minding the Spirit: The Study of Christian Spirituality*, edited by Elizabeth A. Dreyer and Mark S. Burrows, xxi–xxvii. Baltimore: Johns Hopkins University Press, 2005.

Caciola, Nancy. *Discerning Spirits: Divine and Demonic Possession in the Middle Ages.* Ithaca, NY: Cornell University Press, 2006.

Calvin, John. *Institutes of the Christian Religion.* Translated by Henry Beveridge. Peabody, MA: Hendrickson, 2008.

Carthusian. *The Call to Silent Love.* Herefordshire, UK: Gracewing, 2006.

Case-Winters, Anna. "Rethinking the Image of God." *Zygon* 39 (2004) 813–26.

Casey, Michael. "*Suspensa expectatio*: Guerric of Igny on Waiting for God." *Studies in Spirituality* 9 (1999) 78–92.

Cassian, John. *The Conferences.* Translated by Boniface Ramsey. New York: Newman, 1997.

Catherine of Siena. *Catherine of Siena: The Dialogue.* Translated by Suzanne Noffke. Classics of Western Spirituality. New York: Paulist, 1980.

Challies, Tim. *The Discipline of Spiritual Discernment.* Wheaton, IL: Crossway, 2007.

Chan, Simon. "Spiritual Theology." In *Dictionary of Christian Spirituality*, edited by Glen G. Scorgie, 52–57. Grand Rapids: Zondervan, 2011.

———. *Spiritual Theology: A Systematic Study of the Christian Life.* Downers Grove, IL: InterVarsity, 1998.

Chandler, Diane J. *Christian Spiritual Formation: An Integrated Approach for Personal and Relational Wholeness.* Downers Grove, IL: InterVarsity, 2014.

Chang, Hae-Kyung. "The Christian Life in a Dialectical Tension? Romans 7:7–23 Reconsidered." *Novum Testamentum* 49 (2007) 257–80.

Charry, Ellen T. "Experience." In *The Oxford Handbook of Systematic Theology*, edited by John Webster et al., 413–34. New York: Oxford University Press, 2007.

Chisholm, Robert R., Jr. "When Prophecy Appears to Fail, Check Your Hermeneutic." *Journal of the Evangelical Theological Society* 53 (2010) 561–77.

Clark, David K. *To Know and Love God: Method for Theology.* Wheaton, IL: Crossway, 2003.

Climacus, John. *John Climacus: The Ladder of Divine Ascent.* Translated by Colm Luibheid and Norman Russell. Classics of Western Spirituality. Mahwah, NJ: Paulist, 1982.
Clines, D. J. A. "The Image of God in Man." *Tyndale Bulletin* 19 (1968) 53–103.
Coe, John H. "Approaches to the Study of Christian Spirituality." In *Dictionary of Christian Spirituality*, edited by Glen G. Scorgie, 34–39. Grand Rapids: Zondervan, 2011.
———. "Spiritual Theology: A Theological-Experiential Methodology for Bridging the Sanctification Gap." *Journal of Spiritual Formation & Soul Care* 2 (2009) 4–42.
Congar, Yves. *I Believe in the Holy Spirit.* Translated by David Smith. New York: Crossroad, 1997.
Conroy, Maureen. *The Discerning Heart: Discovering a Personal God.* Chicago: Loyola, 1993.
———. "Spirituality: A Resource for Theology." *Proceedings of the Catholic Theological Society of America* 35 (1980) 124–37.
Cornelius, Randolph R. *The Science of Emotion: Research and Tradition in the Psychology of Emotion.* Upper Saddle River, NJ: Prentice Hall, 1996.
Cortez, Marc. *Resourcing Theological Anthropology: A Constructive Account of Humanity in the Light of Christ.* Grand Rapids: Zondervan, 2017.
———. *Theological Anthropology: A Guide for the Perplexed.* New York: T&T Clark, 2010.
Crisp, Oliver D. "A Christological Model of the *Imago Dei*." In *The Ashgate Research Companion to Theological Anthropology*, edited by Joshua R. Farris and Charles Taliaferro, 217–32. New York: Routledge, 2016.
Crisp, Oliver D., and Fred Sanders, eds. *The Christian Doctrine of Humanity: Explorations in Constructive Dogmatics.* Grand Rapids: Zondervan, 2018.
Cunningham, Lawrence. "*Extra Arcam Noe*: Criteria for Christian Spirituality." In *Minding the Spirit: The Study of Christian Spirituality*, edited by Elizabeth A. Dreyer and Mark S. Burrows, 171–78. Baltimore: Johns Hopkins University Press, 2005.
Cyril of Jerusalem. *Catechetical Lectures.* Translated by Edwin Hamilton Gifford. In *The Nicene and Post-Nicene Fathers*, edited by Philip Schaff and Henry Wace, 7:1–202. Buffalo, NY: Christian Literature, 1894.
Danker, Frederick W., et al. *A Greek-English Lexicon of the New Testament and Other Early Christian Literature.* 3rd Ed. Chicago: University of Chicago Press, 2000.
Davis, Caroline Franks. *The Evidential Force of Religious Experience.* Oxford: Clarendon, 1999.
Davison, Andrew. *Participation in God: A Study in Christian Doctrine and Metaphysics.* New York: Cambridge University Press, 2019.
De Wit, Han F. *The Spiritual Path: An Introduction to the Psychology of the Spiritual Traditions.* Pittsburgh: Duquesne University Press, 1999.
Demarest, Bruce. "Human Personhood." In *Dictionary of Christian Spirituality*, edited by Glen G. Scorgie, 71–76. Downers Grove, IL: Zondervan, 2011.
———. *Satisfy Your Soul: Restoring the Heart of Christian Spirituality.* Colorado Springs: NavPress, 1999.
Dempster, Stephen G. *Dominion and Dynasty: A Theology of the Hebrew Bible.* Downers Grove, IL: InterVarsity, 2003.

Denifle, Heinrich Seuse, ed. *Das Buch von geistlicher Armuth.* Munich: Literarisches Institut von Dr. Max Suttler. 1877.

Denis the Carthusian. *Discretione et examinatione spirituum.* In *Doctoris Ecstatici Dionysii Cartusiani Opera Omnia*, 40:261–320. Tornaci: Typis Cartusiae S. M. de Pratis, 1911.

———. *Doctoris Ecstatici D. Dionysii Cartusiani Opera Omnia.* Vol. 27, *Translatio librorum Joannis Cassiani Presbyteri.* Tornaci: Typis Cartusiae S. M. de Pratis, 1904.

Diadochos of Photiki. "On Spiritual Knowledge and Discrimination: One Hundred Texts." In *The Philokalia*, edited and translated by G. E. H. Palmer et al., 1:253–96. Boston: Faber and Faber, 1979.

Dockery, David S. "An Outline of Paul's View of the Spiritual Life: Foundation for an Evangelical Spirituality." In *Exploring Christian Spirituality: An Ecumenical Reader*, edited by Kenneth J. Collins, 339–52. Grand Rapids: Baker, 2000.

Donahue, John R. "The Quest for Biblical Spirituality." In *Exploring Christian Spirituality: Essays in Honor of Sandra M. Schneiders*, edited by Bruce H. Lescher and Elizabeth Liebert, 73–97. New York: Paulist, 2006.

Doran, Robert M. "Affect, Affectivity." In *The New Dictionary of Catholic Spirituality*, edited by Michael Downey, 12–14. Collegeville, MN: Liturgical Press, 1993.

Dougherty, Rose Mary. *Discernment: A Path to Spiritual Awakening.* Mahwah, NJ: Paulist, 2009.

———. *Group Spiritual Direction: Community for Discernment.* Mahwah, NJ: Paulist, 1995.

Downey, Michael, ed. *The New Dictionary of Catholic Spirituality.* Collegeville, MN: Liturgical Press, 1993.

———. *Understanding Christian Spirituality.* New York: Paulist, 1997.

Dreyer, Elizabeth. "Afterword: Emerging Issues and New Trajectories in the Study of Christian Spirituality." In *Minding the Spirit*, edited by Elizabeth A. Dreyer and Mark S. Burrows, 363–72. Baltimore: Johns Hopkins University Press, 2005.

———. "Spirituality as a Resource for Theology: The Holy Spirit in Augustine." In *Minding the Spirit*, edited by Elizabeth A. Dreyer and Mark S. Burrows, 179–99. Baltimore: Johns Hopkins University Press, 2005.

Dubay, Thomas. *Authenticity: A Biblical Theology of Discernment.* San Francisco: Ignatius, 1997.

Dunn, James D. G. "Discernment of Spirits—A Neglected Gift." In *Witness to the Spirit*, edited by W. Harrington, 79–96. Dublin: Irish Biblical Association, 1979.

———. *The Theology of Paul the Apostle.* Edinburgh: T&T Clark, 1998.

Dunne, Tad. "Experience." In *The New Dictionary of Catholic Spirituality*, edited by Michael Downey, 365–77. Collegeville, MN: Liturgical Press, 1993.

———. "Three Models of Discernment." *The Way Supplement* 23 (1974) 18–26.

Dyrness, William A. "Poised Between Life and Death: The *Imago Dei* After Eden." In *The Image of God in an Image Driven Age: Explorations in Theological Anthropology*, edited by Beth Felker Jones and Jeffrey W. Barbeau, 47–65. Downers Grove, IL: IVP Academic, 2016.

Eckhart, Meister. *The Complete Mystical Works of Meister Eckhart.* Edited and translated by Maurice O'C. Walshe. New York: Crossroad, 2009.

———. *Meister Eckhart: Teacher and Preacher.* Edited by Bernard McGinn. Classics of Western Spirituality. New York: Paulist, 1986.

Edgar, William. *Created and Creating: A Biblical Theology of Culture*. Downers Grove, IL: IVP Academic, 2016.

Edwards, Jonathan. *Distinguishing Marks of a Work of the Spirit of God*. In *The Works of Jonathan Edwards*, edited by Edward Hickman, 2:257–77. London: William Ball, 1839.

———. *A Treatise Concerning the Religious Affections*. Boston: S. Kneeland and T. Green, 1746.

Elliott, Matthew A. "Affections." In *Dictionary of Christian Spirituality*, edited by Glen G. Scorgie, 248–49. Grand Rapids: Zondervan, 2011.

———. "Emotions." In *Dictionary of Christian Spirituality*, edited by Glen G. Scorgie, 424–25. Grand Rapids: Zondervan, 2011.

Endean, Philip. "Spirituality and Theology." In *The New Westminster Dictionary of Christian Spirituality*, edited by Philip Sheldrake, 74–80. Louisville: Westminster John Knox, 2013.

———. "Spirituality and the University." *The Way Supplement* 84 (1995) 87–99.

———. "Theology out of Spirituality: The Approach of Karl Rahner." *Christian Spirituality Bulletin* 3 (1995) 6–8.

English, John. *Spiritual Freedom: From an Experience of the Ignatian Exercises to the Art of Spiritual Direction*. Chicago: Loyola, 1995.

Erickson, Millard J. *Christian Theology*. Grand Rapids: Baker Academic, 2013.

Etzelmüller, Gregor. *Gottes verkörpertes Ebenbild: Eine theologische Anthropologie*. Tübingen: Mohr Siebeck, 2021.

Evdokimov, Paul. *The Struggle with God*. Translated by Sister Gertrude. Glen Rock, NY: Paulist, 1966.

Farmer, Thomas A., and Margaret W. Matlin. *Cognition*. Malden, MA: Wiley-Blackwell, 2019.

Farnham, Suzanne G., et al. *Listening Hearts: Discerning Call in Community*. Harrisburg, PA: Morehouse, 1991.

Farrington, Debra K. *Hearing with the Heart: A Gentle Guide to Discerning God's Will in Your Life*. San Francisco: Jossey-Bass, 2003.

Farris, Joshua R. *Introduction to Theological Anthropology*. Grand Rapids: Baker Academic, 2020.

Farrow, Jo. "Discernment in the Quaker Tradition." *The Way Supplement* 64 (1989) 51–62.

Fee, Gordon D. *Pauline Christology: An Exegetical-Theological Study*. Grand Rapids: Baker Academic, 2013.

Finnegan, Jack. *The Audacity of Spirit: The Meaning and Shaping of Spirituality Today*. Dublin: Veritas, 2008.

Frith, Chris. "The Psychology of Volition." *Experimental Brain Research* 229 (2013) 289–99.

Fisher, Christopher L. "Animals, Humans and X-Men: Human Uniqueness and the Meaning of Personhood." *Theology and Science* 3 (2005) 291–314.

Fitzgerald, Patrick T. *Criteria and Method for Discernment of the Holy Spirit: An Ethnographic Study*. MA Thesis, University of Dayton, 2021.

Floristan, Casiano, and Christian DuQuoc, eds. *Discernment of the Spirit and of Spirits*. New York: Seabury, 1979.

Foster, Richard. *Streams of Living Water: Celebrating the Great Traditions of Christian Faith*. New York: HarperCollins, 1998.

Fox, George. *A Collection of Many Select and Christian Epistles, Letters, and Testimonies.* 2 vols. New York: Isaac T. Hopper, 1831.

———. *The Journal of George Fox: Being an Historical Account of His Life, Travels, Sufferings, and Christian Experiences.* 2 vols. Edited by Norman Penney. London: Headley Brothers, 1901.

Frank, S. L. *Man's Soul: An Introductory Essay in Philosophical Psychology.* Athens: Ohio University Press, 1993.

Fransen, Piet. "Divine Revelation: Source of Man's Faith." In *Faith: Its Nature and Meaning,* edited by Paul Surlis, 18–52. Dublin: Gill and Macmillan, 1972.

Fretheim, Terrence. *Jeremiah.* Smyth & Helwys Bible Commentary. Macon, GA: Smyth & Helwys, 2002.

Friesen, Garry, and Robin Maxson. *Decision Making and the Will of God: A Biblical Alternative to the Traditional View.* Portland, OR: Multnomah, 1980.

Frohlich, Mary. "Spiritual Discipline, Discipline of Spirituality: Revisiting Questions of Definition and Method." *Spiritus* 1(2001) 69–70.

Galilea, Segundo. *Temptation and Discernment.* Translated by Stephen-Joseph Ross. Washington, DC: ICS, 1996.

Gallagher, Timothy M. *Discerning the Will of God: An Ignatian Guide to Decision Making.* New York: Crossroad, 2009.

———. *The Discernment of Spirits: An Ignatian Guide for Everyday Living.* New York: Crossroad, 2005.

Garr, W. Randall. *In His Own Image and Likeness: Humanity, Divinity, and Monotheism.* Boston: Brill, 2003.

Garrigou-Lagrange, Reginald. *Christian Perfection and Contemplation: According to St. Thomas Aquinas and St. John of the Cross.* St. Louis, MO: B. Herder, 1946.

Gathercole, Simon. "'Sins' in Paul." *New Testament Studies* 64 (2018) 143–61.

Gavrilyuk, Paul L. "Encountering God: Spiritual Perception in the Bible, Tradition, and Film." *International Journal of Orthodox Theology* 10 (2019) 41–61.

Gay, Robert M. *Vocation et discernment des esprits.* Montreal: Fieds, 1959.

Gelpi, Donald L. *Charism and Sacrament: A Theology of Christian Conversion.* New York: Paulist, 1976.

———. *The Gracing of Human Experience: Rethinking the Relationship Between Nature and Grace.* Collegeville, MN: Liturgical Press, 2001.

———. *The Turn to Experience in Contemporary Theology.* Mahwah, NJ: Paulist, 1994.

Gerhard, Johann. *On Creation and Predestination.* St. Louis: Concordia, 2013.

Gerson, Jean. *Collation Factum est.* In *Oeuvres complètes de Jean Gerson,* edited by P. Glorieux, 5:309–25. Paris: Desclée, 1963.

———. *On Distinguishing True from False Revelations.* In *Jean Gerson: Early Works,* translated by Brian Patrick McGuire, 334–64. Classics of Western Spirituality. New York: Paulist, 1998.

———. *De probatione spirituum.* In *Oeuvres complètes de Jean Gerson,* edited by P. Glorieux, 9:177–85. Paris: Desclée, 1973.

———. *De signis bonis et malis.* In *Oeuvres complètes de Jean Gerson,* edited by P. Glorieux, 9:162–66. Paris: Desclée, 1973.

Goetz, Stewart. "Substance Dualism." In *In Search of the Soul: Four Views of the Mind-Body Problem,* edited by Joel B. Green and Stuart L. Palmer, 33–60. Downers Grove, IL: IVP Academic, 2005.

Goodwin, Thomas. *The Works of Thomas Goodwin.* Vol. 4. Edited by John C. Miller. Edinburgh: James Nichol, 1862.

Green, Thomas H. *Weeds Among Wheat: Discernment: Where Prayer and Action Meet.* Notre Dame, IN: Ave Maria, 1984.

Grenz, Stanley J. *The Social God and the Relational Self: A Trinitarian Theology of the Imago Dei.* Louisville: Westminster John Knox, 2001.

———. *Theology for the Community of God.* Nashville: Broadman & Holman, 1994.

Groeschel, Benedict J. *Spiritual Passages: The Psychology of Spiritual Development.* New York: Crossroad, 1984.

Grossmann, Walter. "Gruber on the Discernment of True and False Inspiration." *Harvard Theological Review* 81 (1988) 363–87.

Gruber, Eberhard Ludwig. *Kurtze/doch gründliche/Unterweisung von dem iñeren Wort Gottes. Um der Einfältigen willen in Frag und Antwort gestellet von einem Liebhaber desselbigen/und nun zum andern mal in Druck gegeben.* (1713).

———. *Unterschiedliche Erfahrungsvolle Zeugnisse, welche einige in Gott verbundene Freunde von der so sehr verhassten und verschreyten Inspirations-Sache nach ihrem Gewissen . . . Jederman zur gründlichen und unpartheyischen Prüfung und Einsicht hiermit offentlich dargeleget haben.* (1715).

Grudem, Wayne. *The Gift of Prophecy in 1 Corinthians.* Lanham, MD: University Press of America, 1982.

Guibert, Joseph de. *The Theology of the Spiritual Life.* Translated by Paul Barrett. New York: Sheed and Ward, 1953.

Gunton, Colin. *The Triune Creator: A Historical and Systematic Study.* Grand Rapids: Eerdmans, 1998.

Habermas, Gary. *The Risen Jesus and Future Hope.* Lanham, MD: Rowman & Littlefield, 2003.

Hall, Todd W. *Relational Spirituality: A Psychological-Theological Paradigm for Transformation.* Downers Grove, IL: IVP Academic, 2021.

Hammett, John S., and Katie J. McCoy. *Humanity.* Brentwood, TN: B&H Academic, 2023.

Hanson, Bradley C., ed. *Modern Christian Spirituality: Methodological and Historical Essays.* Atlanta, GA: Scholars, 1990.

———. "Spirituality as Spiritual Theology." In *Exploring Christian Spirituality: An Ecumenical Reader*, edited by Kenneth J. Collins, 242–48. Grand Rapids: Baker, 2000.

———. "Theological Approaches to Spirituality: A Lutheran Perspective." *Christian Spirituality Bulletin* (1994) 5–8.

Harper, J. Steven. "Old Testament Spirituality." In *Exploring Christian Spirituality: An Ecumenical Reader*, edited by Kenneth J. Collins, 311–27. Grand Rapids: Baker, 2000.

Harrison, Nonna Verna. *God's Many-Splendored Image: Theological Anthropology for Christian Formation.* Grand Rapids: Baker Academic, 2010.

Hastings, W. Ross. *Theological Ethics: The Moral Life of the Gospel in Contemporary Context.* Grand Rapids: Zondervan, 2021.

Hay, David. "Experience." In *The Blackwell Companion to Christian Spirituality*, edited by Arthur Holder, 419–41. Malden, MA: Blackwell, 2005.

Healey, Charles J. *Christian Spirituality: An Introduction to the Heritage.* New York: Alba House, 1999.

Hehn, J. "Zum Terminus 'Bild Gottes.'" In *Festschrift Eduard Sachau zum siebzigsten Geburtstage*, edited by Gotthold Weil, 36–52. Berlin: Reimer, 1915.
Henry of Friemar. *De quattuor instinctibus*. In *Der Traktat Heinrichs von Friemar über die Unterscheidung der Geister*, edited by Robert G. Wamock and Adolar Zumkeller, 1–238. Würzburg: Augustinus-Verlag, 1977.
Henry of Langenstein. *De discretione spirituum*. In *Heinrichs von Langenstein: Unterscheidung der Geister: Lateinisch und Deutsch: Texte und Untersuchungen zur Übersetzungsliteratur aus der Wiener Schule*, edited by Thomas Hohmann, 51–125. Munich: Artemis Verlag, 1997.
Hense, Elisabeth. *Frühchristliche Profilierungen der Spiritualität: Unterscheidung der Geister in ausgewählten Schriften: Didache, Erster Clemensbrief, Barnabasbrief, Hirt des Hermas, Erster Johannesbrief, De principiis und Vita Antonii*. Munster: LIT, 2010.
Hick, John. *An Interpretation of Religion: Human Responses to the Transcendent*. New Haven: Yale University Press, 2004.
Hilton, Walter. *Walter Hilton: The Scale of Perfection*. Translated by John P. H. Clark and Rosemary Dorward. Classics of Western Spirituality. New York: Paulist, 1991.
Hindmarsh, D. Bruce. *The Spirit of Early Evangelicalism: True Religion in a Modern World*. New York: Oxford University Press, 2018.
Hobson, George. *Imago Dei: Man/Woman Created in the Image of God: Implications for Theology, Pastoral Care, Eucharist, Apologetics, Aesthetics*. Eugene, OR: Wipf & Stock, 2019.
Hoekema, Anthony A. *Created in God's Image*. Grand Rapids: Eerdmans, 1986.
Hoffman, Bengt, ed. *The Theologia Germanica of Martin Luther*. Translated by Bengt Hoffman. Mahwah, NJ: Paulist, 1980.
Holder, Arthur. "Introduction." In *The Blackwell Companion to Christian Spirituality*, edited by Arthur Holder, 1–12. Malden, MA: Blackwell, 2005.
———. "Spirituality, Christian Forms of." In *Cambridge Dictionary of Christianity*, edited by Daniel Patte, 1183–84. New York: Cambridge University Press, 2010.
Holder, Arthur, and Lisa Dahill. "Teaching Christian Spirituality in Seminaries Today." *Christian Spirituality Bulletin* 7 (1999) 7–12.
Hollywood, Amy. "Feminist Studies." In *The Blackwell Companion to Christian Spirituality*, edited by Arthur Holder, 363–86. Malden, MA: Blackwell, 2005.
Houdek, Frank J. *Guided by the Spirit: A Jesuit Perspective on Spiritual Direction*. Chicago: Loyola, 1996.
Houston, James M. "Spiritual Life Today. An Appropriate Spirituality for a Post-Modern World." In *The Gospel in the Modern World: A Tribute to John Stott*, edited by Martyn Eden and David F. Wells, 179–97. Downers Grove, IL: InterVarsity, 1991.
Howard, Evan B. *Affirming the Touch of God: A Psychological and Philosophical Exploration of Christian Discernment*. Lanham, MD: University Press of America, 2000.
———. "The Beguine Option: A Persistent Past and a Promising Future of Christian Monasticism." *Religions* 10 (2019) 93–116.
———. *The Brazos Introduction to Christian Spirituality*. Grand Rapids: Brazos, 2008.
———. "Experience." In *Dictionary of Christian Spirituality*, edited by Glen G. Scorgie, 173–78. Grand Rapids: Zondervan, 2011.
———. *A Guide to Christian Spiritual Formation: How Scripture, Spirit, Community and Mission Shape Our Souls*. Grand Rapids: Baker Academic, 2018.

Howard, Philip T. "Vocational Formation: Navigating Leadership Disorientation." In *The Holy Spirit and Christian Formation: Multidisciplinary Perspectives*, edited by Diane J. Chandler, 167–84. Cham, Switzerland: Palgrave Macmillan, 2016.
Hoye, William J. *Gotteserfahrung? Klarung eines Grundbegriffes der gegenwärtigen Theologie*. Zurich: Benzinger, 1993.
Hubmaier, Balthasar. *Theologian of Anabaptism*. Edited and translated by H. Wayne Pipkin and John H. Yoder. Kitchener, ON: Herald Press, 1989.
Hudnut, Robert K. *Call Waiting: How to Hear God Speak*. Downers Grove, IL: InterVarsity, 1999.
Huggett, Joyce. *The Joy of Listening to God: Hearing the Many Ways God Speaks to Us*. Downers Grove, IL: InterVarsity, 1986.
Hughes, G. J. "Ignatian Discernment: A Philosophical Analysis." *Heythrop Journal* 31 (1990) 419–38.
Hughes, Philip Edgcumbe. *The True Image: Christ as the Origin and Destiny of Man in Christ*. Grand Rapids: Eerdmans, 1989.
Ignatius of Loyola. *The Spiritual Exercises of Saint Ignatius: A Translation and Commentary*. Translated by George E. Ganss. St. Louis, MO: Institute of Jesuit Sources, 1992.
Imes, Carmen Joy. *Being God's Image: Why Creation Still Matters*. Downers Grove, IL: InterVarsity, 2023.
Izard, Carroll E. "Basic Emotions, Natural Kinds, Emotion Schemas, and a New Paradigm." *Perspectivees on Psychological Science* 2 (2003) 260–80.
Jantzen, Grace. "Epistemology, Religious Experience, and Religious Belief." *Modern Theology* 3 (1987) 277–91.
Jaquette, James L. *Discerning What Counts: The Function of the* Adiaphora *Topos in Paul's Letters*. SBL Dissertation Series 146. Atlanta, GA: Scholars, 1995.
Jastram, Nathan. "Man as Male and Female: Created in the Image of God." *Concordia Theological Quarterly* 68 (2004) 5–96.
Jenson, Robert W. *Systematic Theology: Volume 2—The Works of God*. New York: Oxford University Press, 1999.
Jewett, Paul K. *Who We Are: Our Dignity as Human: A Neo-Evangelical Theology*. Grand Rapids: Eerdmans, 1996.
Job, Reuben. *A Guide to Spiritual Discernment*. Nashville, TN: Upper Room, 1996.
John of Ruysbroeck. *The Adornment of the Spiritual Marriage; The Sparkling Stone; The Book of Supreme Truth*. Edited by Evelyn Underhill. Translated by C. A. Wynschenk Dom. New York: E. P. Dutton, 1916.
———. *De Quatuor Tentationibus*. In *Opera Omnia: Carthusiano, ex Belgico idiomatein latinum conuersa, & denuo quam diligentissime recusa*, edited by Laurentius Surius, 356–64. Cologne: Arnoldum Quentelium, 1609.
———. *The Spiritual Espousals*. Translated by Eric Colledge. London: Faber and Faber, 1952.
John of the Cross. *The Ascent of Mount Carmel*. In *The Collected Works of St. John of the Cross*, translated by Kieran Kavanaugh and Otilio Rodriguez, 65–292. Washington, DC: ICS, 1979.
———. *The Dark Night*. In *The Collected Works of St. John of the Cross*, translated by Kieran Kavanaugh and Otilio Rodriguez, 293–390. Washington, DC: ICS, 1979.
Johnson, Ben Campbell. *Discerning God's Will*. Louisville: John Knox, 1990.

Johnson, Luke Timothy. *Religious Experience in Earliest Christianity*. Philadelphia: Fortress, 1998.

———. *Scripture and Discernment: Decision Making in the Early Church*. Nashville: Abingdon, 1996.

Johnston, Mark. "The Authority of Affect." *Philosophy and Phenomenological Research* 63 (2001) 181–214.

Jones, Beth Felker, and Jeffery W. Barbeau, eds. *The Image of God in an Image Driven Age: Explorations in Theological Anthropology*. Downers Grove, IL: InterVarsity, 2016.

Kelsey, David H. *Eccentric Existence: A Theological Anthropology*. 2 vols. Louisville: Westminster John Knox, 2009.

Kelsey, Morton. *Discernment: A Study in Ecstasy and Evil*. Mahwah, NJ: Paulist, 1978.

Kempis, Thomas à. *The Imitation of Christ*. Translated by Aloysius Croft and Harry F. Bolton. Milwaukee, WI: Bruce, 1940.

Kereszty, Roch. "Theology and Spirituality: The Task of Synthesis." *Communio* 10 (1983) 314–31.

Kidwell, Jeremy. "Elucidating the Image of God: An Analysis of the *Imago Dei* in the Work of Colin E. Gunton and John Zizioulas." MA thesis, Regent College, 2009. Theological Research Exchange Network.

Kiechle, Stefan. *The Art of Discernment: Making Good Decisions in Your World of Choices*. Notre Dame, IN: Ave Maria, 2005.

Kilner, John F. *Dignity and Destiny: Humanity in the Image of God*. Grand Rapids: Eerdmans, 2015.

Kinerk, Edward. "Toward a Method for the Study of Spirituality." *Review for Religious* 40 (1981) 3–19.

King, Jonathan. *The Beauty of the Lord: Theology as Aesthetics*. Bellingham, WA: Lexham, 2018.

King, Norman. *Experiencing God All Ways and Every Day*. Minneapolis, MN: Winston, 1982.

King, Rachel Hadley. *George Fox and the Light Within, 1650–1660*. Philadelphia: Friends Book Store, 1940.

Kline, Meredith. *Images of the Spirit*. Eugene, OR: Wipf & Stock, 1999.

Knitter, Paul. *Without Buddha I Could Not Be a Christian*. Oxford: One World, 2009.

Kourie, Celia. "Spirituality and the University." *Verbum et Ecclesia* 30 (2009) 148–73.

———. "The Turn to Spirituality" *Acta Theologica Supplementum* 8 (2006) 19–38.

Kourie, Celia, and Trevor Ruthenberg. "Contemporary Christian Spirituality: An 'Encompassing Field.'" *Acta Theologica Supplementum* 11 (2008) 76–93.

———. "Experience: Its Significance in Contemporary Christian Spirituality." *Alternation* Special Edition 3 (2009) 177–98.

Kuhn, Thomas S. *The Structure of Scientific Revolutions*. Chicago: University of Chicago Press, 1996.

Laato, Timo. "*Simul Iustus et Peccator*: Through the Lenses of Paul," *Journal of the Evangelical Theological Society* 61 (2018) 735–66.

LaCugna, Catherine. "The Practical Trinity." In *Exploring Christian Spirituality: Essays in Honor of Sandra M. Schneiders*, edited by Bruce H. Lescher and Elizabeth Liebert, 273–82. New York: Paulist, 2006.

LaCugna, Catherine, and Michael Downey. "Trinitarian Spirituality." In *New Dictionary of Catholic Spirituality*, edited by Michael Downey, 968–71. Collegeville, MN: Liturgical Press, 1993.

Lane, Anthony N. S. "Lust: The Human Person as Affected by Disordered Desires." *Evangelical Quarterly* 78 (2006) 21–35.

Lane, Dermot. *The Experience of God*. Dublin: Veritas, 1985.

LaPierre, Lawrence L. "A Model for Describing Spirituality." In *Exploring Christian Spirituality: An Ecumenical Reader*, edited by Kenneth J. Collins, 74–82. Grand Rapids: Baker, 2000.

Larkin, Ernest. *Silent Presence: Discernment as Process and Problem*. Danville, NJ: Dimension Books, 1998.

Lash, Nicholas. *Easter in Ordinary: Reflections on Human Experience and the Knowledge of God*. Notre Dame: University of Notre Dame Press, 1988.

Leech, Kenneth. *Experiencing God: Theology as Spirituality*. Eugene, OR: Wipf & Stock, 1985.

Letham, Robert. *The Work of Christ*. Downers Grove, IL: InterVarsity, 1993.

Levenson Jon Douglas. *Creation and the Persistence of Evil: The Jewish Drama of Divine Omnipotence*. Princeton: Princeton University Press, 1994.

Levering, Matthew. *Engaging the Doctrine of Creation: Cosmos, Creatures, and the Wise and Good Creator*. Grand Rapids: Baker Academic, 2017.

Libanio, J. B. *Spiritual Discernment and Politics: Guidelines for Religious Communities*. Eugene, OR: Wipf & Stock, 2003.

Liebert, Elizabeth. "Linking Faith and Justice: Working with Systems and Structures as a Spiritual Discipline." *Christian Spirituality Bulletin* 5 (1997) 19–21.

———. *The Soul of Discernment: A Spiritual Practice for Communities and Individuals*. Louisville: Westminster John Knox, 2015.

———. "Supervisions as Widening the Horizons." In *Supervision of Spiritual Directors: Engaging in Holy Mystery*, edited by Mary Rose Bumpus and Rebecca Bradburn Langer, 125–45. Harrisburg, PA: Morehouse, 2005.

———. *The Way of Discernment: Spiritual Practices for Decision Making*. Louisville: Westminster John Knox, 2010.

Lienhard, Joseph T. "On 'Discernment of the Spirits' in the Early Church." *Theological Studies* 41 (1980) 505–29.

Lints, Richard. *Identity and Idolatry: The Image of God and Its Inversion*. Downers Grove, IL: IVP Academics, 2015.

Lonergan, Bernard *Insight: A Study of Human Understanding*. New York: Harper and Row, 1958.

———. *Method in Theology*. New York: Seabury, 1972.

———. "Religious Experience." In *A Third Collection*, edited by F. Crowe, 115–28. New York: Paulist, 1985.

Lonsdale, David. "The Church as Context for Christian Spirituality." In *The Blackwell Companion to Christian Spirituality*, edited by Arthur Holder, 239–53. Malden, MA: Blackwell, 2005.

———. *Listening to the Music of the Spirit: The Art of Discernment*. Notre Dame, IN: Ave Maria, 1993.

Lossky, Vladimir. *In the Image and Likeness of God*. Crestwood, NY: St. Vladimir's Seminary Press, 1974.

Louth, Andrew. *Discerning the Mystery: An Essay on the Nature of Theology*. New York: Oxford University Press, 1983.

———. *Theology and Spirituality*. London: Fairacres, 1978.

Lovelace, Richard. *Dynamics of Spiritual Life: An Evangelical Theology of Renewal*. Downers Grove, IL: InterVarsity, 1979.

———. "Evangelical Spirituality: A Church Historian's Perspective." In *Exploring Christian Spirituality: An Ecumenical Reader*, edited by Kenneth J. Collins, 214–26. Grand Rapids: Baker, 2000.

———. "The Sanctification Gap." *Theology Today* 29 (1973) 363–69.

Luhrmann, Tanya. *When God Talks Back: Understanding the American Evangelical Relationship with God*. New York: Vintage Books, 2012.

Luther, Martin. *The Sermon on the Mount (Sermons) and the Magnificat. Luther's Works: Volume 21*. Edited by Jaroslav Pelikan. St. Louis: Concordia, 1956.

———. *Sermons on the Gospel of St. John Chapters 14–16. Luther's Works: Volume 24*. Edited by Jaroslav Pelikan. St. Louis: Concordia, 1961.

———. *Lectures on Galatians 1535, Chapters 1–4. Luther's Works: Volume 26*. Edited by Jaroslav Pelikan. St. Louis: Concordia, 1963.

———. "Preface to the Complete Edition of Luther's Latin Writings, 1545." In *Martin Luther: Selections from His Writings*, edited by John Dillenberger, 3–12. Garden City, NY: Anchor Books, 1962.

Macchia, Frank D. "Prophetic Jesus, Prophetic Church: A Response to Luke Timothy Johnson." *Journal of Pentecostal Theology* 22 (2013) 26–30.

———. *The Spirit-Baptized Church: A Dogmatic Inquiry*. New York: T&T Clark, 2020.

———. *Tongues of Fire: A Systematic Theology of the Christian Faith*. Eugene, OR: Cascade, 2023.

Macchia, Stephen. *The Discerning Life: An Invitation to Notice God in Everything*. Grand Rapids: Zondervan, 2022.

MacDonald, Nathan, et al., eds. *Genesis and Christian Theology*. Grand Rapids: Eerdmans, 2012.

Macquarrie, John. *In Search of Humanity: A Theological and Philosophical Approach*. Cardiff, Wales: Hymn Ancient and Modern, 1993.

———. "Spirit and Spirituality." In *Exploring Christian Spirituality: An Ecumenical Reader*, edited by Kenneth J. Collins, 63–73. Grand Rapids: Baker, 2000.

Maiese, Michelle. "How Can Emotions Be Both Cognitive and Bodily?" *Phenomenology and the Cognitive Sciences* 13 (2014) 513–31.

Malatesta, Edward, ed. *Discernment of Spirits*. Collegeville, MN: Liturgical Press, 1970.

Marcel, Gabriel. *Being and Having: An Existentialist Diary*. New York: Harper & Row, 1965.

Marpeck, Pilgram. *Writings of Pilgrim Marpeck*. Edited and translated by William Klassen and Walter Klassen. Scottdale, PA: Herald, 1978.

Marshall, I. Howard. "Being Human: Made in the Image of God." *Stone-Campbell Journal* 4 (2001) 47–67.

Martínez, Mariano. *Discernimiento personal y communitario: Necessidad, claves, ejercicio*. Madrid: San Pablo, 2001.

McAlpine, Thomas H. *Facing the Powers: What Are the Options?* Eugene, OR: Wipf & Stock, 2003.

McConville, J. Gordon. *Being Human in God's World: An Old Testament Theology of Humanity*. Grand Rapids: Baker, 2016.

McDermott, Gerald R. *Seeing God: Twelve Reliable Signs of True Spirituality*. Downers Grove, IL: InterVarsity, 1995.

McDonough, Sean. "The Fall and Fallenness in the NT." *Trinity Journal* 40 (2019) 185–95.

McDowell, Catherine. "In the Image of God He Created Them." In *The Image of God in an Image Driven Age*, edited by Beth Felker Jones and Jeffery W. Barbeau, 29–46. Downers Grove, IL: InterVarsity, 2016.

McFarland, Ian A. *Difference and Identity: A Theological Anthropology*. Cleveland, OH: Pilgrim, 2001.

———. *The Divine Image: Envisioning the Invisible God*. Minneapolis, MN: Fortress, 2005.

McGinn, Bernard. *The Flowering of Mysticism: Men and Women in the New Mysticism (1200–1350)*. The Presence of God: A History of Western Christian Mysticism 3. New York: Crossroad, 1998.

———. "The Letter and the Spirit: Spirituality as an Academic Discipline." *The Cresset* 56 (1993) 13–22.

McGrath, Alister. *Christian Spirituality: An Introduction*. Malden, MA: Blackwell, 1999.

———. *For All the Saints: Evangelical Theology and Christian Spirituality*. Edited by Timothy George and Alister McGrath. Louisville: Westminster John Knox, 2003.

———. *Reformation Thought: An Introduction*. New York: Wiley & Sons, 2021.

———. *Studies in Doctrine*. Grand Rapids: Zondervan, 1997.

———. "Theology and Experience: Reflections on Cogntive and Experiential Approaches to Theology." *European Journal of Theology* 2 (1993) 65–74.

McIntosh, Mark. *Discernment and Truth: The Spirituality and Theology of Knowledge*. New York: Crossroad-Herder and Herder, 2004.

———. *Mystical Theology: The Integrity of Spirituality and Theology*. Malden, MA: Blackwell, 1998.

———. "Trinitarian Perspectives on Christian Spirituality." In *The Blackwell Companion to Christian Spirituality*, edited by Arthur Holder, 177–89. Malden, MA: Blackwell, 2005.

McKinney, Mary Benet. *Sharing Wisdom: A Process for Group Decision Making*. Allen, TX: Tabor, 1987.

McNamara, Martin. "Discernment Criteria in Israel: True and False Prophets." In *Discernment of the Spirit and of Spirits*, edited by Casiano Floristan and Christian Duquoc, 2–13. New York: Seabury, 1979.

McRorie, Christina G. "Moral Reasoning in the 'World.'" *Theological Studies* 82 (2021) 213–37.

Megyer, Eugene. "Spiritual Theology Today." *The Way* 21 (1981) 55–67.

Middleton, J. Richard. *The Liberating Image: The* Imago Dei *in Genesis 1*. Grand Rapids: Brazos, 2005.

Moberly, R. W. L. *Prophecy and Discernment*. New York: Cambridge University Press, 2008.

Moreland, J. P. *Love Your God with All Your Mind*. Colorado Springs: NavPress, 2012.

———. *The Recalcitrant* Imago Dei: *Human Persons and the Failure of Naturalism*. London: SCM, 2009.

Morgan, Christopher W., ed. *Biblical Spirituality*. Wheaton, IL: Crossway, 2019.

Morgan, Christopher W. and Justin L. McLendon. "A Trajectory of Spirituality." In *Biblical Spirituality*, edited by Christopher W. Morgan, 19–54. Wheaton, IL: Crossway, 2019.

Morneau, Robert F. "Principles of Discernment." *Review for Religious* 41 (1982) 161–85.

Morris, Danny E., and Charles M. Olsen. *Discerning God's Will Together: A Spiritual Practice for the Church*. Bethesda, MD: Alban Institute, 1997.

Moser, Paul. *The Elusive God: Reorienting Religious Epistemology*. New York: Cambridge University Press, 2008.

———. *Understanding Religious Experience: from Conviction to Life's Meaning*. New York: Cambridge University Press, 2020.

Moses, Sarah. "'Keeping the Heart': Natural Affection in Joseph Butler's Approach to Virtue." *Journal of Religious Ethics* 37 (2009) 613–29.

Mouroux, Jean. *The Christian Experience: An Introduction to a Theology*. Translated by George Lamb. New York: Sheed and Ward, 1954.

Mulholland, M. Robert. *Invitation to a Journey: A Road Map for Spiritual Formation*. Downers Grove, IL: InterVarsity, 2016.

Mumford, Bob. *Take Another Look at Guidance: A Study of Divine Guidance*. Raleigh, NC: Lifechangers, 1993.

Munzinger, Andre. *Discerning the Spirits: Theological and Ethical Hermeneutics in Paul*. New York: Cambridge University Press, 2007.

Muto, Susan. "Formative Spirituality." *Epiphany International* 6 (2000) 8–16.

Netland, Harold A. *Encountering Religious Pluralism: The Challenge to Christian Faith and Mission*. Downers Grove, IL: InterVarsity, 2001.

———. *Religious Experience and the Knowledge of God: The Evidential Force of Divine Encounters*. Grand Rapids: Baker Academic, 2022.

Neufelder, Jerome M., and Coelho, Mary C. *Writings on Spiritual Direction by Great Masters*. Minneapolis, MN: Seabury, 1982.

Nichols, Aidan. *The Word Invites: A Spiritual Theology*. Herefordshire, UK: Gracewing, 2019.

Nissen, P. *Eene zachte aanraking van zijn zieleleven: Over 'ware' en 'valse' mystiek rond 1900*. Nijmegen: Vantilt, 2008.

Nouwen, Henri J. *Discernment: Reading the Signs of Daily Life*. New York: HarperOne, 2013.

———. *Spiritual Direction: Wisdom for the Long Walk of Faith*. New York: HarperCollins, 2006.

———. *Spiritual Formation: Following the Movements of the Spirit*. San Francisco: HarperOne, 2010.

Nugent, John C. *The Fourfold Office of Christ: A New Typology for Relating Church and World*. Eugene, OR: Cascade, 2024.

Nussbaum, Martha C. *Upheavals of Thought: The Intelligence of Emotions*. New York: Cambridge University Press, 2001.

Nuttall, Geoffrey. *The Holy Spirit in Puritan Faith and Experience*. Chicago: University of Chicago Press, 1992.

O'Brien, Glen. "John Wesley and Athanasius on Salvation in the Context of the Debate over Wesley's Debt to Eastern Orthodoxy." *Phronema* 28 (2013) 35–53.

Oden, Thomas C. *Life in the Spirit*. Systematic Theology 3. San Francisco: HarperCollins, 1992.

———. *The Word of Life*. Systematic Theology 2. San Francisco: HarperCollins, 1992.

Origen, *On First Principles*. Translated by G. W. Butterworth. Gloucester, MA: Peter Smith, 1973.

Orsy, Ladislas. *Discernment*. Collegeville, MN: Liturgical Press, 2020.

———. *Probing the Spirit: A Theological Evaluation of Communal Discernment*. Denville, NJ: Dimension Books, 1976.

Ortiz, Hector. *Discernment: A Theological Process in Ecclesial Decision Making*. Decatur, GA: Columbia Theological Seminary, 2000.

O'Sullivan, Michael. "Spirituality: A New Academic Discipline." *Melita Theologica* 59 (2008) 71–77.

Oswald, Roy M., and Robert E. Friedrich Jr. *Discerning Your Congregation's Future: A Strategic and Spiritual Approach*. Bethesda, MD: Alban Institute, 1996.

Ota, Koji. "Neuroscientific Threat to Free Will as Non-Veridicality of Agentive Experience." *Journal of Mind and Behavior* 41 (2020) 109–30.

Otto, Randall E. "Baptism and the *Munus Triplex*." *Evangelical Quarterly* 76 (2004) 217–25.

Owen, John. *Πνευματολογία: Or, a Discourse Concerning the Holy Spirit*. 2 vols. Glasgow: W. & E. Miller, 1791.

Packer, J. I. "An Introduction to Systematic Spirituality." *Crux* 26 (1990) 1–8.

———. "The Ministry of the Spirit in Discerning the Will of God." In *Who's Afraid of the Holy Spirit? An Investigation into the Ministry of the Spirit of God Today*, edited by M. James Sawyer and Daniel B. Wallace, 95–110. Dallas, TX: Biblical Studies, 2005.

———. "Towards a Systematic Spirituality." *Criswell Theological Review* 7 (1994) 1–14.

Panikkar, Raimundo. *The Unknown Christ of Hinduism: Towards an Ecumenical Christophany*. London: Dartman, Longman and Todd, 1981.

Pannenberg, Wolfhart. *Christian Spirituality and Sacramental Community*. Maryknoll, NY: Darton, Longman and Todd, 1983.

Parker, Stephen E. *Led by the Spirit: Toward a Practical Theology of Pentecostal Discernment and Decision Making*. Sheffield: Sheffield Academic Press, 1996.

Paz, Jacobo Àlvarez de. *De perfecta contemplatione*. In *Opera*, edited by Ludovicum Vives, 385–686. Paris: Bibliopolam, 1876.

Penn, William. *A Collection of the Works of William Penn*. 2 vols. London: J. Sowle, 1726.

Peppiatt, Lucy. *The Imago Dei: Humanity Made in the Image of God*. Eugene, OR: Wipf & Stock, 2022.

Perlman, Helen Harris. *Relationship: The Heart of Helping People*. Chicago: University of Chicago Press, 1979.

Perrin, David. *Studying Christian Spirituality*. New York: Routledge, 2007.

Peters, Ted. *God—The World's Future: Systematic Theology for a New Era*. Philadelphia: Fortress, 2015.

Peterson, Eugene H. *Christ Plays in Ten Thousand Places: A Conversation in Spiritual Theology*. Grand Rapids: Eerdmans, 2005.

———. "Saint Mark: The Basic Text for Christian Spirituality." In *Exploring Christian Spirituality: An Ecumenical Reader*, edited by Kenneth J. Collins, 327–38. Grand Rapids: Baker, 2000.

———. *Under the Unpredictable Plant: An Exploration in Vocational Holiness*. Grand Rapids: Eerdmans, 1992.

Peterson, Ryan S. "Emotions in the Image of God? The Holistic Vision of Classical Christian Anthropology." *Journal of Spiritual Formation and Soul Care* 16 (2023) 189–203.

———. *The* Imago Dei *as Human Identity: A Theological Interpretation*. University Park, PA: Eisenbrauns, 2016.
Plantinga, Alvin. *Warranted Christian Belief*. New York: Oxford University Press, 2000.
Plantinga, Cornelius, Jr. *Not the Way It's Supposed to Be: A Breviary of Sin*. Grand Rapids: Eerdmans, 1995.
Plantinga, Richard J., et al. *An Introduction to Christian Theology*. New York: Cambridge University Press, 2010.
Poling, James, and Donald Miller. *Foundations for a Practical Theology of Ministry*. Nashville: Abingdon, 1985.
Pollock, John L. "Evaluative Cognition." *NOÛS* 35 (2001) 625–64.
Porter, Steven L. "The Gradual Nature of Sanctification: Σάρξ as Habituated, Relational Resistance to the Spirit." *Themelios* 39 (2014) 470–83.
———. "Will/Heart/Spirit: Discipleship That Forms the Christian Character." *Christian Education Journal* 16 (2019) 79–94.
Poulain, Augustin. *The Graces of Interior Prayer: A Treatise on Mystical Theology*. Jeffersonville, IN: Caritas, 2016.
Principe, Walter. "Pluralism in Christian Spirituality." *The Way* 32 (1992) 54–61.
———. "Spirituality, Christian." In *The New Dictionary of Catholic Spirituality*, edited by Michael Downey, 931–8. Collegeville, MN: Liturgical Press, 1993.
———. "Toward Defining Spirituality." In *Exploring Christian Spirituality: An Ecumenical Reader*, edited by Kenneth J. Collins, 43–60. Grand Rapids: Baker, 2000. Originally published in *Sciences Religieuses* 12 (1983) 127–41.
Protera, Michael. *Homo spiritualis nititur fide: Martin Luther and Ignatius of Loyola: An Analytical and Comparative Study of a Hermeneutic Based on the Heuristic Structure of Discretio*. Lanham, MD: University Press of America, 1983.
Quarles, Charles L. "New Creation: Spirituality According to Jesus." In *Biblical Spirituality*, edited by Christopher W. Morgan, 79–106. Wheaton, IL: Crossway, 2019.
Rad, Gerhard von. *Genesis: A Commentary*. Translated by John H. Marks. Philadelphia: Westminster, 1972.
Rahner, Karl. "The Logic of Concrete Individual Knowledge in Ignatius Loyola." In *The Dynamic Element in the Church*. Translated by W. J. O'Hara, 85–170. New York: Herder and Herder, 1964.
———. *The Practice of Faith: A Handbook of Contemporary Spirituality*. Edited by Karl Lehmann and Albert Raffelt. New York: Crossroad, 1992.
———. "The Theology of Mysticism." In *The Practice of Faith: A Handbook of Contemporary Spirituality*, edited by K. Lehmann and L. Raffelt, 70–77. New York: Crossroad, 1986.
Rakoczy, Susan. "The Structures of Discernment Processes and the Meaning of Discernment Language in Published U.S. Catholic Literature 1965–1978." PhD diss., Catholic University of America, 1980.
Rauschenbusch, Walter. *A Theology for the Social Gospel*. New York: Macmillan, 1917.
Rea, Michael C. *The Hiddenness of God*. New York: Oxford University Press, 2018.
Records of the Churches of Christ, Gathered at Fenstanton, Warboys, and Hexham, 1644–1729. Edited by E. B. Underhill. London: Haddon Brothers, 1854.
The Register of the Parish of Hackness, Co. York., 1557–1783. Vol. 25. Leeds: Yorkshire Parish Register Society, 1906.

Reguera, Emmanuel de la. *Praxis theologiae mysticae, opusculum selectum auctore P. Michaele Godinez.* Vol. 2. Rome: Antonii de Rubeis, 1745.

Rescher, Nicholas. "Evidentiating Free Will." *Journal of Speculative Philosophy* 28 (2014) 79–106.

Rigoni, David, et al. "Inducing Disbelief in Free Will Alters Brain Correlates of Preconscious Motor Preparation: The Brain Minds Whether We Believe in Free Will or Not." *Pyschological Science* 22 (2011) 613–18.

Roberts, Laura Schmidt. "Toward a Theological Anthropology: A Study of Genesis 1–3." *Direction* 45 (2016) 136–48.

Roberts, Robert C. *Spiritual Emotions: A Psychology of Christian Virtues.* Grand Rapids: Eerdmans, 2007.

Robinson, Denis. "Encounter with God: The Primary Task of Applied Spirituality." In *With Wisdom Seeking God: The Academic Study of Spirituality*, edited by Una Agnew, et al., 173–86. Leuven: Peeters, 2008.

Rodrigues, Adriani M. "Thinking Systematically with the Scriptural Christology of Hebrews: Contributions to the Theology of Christ's Threefold Office." *Andrews University Seminary Studies* 58 (2020) 33–63.

Rohr, Richard. *The Universal Christ: How a Forgotten Reality Can Change Everything We See, Hope for, and Believe.* New York: Convergent, 2019.

Rosenberg, Stanley. *Finding Ourselves after Darwin: Conversations on the Image of God, Original Sin, and the Problem of Evil.* Grand Rapids: Baker Academic, 2018.

Roy, Louis. *Transcendent Experiences: Phenomenology and Critique.* Toronto: University of Toronto Press, 2001.

Rulla, Luigi M. "The Discernment of Spirits and Christian Anthropology." *Gregorianum* 59 (1978) 537–69.

Rupnik, Marko Ivan. *Discernment: Acquiring the Heart of God.* Boston: Pauline Books & Media, 2006.

Salamon, Janusz. "On Cognitive Validity of Religious Experience." *Forum Philosophicum* 9 (2004) 7–24.

Sands, Paul. "The *Imago Dei* as Vocation." *Evangelical Quarterly* 82 (2010) 28–41.

Scaramelli, Giovanni Battista. *Discernimento de' spiriti: Per il retto regolamento delle azioni proprie ed altrui.* Venice: Simone Occhi, 1764.

Schaeffer, Francis. *The Complete Works of Francis A. Schaeffer: A Christian Worldview.* 5 vols. Westchester, IL: Crossway, 1982.

Schleiermacher, Friedrich. *The Christian Faith.* New York: Bloomsbury, 2016.

Schlosser, Markus E. "The Neuroscientific Study of Free Will: A Diagnosis of the Controversy." *Synthese* 191 (2014) 245–62.

Schmidt, Hans P. "Scheidung der Geister." In *Der Geist und die Geister*, edited by H. P. Schmidt, et al., 5–38. Konstanz: Friedrich Bahn Verlag, 1976.

Schneiders, Sandra M. "Approaches to the Study of Christian Spirituality." In *The Blackwell Companion to Christian Spirituality*, edited by Arthur Holder, 15–34. Oxford: Blackwell, 2005.

———. "Christian Spirituality: Definition, Method and Types." In *The New Westminster Dictionary of Christian Spirituality*, edited by Philip Sheldrake, 1–6. Louisville: Westminster John Knox, 2013.

———. "The Future of Christian Spirituality as an Academic Discipline." *Offerings* 14 (2021) 19–36.

———. "A Hermeneutical Approach to the Study of Christian Spirituality." In *Minding the Spirit*, edited by Elizabeth A. Dreyer and Mark S. Burrows, 49–60. Baltimore: Johns Hopkins University Press, 2005.

———. "The Interpretive Dialogue Between Experience and Explanation in Bernard McGinn's Study of the Mystical Tradition." *Theological Studies* 82 (2021) 690–94.

———. "Spirituality as an Academic Discipline: Reflections from Experience." *Christian Spirituality Bulletin* 1 (1993) 10–15.

———. "Spirituality in the Academy." *Theological Studies* 50 (1989) 676–97.

———. "The Study of Christian Spirituality and Catholic Theology." In *Exploring Christian Spirituality: Essays in Honor of Sandra M. Schneiders*, edited by Bruce H. Lescher and Elizabeth Liebert, 196–212. New York: Paulist, 2006.

———. "The Study of Christian Spirituality: Contours and Dynamics of a Discipline." In *Minding the Spirit*, edited by Elizabeth A. Dreyer and Mark S. Burrows, 5–24. Baltimore: Johns Hopkins University Press, 2005. Originally published in *Studies in Spirituality* 8 (1998) 38–57.

———. "Theology and Spirituality: Strangers, Rivals or Partners." *Horizons* 13 (1986) 253–74.

Schreiner, Susan. *Are You Alone Wise? The Search for Certainty in the Early Modern Era*. Oxford: Oxford University Press, 2011.

Scorgie, Glen G. "Preface" In *Dictionary of Christian Spirituality*, edited by Glen G. Scorgie, 7–9. Grand Rapids: Zondervan, 2011.

Scougal, Henry. *The Life of God in the Soul of Man*. Boston: Nichols and Noyes, 1868.

Senn, Frank C. *Protestant Spiritual Traditions*. 2 vols. Eugene, OR: Cascade, 2020.

Sheeran, Michael J. *Beyond Majority Rule: Voteless Decisions in the Religious Society of Friends*. Philadelphia: Philadelphia Yearly Meeting, 1983.

———. "Ignatius and the Quakers." *The Way Supplement* 68 (1990) 86–97.

Sheets, John R. "Profile of the Spirit: A Theology of Discernment of Spirits." *Review for Religious* 30 (1971) 363–76.

Sheldrake, Philip, ed. *The New SCM Dictionary of Christian Spirituality*. London: SCM, 2005.

———. "Spirituality and Its Critical Methodology." In *Exploring Christian Spirituality: Essays in Honor of Sandra M. Schneiders*, edited by Bruce H. Lescher and Elizabeth Liebert, 15–34. New York: Paulist, 2006.

———. "Spirituality and the Integrity of Theology." *Spiritus* 7 (2007) 93–8.

———. *Spirituality and Theology: Christian Living and the Doctrine of God*. Maryknoll, NY: Darton, Longman and Todd, 1998.

———. "Spirituality as an Academic Discipline." In *Spirituality and the Curriculum*, edited by A. Thatcher, 55–78. London: Cassell, 1999.

———. "The Study of Spirituality." *The Way* 39 (1999) 162–72.

Sherlock, Charles. *The Doctrine of Humanity: Contours of Christian Theology*. Downers Grove, IL: IVP Academic, 1997.

Shuler, Bryan. "Conscious of Christ: Toward a Doctrinal Mysticism in Dialogue with Bernard McGinn, John Calvin, and Meister Eckhart." *Journal of Spiritual Formation and Soul Care* 17 (2024) 155–69.

Sibbes, Richard. *The Complete Works of Richard Sibbes*. 7 vols. Edited by Alexander Balloch Grosart. Edinburgh: James Nichol, 1862–1864.

Silf, Margaret. *Wise Choices: A Spiritual Guide to Life Decisions*. New York: Bluebridge, 2007.

Sire, James W. *The Universe Next Door: A Basic Worldview Catalog.* Downers Grove, IL: InterVarsity, 2009.
Skaug, Benjamin M. and Christopher W. Morgan. "Tensions in Spirituality: Spirituality According to Paul." In *Biblical Spirituality*, edited by Christopher W. Morgan, 107-36. Wheaton, IL: Crossway, 2019.
Smith, Gordon T. "Discernment." In *Dictionary of Christian Spirituality*, edited by Glen G. Scorgie, 405-6. Downers Grove, IL: Zondervan, 2011.
———. *Listening to God in Times of Choice: The Art of Discerning God's Will.* Downers Grove, IL: InterVarsity, 1997.
———. *The Voice of Jesus: Discernment, Prayer and the Witness of the Spirit.* Downers Grove, IL: InterVarsity, 2003.
Smith, James K. A. *Desiring the Kingdom: Worship, Worldview, and Cultural Formation.* Grand Rapids: Baker Academic, 2009.
———. "Questions About the Perception of 'Christian Truth': On the Affective Effects of Sin." *New Blackfriars* 88 (2007) 585-93.
Smith, John E. *Experience and God.* New York: Oxford University Press, 1968.
Sobrino, Jon. *Christology at the Crossroads: A Latin American Approach.* Maryknoll, NY: Orbis Books, 1978.
———. "Following Jesus as Discernment." In *Discernment of the Spirit and of Spirits*, edited by Casiano Floristan and Christian Duquoc, 14-24. New York: Seabury, 1979.
Soulen, R. Kendall, and Linda Woodhead, eds. *God and Human Dignity.* Grand Rapids: Eerdmans, 2006.
Spencer, F. Scott. *Passions of the Christ: The Emotional Life of Jesus in the Gospels.* Grand Rapids: Baker Academic, 2021.
Spohn, William C. "Charismatic Communal Discernment and Ignatian Communities." *The Way Supplement* 20 (1973) 38-54.
———. "The Reasoning Heart: An American Approach to Christian Discernment." *Theological Studies* 44 (1983) 30-52.
Steggink, Otger. "Study in Spirituality in Retrospect: Shifts in Methodological Approach." *Studies in Spirituality* 1 (1991) 5-23.
Sterry, Peter. *The Spirit Convincing of Sinne.* London: Matth. Simmons, 1645.
Stewart, Robert B. "Can Only One Religion Be True? Considering This Question." In *Can Only One Religion Be True? Paul Knitter and Harold Netland in Dialogue.* Edited by Robert B. Stewart. Philadelphia: Fortress, 2013.
Studzinski, Raymond. "Feelings." In *The New Dictionary of Catholic Spirituality*, edited by Michael Downey, 392-24. Collegeville, MN: Liturgical Press, 1993.
Suarez, Francisco. *De divina gratia.* Venice: Balleoni, 1740.
Sumner, George R. "'You Have Not Yet Considered the Gravity of Sin': A Key Retrieval for Our Time." *Pro Ecclesia* 25 (2016) 261-73.
Suso, Henry. *The Life of the Servant.* In *Henry Suso: The Exemplar, with Two German Sermons*, edited and translated by Frank Tobin, 61-204, Classics of Western Spirituality. New York: Paulist, 1989.
———. *Little Book of Truth.* In *Henry Suso: The Exemplar, with Two German Sermons*, edited and translated by Frank Tobin, 305-32, Classics of Western Spirituality. New York: Paulist, 1989.
Sutanto, N. Gray. "Cultural Mandate and the Image of God: Human Vocation Under Creation, Fall, and Redemption." *Themelios* 48 (2023) 592-604.

———. "Questioning Bonaventure's Augustinianism? On the Noetic Effects of Sin." *New Blackfriars* 102 (2021) 401–17.
Svigel, Michael, and Caroline Buie. *The Shepherd of Hermas: A New Translation and Commentary*. Eugene, OR: Cascade, 2023.
Swann, John Thomas. *The Imago Dei: A Priestly Calling for Humankind*. Eugene, OR: Wipf & Stock, 2017.
Swinburne, Richard. *The Existence of God*. Oxford: Clarendon, 2004.
Tanner, Kathryn. *Christ the Key*. New York: Cambridge University Press, 2010.
Tanquerey, Adolphe. *The Spiritual Life: A Treatise on Ascetical and Mystical Theology*. Translated by Herman Branderis. Paris: Desclée, 1930
Tauler, Johannes. *Johannes Tauler: Sermons*. Translated by Maria Shrady. Classics of Western Spirituality. New York: Paulist, 1985.
———. *Die Predigten Taulers*. Edited by Ferdinand Vetter. Berlin: Weidmannsche Buchhandlung, 1910.
Teresa of Avila. *The Book of Her Life*. In *The Collected Works of St. Teresa of Avila*, translated by Kieran Kavanaugh and Otilio Rodriguez, 1:1–308. Washington, DC: ICS, 1976.
———. *The Interior Castle*. In *The Collected Works of St. Teresa of Avila*, translated by Kieran Kavanaugh and Otilio Rodriguez, 2:263–454. Washington, DC: ICS, 1980.
———. *The Way of Perfection*. In *The Collected Works of St. Teresa of Avila*, translated by Kieran Kavanaugh and Otilio Rodriguez, 2:15–206. Washington, DC: ICS, 1980.
Thagard, Paul. "The Moral Psychology of Conflicts of Interest: Insights from Affective Neuroscience." *Journal of Applied Philosophy* 24 (2007) 367–80.
Therrien, Gérard. *Le discernement dans les écrits pauliniens*. Paris: Gabalda, 1973.
———. "Le discernement spirituel." *Il est vivant* 8 (1976) 16–25.
Thibodeaux, Mark E. *God's Voice Within: The Ignatian Way to Discover God's Will*. Chicago: Loyola, 2010.
Thiselton, Anthony C. *The Two Horizons: New Testament Hermeneutics and Philosophical Description*. Grand Rapids: Eerdmans, 1980.
Thompson, Heather. "Fallen Image and Redeemed Dust: Being Human in God's Creation." *St. Mark's Review* 212 (2010) 65–74.
Tillich, Paul. *Systematic Theology*. Vol. 1. Chicago: University of Chicago Press, 1973.
Toner, Jules J. *A Commentary on Saint Ignatius' Rules for the Discernment of Spirits*. St. Louis, MO: Institute of Jesuit Sources, 1982.
———. *Discerning God's Will: Ignatius of Loyola's Teaching on Christian Decision Making*. St. Louis, MO: Institute of Jesuit Sources, 1991.
———. "A Method for Communal Discernment of God's Will." *Studies in the Spirituality of Jesuits* 3 (1971) 121–52.
———. *Spirit of Light or Darkness: A Casebook for Studying Discernment of Spirits*. St. Louis, MO: Institute of Jesuit Sources, 1995.
Tracy, David. *Blessed Rage for Order*. New York: Seabury, 1975.
Trueman, Carl. *The Rise and Triumph of the Modern Self: Cultural Amnesia, Expressive Individualism, and the Road to Sexual Revolution*. Wheaton, IL: Crossway, 2020.
Turner, James T., Jr. "Temple Theology, Holistic Eschatology, and the *Imago Dei*: An Analytic Prolegomenon." *TheoLogica* 2 (2018) 95–114.
Upkong, Justin. "Pluralism and the Discernment of Spirits." *Ecumenical Review* 41 (1989) 416–25.

Vandici, Gratian. "Reading the Rules of Knowledge in the Story of the Fall: Calvin and Reformed Epistemology on the Noetic Effects of Original Sin." *Journal of Theological Interpretation* 10 (2016) 173–91.

Vanhoozer, Kevin J. "Putting on Christ: Spiritual Formation and the Drama of Discipleship." *Journal of Spiritual Formation and Soul Care* 8 (2015) 147–71.

van Huyssteen, J. Wentzel. *Alone in the World? Human Uniqueness in Science and Theology*. Grand Rapids: Eerdmans, 2004.

Visala, Aku. "Human Cognition and the Image of God." In *The Christian Doctrine of Humanity: Explorations in Constructive Dogmatics*, edited by Oliver D. Crisp and Fred Sanders, 91–109. Grand Rapids: Zondervan, 2018.

Voaden, Rosalynn. *God's Words, Women's Voices: The Discernment of Spirits in the Writing of Late-Medieval Women Visionaries*. York: York Medieval, 1999.

Volf, Miroslav. *Work in the Spirit: Toward a Theology of Work*. Eugene, OR: Wipf & Stock, 2001.

Voorwinde, Stephen. *Jesus' Emotions in the Gospels*. London: Continuum International, 2011.

Vorster, Nico. *Created in the Image of God: Understanding God's Relationship with Humanity*. Eugene, OR: Pickwick, 2011.

Vroom, Hendrik M. "Sin and Decent Society: A Few Untimely Thoughts." *International Journal of Public Theology* 1 (2007) 471–88.

Waaijman, Kees. "Discernment and Biblical Spirituality: An Overview and Evaluation of Recent Research." *Acta Theologica Supplementum* 17 (2013) 1–12.

———. "Discernment—The Compass on the High Sea of Spirituality." *Acta Theologica Supplementum* 17 (2013) 13–24.

———. "A Hermeneutic of Spirituality." *Studies in Spirituality* 5 (1995) 5–39.

———. "Spirituality: A Multifaceted Phenomenon—Interdisciplinary Explorations." *Studies in Spirituality* 17 (2007) 1–113.

———. "Spirituality as Theology." *Studies in Spirituality* 21 (2011) 1–43.

———. *Spirituality: Forms, Foundations, Methods*. Translated by John Vriend. Leuven: Peeters, 2002.

———. "Toward a Phenomenological Definition of Spirituality." *Studies in Spirituality* 3 (1993) 5—57.

Wallace, Daniel, and James M. Sawyer. *Who's Afraid of the Holy Spirit? An Investigation into the Ministry of the Spirit of God Today*. Dallas, TX: Biblical Studies, 2013.

Watson, Francis. *Text and Truth: Redefining Biblical Theology*. Grand Rapids: Eerdmans, 1997.

Webb, Mark. "Religious Experience." In *The Stanford Encyclopedia of Philosophy*, edited by Edward N. Zalta and Uri Nodelman. Stanford, CA: Stanford University, 2022.

Wellum, Stephen J. *God the Son Incarnate: The Doctrine of Christ*. Wheaton, IL: Crossway, 2016.

Wesley, John. *A Farther Appeal to Men of Reason and Religion*. London: W. Strahan, 1745.

———. *A Plain Account of Christian Perfection: As Believed and Taught by Rev. John Wesley*. New York: Eaton & Mains, 1900.

———. "Sermon I: Salvation by Faith." In *The Works of John Wesley*, edited by Thomas Jackson, 5:7–16. Grand Rapids: Zondervan, 1958.

———. "Sermon X: The Witness of the Spirit: Discourse I." In *The Works of John Wesley*, edited by Thomas Jackson, 5:111–22. Grand Rapids: Zondervan, 1958.

———. "Sermon XI: The Witness of the Spirit: Discourse II." In *The Works of John Wesley*, 5:123–33. Grand Rapids: Zondervan, 1958.

White, Wesley J. "The Personality of Sin: Anxiety, Pride, and Self-Contempt." *Mid-America Journal of Theology*, 27 (2016) 85–97.

Whitehead, Alfred N. *Process and Reality: An Essay in Cosmology*. New York: Macmillan, 1960.

Wiebe, Phillip H. *Visions of Jesus: Direct Encounters from the New Testament to Today*. New York: Oxford University Press, 1997.

Wilkins, Michael J. *In His Image: Reflecting Christ in Everyday Life*. Eugene, OR: Wipf & Stock, 2020.

Willard, Dallas. *The Divine Conspiracy: Rediscovering Our Hidden Life in God*. San Francisco: Harper, 1998.

———. *The Great Omission: Reclaiming Jesus's Essential Teachings on Discipleship*. San Francisco: Harper, 2006.

———. *Hearing God: Developing a Conversational Relationship with God*. Downers Grove, IL: InterVarsity, 1999.

———. *Renovation of the Heart: Putting on the Character of Christ*. Colorado Springs: NavPress, 2021.

Williams, Rowan. *The Wound of Knowledge: A History of Christian Spirituality from the New Testament to John of the Cross*. Boston: Cowley, 1987.

Wilson, Stephen J. *The Communal Nature of Man in the Image of God*. ThM Thesis, Biola University, 2008. Theological Research Exchange Network.

Wink, Walter. *Engaging the Powers: Discernment and Resistance in a World of Domination*. Philadelphia: Fortress, 1992.

Wolff, Pierre. *Discernment: The Art of Choosing Well*. Liguori, MO: Triumph Books, 1993.

Wolters, Albert M. *Creation Regained: Biblical Basics for a Reformational Worldview*. Grand Rapids: Eerdmans, 2005.

Wolterstorff, Nicholas. *Reason Within the Bounds of Religion*. Grand Rapids: Eerdmans, 1988.

Woolman, John. *The Journal of John Woolman*. New York: Houghton Mifflin, 1909.

Wright, N. T. *The New Testament and the People of God*. Philadelphia: Fortress, 1992.

Wynn, Mark. "Towards a Broadening of the Concept of Religious Experience: Some Phenomenological Considerations." *Religious Studies* 45 (2009): 147–66.

Yandell, Keith E. *The Epistemology of Religious Experience*. New York: Cambridge University Press, 1994.

Yeo, Ray S. "Emotional Formation: A Trinitarian Interaction." In *The Holy Spirit and Christian Formation: Multidisciplinary Perspectives*, edited by Diane J. Chandler, 33–48. Cham, Switzerland: Palgrave Macmillan, 2016.

Zahl, Simeon. *The Holy Spirit and Christian Experience*. New York: Oxford University Press, 2020.

Zhong, Jimmy Y. "What Does Neuroscience Research Tell Us About Human Consciousness? An Overview of Benjamin Libet's Legacy." *Journal of Mind and Behavior* 37 (2016) 287–310.

Zhu, Jing. "Intention and Volition." *Canadian Journal of Philosophy* 34 (2004) 175–93.